FIGHTING
GOD

FIGHTING
GOD

AN ATHEIST MANIFESTO
FOR A RELIGIOUS WORLD

David Silverman

Thomas Dunne Books St. Martin's Press New York

THOMAS DUNNE BOOKS.
An imprint of St. Martin's Press.

FIGHTING GOD. Copyright © 2015 by David Silverman. Foreword copyright © 2015 by Cara Santa Maria. All rights reserved. Printed in the United States of America. For information, address St. Martin's Press, 175 Fifth Avenue, New York, N.Y. 10010.

www.thomasdunnebooks.com
www.stmartins.com

Designed by Steven Seighman

The Library of Congress Cataloging-in-Publication Data is available upon request.

ISBN 978-1-250-06484-4 (hardcover)
ISBN 978-1-4668-7128-1 (e-book)

Our books may be purchased in bulk for promotional, educational, or business use. Please contact your local bookseller or the Macmillan Corporate and Premium Sales Department at (800) 221-7945, extension 5442, or by e-mail at MacmillanSpecialMarkets@macmillan .com.

First Edition: December 2015

10 9 8 7 6 5 4 3 2 1

For Hildy.
Our love is like a storybook story.

CONTENTS

ACKNOWLEDGMENTS

I've been influenced by many and helped along the way by many more. I need to acknowledge with deep appreciation Carl Sagan, James Randi, Richard Dawkins, Robert Green Ingersoll, Madalyn Murray O'Hair, and Christopher Hitchens, all of whose work continues to influence me today.

Additionally, past American Atheists presidents Ellen Johnson and Ed Buckner, and longtime employee Conrad Goeringer were major players in my growth in activism. I would not be where I am today without them.

I'd like to thank my agent, Jane Dystel at Dystel & Goderich Literary Management, and my editor, Rob Kirkpatrick at Macmillan/ St. Martin's Press, whose support helped me bring this book to a new level, and to Cara Santa Maria for her foreword. I'd also like to thank readers Amanda Knief, Erica Cohn, Walter Mattingly, and Dennis Horvitz, all of whom provided great insight during the book's final stages.

My mother, Janice Silverman, had constantly urged me to write a book ever since I first became an activist. The good news is she knew I was writing one before she died. The bad news is she never saw it published. Although she made me do oh-so-many "Jewy" things as a child, her love for me never wavered—nor mine for her.

By far, my greatest acknowledgment must go to my biggest

supporter, my lovely wife, Hildy. She's my writing coach and in-vested many hours in this book and is a great source of information. She is by far my greatest influence, and I am happy and honored to dedicate this book to her.

FOREWORD

I was raised Mormon in a comfortable suburb, protected from the urban dangers of impiety. Soon after my eighth birthday, my father baptized me in the font tucked behind an accordion door in the humble church hallway I'd scurried along since I was old enough to walk. I thought everything would change that day. I was, after all, a Latter-day Saint of my own volition now, washed away of the sins I'd accumulated in my childhood. As the song I sang every Sunday morning went, "I want to live the gospel, to know I am heard when I pray, to know that I will be happy, because I have learned to obey." This was my chance to show my parents what a good Mormon girl they'd raised.

Unfortunately for my folks (and the whole lot of unnaturally friendly churchgoers), my obedience wouldn't outweigh the forces of logic and reason brewing within my developing brain.

Suffice it to say, I grew up not knowing other atheists. I often felt that I might be the only person in the world who didn't require the comfort of an almighty being—who scratched her head, perplexed, when she heard others pontificate about personal relationships with the Lord. After brief exposure in an elementary-school class, I began smuggling philosophy books from the library. By fourteen, I'd had enough of the confusion, manipulation, and lies, and I officially broke away from the Church (a defining decision for my own life and my relationship with my family). A decade later, I found myself working in the nascent field of science communication.

I met David Silverman for the first time at the American Atheists Convention in Austin, Texas, in 2013. It was an important gathering, celebrating fifty years of advocacy, education, and activism by and for the atheist community. David invited me to come and speak to the attendees. It was an exciting time for me, as I'd given many talks about science, but I'd never spoken to a live audience about my own atheism.

Of course, I'd known of David—from television and print media. I knew he was the president of American Atheists. And I knew him on Twitter as @MrAtheistPants, a fitting handle if there ever was one.

At the time, I was working as the senior science correspondent for a major news outlet, and I supplemented my income with on-air appearances and speaking opportunities about science communication, women in the sciences, and evidence-based thinking. I had spoken frankly on a small number of television and Web programs about my lack of a belief in god, but my atheism still felt personal— a fight within, a worldview that took years of lonely struggle to cultivate and fully own. I didn't understand the depths of the atheist community that existed outside my comfortable life.

David saw me as a contributor to the cause, and he reached out to me. He asked me to speak and I obliged. Just as his story rings familiar to so many people, mine too resonated with my fellow nonbelievers. Perhaps that's why David asked me to write the foreword to *Fighting God*.

I think this book is important for a number of reasons. But in the interest of time and respect for your patience (you came here to read what David has to say, after all), I will focus on two.

First, it will arm you with a vast array of tools—weapons, if it so pleases you—to face the not-so-hospitable world as an out-loud and proud atheist. I wish I'd had these tools available to me as I struggled to come out as a teenager. I wish the firebrand tactics outlined in this book had reached me way back then. A billboard, a television appearance, some way to see that there was a movement out there, and I could be a part of it.

Second, and perhaps most important, *Fighting God* chronicles the how and the why of David's intense hunger for activism and social change. Make no mistake about it—David is an unapologetic atheist. He will make it known to whoever comes within earshot of him, and he will gladly engage in heated debate or even attempt his brand of "de-indoctrination" of dogged theists who dare approach him on the street.

But to be plain, David is *not a dick*. He is thoughtful, kind, and highly moral. But to those who incorrectly presuppose that the "atheist lifestyle" is one of dickish confrontation, David may just deliver on such prejudices. I myself take a fairly different approach. I speak publicly, yes. But I avoid debate with creationists and the like. I find common ground with the agnostics, skeptics, freethinkers, disbelievers, irreligious, and all the other thesaurus-loving, god-questioning people out there. (But we all do have our limits—I suppress an eye roll every time someone describes him- or herself as "spiritual.")

I've found in my personal conversations with many prominent thinkers, such as Sean Carroll, Richard Dawkins, Sam Harris, the late Chris Hitchens, Lawrence Krauss, Bill Maher, Neil deGrasse Tyson, and even Seth MacFarlane, that it takes all types. We nontheists are as varied as any other group of random people, bound together by the single commonality that we *don't* believe in something. We approach our secular lives as differently as our histories will allow us.

I can't speak for everyone when I say this, but I wouldn't be surprised if it was echoed in the sentiments of many strong thinkers both within and beyond the so-called atheist movement: David Silverman has been instrumental in defending the First Amendment rights and civil liberties of nonreligious Americans who would otherwise fall through the cracks of a political system powered by evangelical crusaders, hell-bent on maintaining a moral majority in this country.

You see, David's fight is not his alone. It's important to all of us—even if we choose to go about it in a different way. He may never have met another person from the Third Ward of the Church of Jesus Christ of Latter-day Saints in Plano, Texas, but he has made the path easier for the next young girl who wakes up one day realizing it's all a bunch of bullshit.

—Cara Santa Maria
Science communicator
Television presenter and producer
Host of the *Talk Nerdy* podcast
Los Angeles, California
December 2014

EDITORIAL NOTE

You will see one word a lot in this book, and the way I write it is going to get me into trouble because my style diverges from the style used by other leaders of the atheist movement, including some of my greatest predecessors.

I spell *atheist* with a lowercase *a*—I don't capitalize it (unless it begins a sentence or is part of a proper noun, such as American Atheists). The arguments for capitalizing the word *atheist* come from the idea of demanding equality and include:

- Christians capitalize *Christian,* and Jews capitalize *Jewish,* so why not capitalize *Atheist* and bring ourselves up to their level?
- It's more "firebrandy" to capitalize. "I'm not just an atheist; I'm an Atheist with a capital *A*!"
- We should demand reverence the way Christians do. To make believers capitalize *atheist* would be a feat in and of itself!

But capitalizing *atheist* would be wrong.

Like *theist, atheist* is a common noun. We may not like it, we may *want* it to be a proper noun, but it's not, and as atheists we need to face and accept the truth (after all, that's what we are all about). And while we are at it, *God* (the primary name of the god to whom the Jews and the Christians pray) is a proper noun. Determining whether to use *God* or *god* in a sentence can at times be subjective depending on context, but categorically refusing to capitalize *God* when referring to this particular god is just as incorrect as refusing to capitalize the names of other fictional characters such as Zeus or Cinderella. Names are proper nouns—they get capitalized.

And, no, I won't deliberately misspell *God* as *gawd* or something like that. Madalyn Murray O'Hair used to do that, and, damnit, she was wrong to do so. The god's name is God. It's a stupid name, I know (like calling a dog *Dog* or a child *Child*), but it's a name, that's how it's spelled, and it's a proper noun.

We not only have to do what is right—we have to do what is correct. If we knowingly do that which is incorrect, we live in a space of denial while opening ourselves up to lots of useless (and quite justifiable) criticism. I get criticized enough for doing right—I don't need to compound that by doing something deliberately wrong. Period.

Finally, I should also mention that I support the LGBTQ community and understand that the traditional gender binary does not fit all people, so I use *they/them* instead of third-person singular pronouns when I can. I think that's the right thing to do.

Okay. Let's get started.

FIGHTING
GOD

INTRODUCTION

Once again, abherrant [sic] groups like you and the homosexuals are com-
plaining that you don't have a golden cup and seat at the table. Listen, in
America, you are allowed to exist without persecution. Any other right that
you request is another step towards the hedonistic values that contributed
to the destruction of Sodom and Gomorrah. The closer America gets as a
society to honoring your seat at the table is yet another step towards the
decline of western civilization, and deep down inside you know it. You are
deviants. —AN E-MAIL TO AMERICAN ATHEISTS, SEPTEMBER 2012

An Atheist loves himself and his fellow man instead of a god. An Atheist
thinks that heaven is something for which we should work for now—here
on earth—for all men together to enjoy. An Atheist knows that a hospital
should be built instead of a church. An Atheist knows that a deed must be
done instead of a prayer said. An Atheist strives for involvement in life
and not escape into death. He wants disease conquered, poverty vanquished,
war eliminated. —MADALYN MURRAY O'HAIR

I wish I were wrong.

I wish all the good guys went to heaven, the bad guys somehow justly paid for their crimes, and everyone (especially my daughter) lived forever. Indeed, not a single person on earth wants people to live forever more than I do. I also wish the World Trade Center still stood, hunger was eradicated, and that my mother had lived long enough to see this book published.

But wishing doesn't make it true. We live in the real world, and I make my living telling the truth.

I'm *that* atheist guy—the guy with the atheist shirt and/or jacket and/or baseball cap in the airport or at a street fair. I'm not talking about subtle clothing that someone might pass by and not notice, either. I wear the word ATHEIST in big letters. I cannot be missed, quite by design. I talk to people who ask about what my clothes say (which happens more and more these days), answer their questions as honestly and clearly as possible, and sometimes even have on-the-spot debates. I'm a walking, talking atheist billboard. I love being "that guy" (you should try it).

I'm also "that atheist guy on TV," often Fox News, who espouses such horrible concepts as religious equality and separation of religion and government (same thing), usually to a talking head or audience that simply does not understand the concept and tries to trip me up rather than actually consider that I might be right.

Some call me a militant atheist. Others call me a dick. I am neither. A militant atheist, like a militant Muslim, Jew, or Christian, would be someone who uses, threatens, or promotes violence; there is nothing violent in anything I do or endorse. A *dick* would be someone who makes people angry for the sake of making people angry. I have much better reasons.

I promote no harm, violence, or vandalism, opting instead to fight for equality of all people through truth and honesty. I think that makes me That Pretty Good Guy Who Gets Called a Dick So Often He Gets Angry and Writes a Book About It. (My publisher thought such a title might be a bit too long for the cover, though.)

I've been a walking, talking atheist billboard for nearly twenty years. I have had many conversations with strangers about atheism, as you would expect, and as I intend. In the early years, most of my on-the-street conversations were confrontational and somewhat less than civil. I've received more than my fair share of the stereotypical "You're going to hell" comments, usually delivered in a hit-and-run style, whereby people deliver their "good news" that I will be spending eternity being tortured and then run away before I can continue the conversation.

However, in more recent years, I've begun receiving more and more positive comments, and the negativity I once received—in every airport, in every city—has fallen silent. Indeed, the hostility that I used to encounter nearly every time I stepped out the door never occurs anymore.

Why?

Because we are *winning.*

In this enduring battle for freedom from the Lie of God (a phrase I use to describe all deities and the lies, empty promises, and threats that surround them), we are finally winning, mainly because, thanks to the Internet, we are finally capable of trying. We, the atheists of America, are on the cusp of achieving equality. We have no money compared to religion. We have no power compared to religion. Yet our numbers are growing while theirs are shrinking, because it's not just about money or power, but about truth. Truth beats money and power, and when it comes to religion, atheists have a monopoly on truth.

Atheists like me are what I call *conclusionary.* We have concluded that gods are myths because we've seen sufficient evidence and heard or read sufficient arguments to convince us there are no gods. But this is not stubbornness. If any god, anywhere, were proven real even once, I would convert, quit my job, and donate all the proceeds of this book to that correct god's religion. Of course, that has never happened, and there is no reason to expect that it will. I am convinced this mentality holds true for almost all atheists everywhere— if there were any proof of any god, there would be practically no atheists anywhere. I search for truth, not just confirmation of preferred belief.

But religion is not just incorrect, it is malevolent. It ruins lives, splits families, and justifies hatred and bigotry, all while claiming to be *the* source of morality. People die and suffer needlessly because of religion; such a waste.

As the late Christopher Hitchens said, "Religion poisons everything," and that seems almost literal when we are talking about the minds it infects. It makes good people do bad things while thinking they are doing good—effectively turning good people into bad people, at least sometimes. Religion deserves to die.

Some (too many?) people call me a dick because I challenge the absurd notion that religion deserves respect by default. But religion is wrong for demanding respect simply for being, and even more wrong for demanding never to be questioned. Indeed, it is my duty as an American, as an atheist, and as a nice person to do what I can to take religion down—not by force, not by law, but by truth.

And the truth is quite simple: all religions are lies, and all believers are victims.

Chapter 1

ATHEIST, KNOW THYSELF

If you say, I'm for equal pay, that's a reform. But if you say, I'm a feminist, that's a transformation of society. —GLORIA STEINEM

Fuck you, you're an atheist. —PENN JILLETTE

It's an unfortunate situation. Even some major sources of information give the wrong—or at least an imperfect—definition of the word *atheist:*

1. Merriam-Webster defines an atheist as "a person who believes that God does not exist."[1] *Wrong.*
2. *The Free Dictionary* describes an atheist as a person who "absolutely denies" the existence of God or any other gods.[2] *Nope.*

How do we win a battle with words when the words we use are wrong? How do we organize atheists when most of the atheists don't even know they *are* atheists because they've been given wrong information?

The Oxford English Dictionary, thankfully, gets it right: an atheist is "a person who disbelieves *or lacks belief* in the existence of God or gods"[3] (emphasis mine).

So we begin this book with three different reliable sources, giving

three different definitions for *atheist*—how do we know which is correct? There is a big difference between "lacks belief" and "absolutely
denies," so we need to look at the word and see its etymology for
support. As stated perfectly at defineatheism.com: "Absence (rather
than opposition) is indicated by the 'a-' prefix, meaning 'without,'
hence 'atheism' can be concisely characterized as 'without theism.'"[4]

Theism is consistently defined as "belief in the existence of a god
or gods,"[5] so *atheism* is therefore "the absence of belief in the existence of a god or gods," which makes it a broad term that has many
implications, not just absolute denial. Atheism is *without* that belief,
not *against* it. Got it?

Let me clarify this point with some helpful tips for determining
if you're an atheist. For this list, *literal god* means a living, thinking,
supernatural being, as opposed to a metaphor such as "god is love"
or "god is the universe":

- If you don't have a belief in any literal god(s), i.e., are without
  theism, you're an atheist.
- If you don't have a belief in any literal god(s) but aren't *sure*
  none exist, you're an atheist.
- If you don't have a belief in any literal god(s) but rather think
  God is a metaphor for love, all humanity, etc., you're an atheist.
- If you don't have a belief in any literal god(s) *because* you think
  the universe is unknowable and we can never know all the answers, you're an atheist (and an agnostic, see below).
- If you don't have a belief in any literal god(s) and you feel you're
  educated enough to think you can say definitively there are
  no god(s), you're an atheist (a conclusionary atheist like me).
- If you don't have a belief in any literal god(s) but you like/
  follow some religious traditions (Jewish, Muslim, Hindu, or
  whatever) in which you were raised and maybe even agree
  with some of the religion's nonsupernatural teachings (e.g.,
  "Love thy neighbor"), you're an atheist.

- If you don't have a belief in any literal god(s), but you *wish* there were a god and maybe still hold out hope for one to show up, you're an atheist (hoping and wishing are not believing).
- If you don't have a belief in any literal god(s), but you consider yourself "on the fence," you're an atheist (until you believe, you're not a theist, and, no, there is no middle ground—you have a belief that a god exists or you don't).
- If you don't have a belief in any literal god(s), but you "like to think" there is a god, because the story is good and wouldn't it be nice if it was true, you're an atheist (and you're literally proclaiming belief in something you know is a fantasy).
- If you don't have any belief in any literal god(s), but you absolutely hate the word *atheist*—tough shit, you're still an atheist.

Is that clear enough? If I've just called you an atheist and you're unhappy about it, don't worry—it's good—you're right! Keep reading!

In one of his most brilliant books, *The God Delusion,* Richard Dawkins describes the categories "weak agnosticism," "strong agnosticism," "weak atheism," and "strong atheism" as different extremes of disbelief along a continuum. I disagree with this definition. Almost all "agnostics" are atheists, and almost all atheists are agnostics, and I strongly feel that this distinction must be properly understood.

Atheist is the broadest term and, again, means only "the absence of a belief in a god or gods." The reasons for the lack of belief, and the convictions behind the reasons, are irrelevant to the term's definition. Agnostics, Secular/Humanistic Jews, Secular Humanists, Brights, some Buddhists, some Hindus, and all "apatheists" are atheists.

Some might counter my assertion by saying that dictionary definitions are not always the way words are used in the English language. They will say that language is ever evolving, and "words have usage, not meaning," and that relying on etymology for a word's definition is fallacious[6]. They will assert that correcting people who use the words incorrectly is fighting an unnecessary, uphill battle.

In this case I disagree. This word confusion is detrimental to our cause and our freedom. It impedes communication such that nobody knows what anyone else is talking about, and this leads to the ignorance of the general population to the detriment of a minority—us. I assert it is necessary to clear up and reaffirm the correct usage of *atheist* and to not let society, which is heavily influenced by those who want the label confusion to persist, redefine us to make us look smaller and therefore less important than we are. Comparing the etymology of the word with the broad list of conflicting definitions (including current use) to determine which is most correct is a perfectly logical way to do so.

Skeptics are atheists, at least the good ones (see Fig. 1), because skepticism applied to religion invariably yields atheism. As a result, the amount of overlap between skepticism and atheism is quite large (larger than what the graphic depicts), but a sliver of atheists are not skeptical (homeopaths and such), and a sliver of "skeptics" will turn their nose up at homeopathy and Bigfoot, but consider the invisible

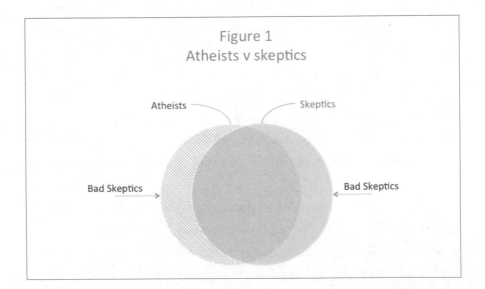

Figure 1
Atheists v skeptics

Atheists   Skeptics

Bad Skeptics   Bad Skeptics

man in the sky a reasonable possibility. The graphic says both slivers are "bad skeptics," but frankly, I wonder if we could call either side skeptical. You can be a skeptic, and you can be a theist, but if you're both, you're bad at skepticism.

Now, some atheists don't like the A-word. They feel it has a negative connotation—indeed, that it is a negative word—so they prefer to use a different descriptor. So silly—is *independent* a negative word? *Unencumbered? Unchained? Atheism* is a positive word—it is *theism* that is negative! Additionally, wishing something to be true doesn't make it so, and changing the descriptor of a thing doesn't change the thing itself. If you do not have an active belief in a god, you're an atheist, and all atheists by any name need to accept that reality. Any other word is sugarcoating at best and an outright lie at worst.

A well-regarded atheist who calls himself a humanist (Humanism is an atheistic lifestance that stresses progressive values and the betterment of humankind) once got angry in a discussion with me on this subject. He told me, "I'm not about what I am *not;* I like to tell people what I *am,*" and behaved as if there was some kind of wisdom behind that statement. I asserted that he was just avoiding the question in a theist-approved way so as not to antagonize the religious majority. Doing so is being nice to the bigots because they've convinced you it's right to do so. It is *avoiding* the truth, not *telling* the truth.

Religion is about belief in a god, not a general philosophy on how we humans should behave or treat each other. If I ask vegetarians what meat they eat, they say, "None." They wouldn't answer that question with "I like lasagna" because that's not what I asked. The question of "Well, if you don't eat meat, what *do* you eat?" may or may not be a follow-up, but it's not the question *at hand.* Similarly, the atheist's answer to the question "Do you believe in god?" is not "I believe in treating all humans well." It's "No." The answer to "What is your religion?" is "None—I'm an atheist."

Identifying as an atheist, as opposed to some other descriptor, is a very important form of activism, in part because it helps those who cannot come out. Atheists who are unable to identify as such are inhibited by the bigotry we all understand, for any number of reasons, and bigotry is based on ignorance. Using *atheist* lets you fight bigotry by associating the word with a face, possibly for the first time (depending on the listener). This promotes an awareness and humanization of atheists, which attacks the church-taught bigotry that keeps others in the closet head-on. So, by specifically using *atheist* as an identifier, you educate the public about atheism, attacking bigotry one listener at a time.

Why not use those other words? Simple—very few people understand them. According to a 2014 quantitative study performed for Openly Secular, most people have no idea what all those euphemisms for atheist (they may have different dictionary definitions, but they are used by atheists as synonyms/substitutes for *atheist*) mean. As you can see in Figure 2, while more than eighty percent of Americans essentially know what an atheist is, less than half of Americans know what *agnostic* means, less than 30 percent understand what it means to be secular, and, as you can see, very few Americans know what

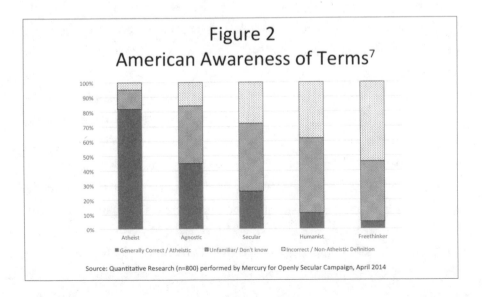

Figure 2
American Awareness of Terms[7]

Legend: ■ Generally Correct / Atheistic   ▨ Unfamiliar/ Don't know   ▨ Incorrect / Non-Atheistic Definition

Categories: Atheist, Agnostic, Secular, Humanist, Freethinker

Source: Quantitative Research (n=800) performed by Mercury for Openly Secular Campaign, April 2014

Humanists and freethinkers (a person who forms their opinions on the basis of reason[8]) are.

Where is the teaching in using these euphemisms? How do they help closeted nonbelievers? If you are asked about your religion and you answer with a term that, while technically correct, has a very high likelihood of being misunderstood, how is that telling the truth?

How is that even honest?

Agnostic is a useless term when used as a religious identifier. It states that gods, the finite details of the universe, etc., are simply unknowable, which as you may notice is not an expression of belief or disbelief, but rather of knowledge. This is a totally useless concept because anyone can say that about everything. We don't know with 100 percent certainty that Santa Claus isn't up there at the North Pole (maybe he's just really good at hiding), or that we aren't part of someone's dream or a computer simulation. Since we don't know everything, agnosticism would tell us we can never use the word *know* at all, since it implies a complete understanding of the universe. This confuses the word *know,* which means "to perceive or understand as fact or truth; to apprehend clearly and with certainty."[9] *Know* does not imply perfect knowledge. I *know* there is no god just as surely as I *know* there is no Santa Claus, of which I am quite certain even though I've never been to the North Pole personally. Again, when Santa lands on my roof, I will believe. Until there is proof, Santa, like God, is a myth.

I am reminded of *The Matrix,* in which we find that all life is a dream, fed into our brains by sentient machines. Since we don't know everything in the universe and cannot mathematically prove the movie false, do we consider the hypothesis put forth in the movie to be viable enough to hedge our bets? Is *The Matrix probably* fiction? But even if I brought Keanu Reeves to your home and he personally told you it was just fiction, even if I brought the scriptwriters to tell you that they had indeed made the whole thing up, this would not prove the movie false with 100 percent certainty. Still, nobody would say they were only "pretty sure" *The Matrix* was fiction, but they couldn't commit to saying it for sure "because no one knows everything in the universe."

Why is God different from other fiction? The odds that a god exists may not be absolute zero, but in the words of British philosopher A. C. Grayling, the possibility is "vanishingly small,"[10] just as it is with unicorns and *The Matrix*. Being a former math geek, I think of it in calculus terms: "the limit as god approaches zero," which is, well, vanishingly close to zero.

Yet religion gets a waiver and is not subjected to the same standards as other fiction. It has no basis in fact (like fiction), cannot hold up to logic (like fiction), yet still earns a "probably not" by way of too many of us.

But again—*probably not* is just another segment of atheism. The word *agnostic* is used by atheists to soften the blow felt by people who don't like atheists (and thereby lessen the anticipated blowback from them). Therefore, atheists who call themselves agnostics use a euphemism to be nice to the people who aren't nice to us. Atheophobes (people who fear/dislike atheists and/or atheism) aren't all bad people— they are just ignorant victims, and they need help. Again, when an atheist uses a label such as *agnostic* or *humanist,* an opportunity to teach is averted, and the atheophobe walks away thinking, "What a nice person. At least they're not an atheist."

Now, consider Christianity. If you walk up to Baptists and ask what their religion is, you'd get one word: *Christian*. If you ask a Methodist, you get *Christian*. Ask a Seventh-day Adventist, you get *Christian*. Now try the other side. Despite that so many people are atheists, few people use the word, even when they know it is accurate. Some atheists will call themselves any of a breadth of descriptors just to avoid *atheist*. Some so-called secular Jews will call atheist, as described by Openly Secular. But as *secular* usually refers to a government or a school, as opposed to a person, *secular person* often gets used as a synonym for *secularist*—a person, religious or not, who supports a secular government.[12] This one word has two very different but confusable definitions.

Unfortunately, but predictably, during *Openly Secular Day* (April 23, 2015, on which the organization encouraged people to come out as "secular people") much of the discussion was about what *secular* meant, not about coming out as a nonbeliever. My Twitter feed was filled with messages including "I'm a Christian and I'm secular!" and "secular =/= Atheist." Even popular blogger (and friend) JT Eberhard wrote "*Religious people can be openly secular. Being secular doesn't mean you're an atheist. Just look at Barry Lynn or Rebecca Florence Miller.*"[13] unaware that his definition for *secular* (secularists) conflicted with the definition given by Openly Secular (atheists).

The intent of Openly Secular Day was to urge people to come out as *secular people* (atheists), but the confusion around the term got in the way of that objective and diverted the conversation. How much more impactful would the event have been if they'd used a word most people understood? What would the conversation on Openly Secular Day have looked like if it was "Openly Atheist Day"? *Secular* may have "better connotations" than *atheist*, but at least people know what you're saying! Campaigns and publicity stunts conducted using euphemisms, like Openly Secular Day, cannot be efficiently effective for the atheist movement if most people don't know that the euphemism means *atheist*.

Yes, some people may have a negative reaction to the word *atheist*, but you can mitigate that reaction for the next atheist by making someone new familiar with it. Your willingness to be the first to introduce yourself as an atheist will make it easier for all the other atheists this person will go on to meet (assuming you make a posi-

themselves *Jews* when asked about their religion, even though it means
the exact opposite of the truth!

So Christians unite themselves despite real differences in theology, while we atheists will go out of our way to divide ourselves by
using different words, despite the fact that we are all the same, religiously. As a result, polls measuring the numbers of Christians and
atheists in the United States show Christianity at 70 percent plus and
atheism in the 2–5 percent range, leaving a huge number of atheists
categorized as *agnostic, secular, none,* or, even worse, Jewish, Muslim, or
Christian. It's not difficult to see how we are perpetuating the myth
that we don't exist in large numbers, because most of us claim to be
something else!

For another example of why it's important to use a word that is clearly
understood, let's take a quick look at my friends at Openly Secular,
who graciously supplied the data above based on research they com-
missioned to find the best euphemism/word choice for *atheist.* They
chose *secular,* even though 70 percent didn't know that the word
secular, in this context, meant *atheist.* They clarified themselves on their
Web page (www.openlysecular.org):

"*The mission of Openly Secular is to eliminate discrimination and increase acceptance by getting secular people—including atheists, freethinkers,
agnostics, humanists and nonreligious people—to be open about their beliefs.*"

Todd Stiefel, Chair of Openly Secular commented for this book:
"*We picked SECULAR specifically because it was a word that could serve
as an umbrella over a wide-swath of self-identities. It simply means 'nonreligious' which applies to a huge group of the nones (pronounced like 'nuns,'
who self-classify as 'none/no religion'), from atheists to those who
simply say 'I am not religious.'*"

The thing is, less than 30 percent of those surveyed understood
the definition of *secular. Secular* refers to things that are separate from
religion,[11] so a *secular person* would be a *person without religion,* aka, an

tive impression, which you should strive to do). Calling yourself an atheist is both activism and Humanism.

I am convinced that euphemisms only have "better connotations" *because* they are not clearly understood to be atheistic—those more "acceptable" terms are only so because people don't know they mean/include atheism. The data shown in Figure 3 supports my assertion (until awareness gets very low). So it appears that it is *atheism*, not the word *atheist*, that is the problem with all these terms.

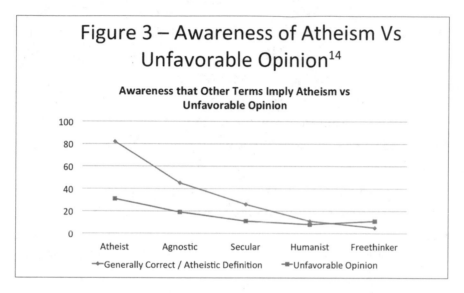

Figure 3 – Awareness of Atheism Vs Unfavorable Opinion[14]

Using *atheist* will prompt questions much more often than will using the sugarcoated terms, as people know what an atheist is and will likely ask follow-up questions, opening the door to real conversation. You will get more opportunity to talk about your ethics and positions if you use the word that prompts questions—*atheist*—than by using a word that confuses the listener, who is therefore more likely to act defensively, walk away, or change the subject. So euphemisms not only give the wrong impression and rob you of a chance to educate, they also stifle your ability to talk about your ethics and agenda by confusing the person to whom you are speaking.

Hiding behind other labels is yielding to bigotry. When atheists use identifiers such as *humanist, freethinker, or secular,* they are effectively saying very little because, again, nearly nobody knows what those words mean (unless they are clarifying themselves by compounding the words like *"I'm an atheist and a Humanist"*). The bigotry goes unchallenged, the teaching opportunity is missed, and the lie that atheists are rare persists. But it's easy, so a lot of people do it, which in my opinion is wrong on many levels.

Another term I'd like to address is one I no longer use: *antitheist*. When I used it, it was meant to deliver the message that I was not only *without* theism, but *against* it. The problem is, like other terms, the listeners don't always get the point because the definition of the word is vague—is an *antitheist* against *theism* or against *theists*? That's a big difference, and the same word describes both positions. I am vehemently against theism, but as you will see in this book, I am not at all against theistic people (I'm actually fighting *for* them). Furthermore, since *antitheist* is also not a position on belief in gods, but rather an attitude toward religion, it does not answer "What is your religion?"—much like the word *Humanist*. *Atheist* is the correct word to use, and I recommend people dump *antitheist* as an identifier, lest you be judged incorrectly.

I also need to define *religion*. For the purpose of this book, religion is *theistic only*. That is, I use the definition on Merriam-Webster.com: "the belief in a god or in a group of gods," with a second definition of "an organized system of beliefs, ceremonies, and rules used to worship a god or a group of gods."[15] Both definitions include the word *god*, which means religion is theistic by definition, so we can envision a solid black line separating atheism and religion—the two never go together.

I should address two counters to this definition:

- There are "secular religions," such as the Humanistic Jews, and they practice all the other trappings of religion, call themselves religions, and the IRS classifies them as religions. I maintain these are *not* religions, but rather secular clubs masquerading as religions. While I have no major problem with secular clubs that look like religions (except for the fact that they legitimize real religion by making it look more prevalent), religions have gods. No god, no religion.

- I summarily dismiss the vaguer definitions of *religion* such as "a cause, principle, or activity pursued with zeal or conscientious devotion" because, well, they're stupid. Not only could atheism be applied to this definition, but so could baseball, politics, thumb-twiddling, or any other activity you could imagine. This definition is so broad as to be meaningless. All the meaningful definitions of the word *religion* include a deity.

Religion is much more than a holy book. Rather it is the interpretation of that book, which is individual yet heavily influenced by the society and the environment (on a micro and macro level), which is itself often heavily influenced by the religion. People created religion, which then evolved (as memes do) into different sects, each of which adapted in ways that benefited that sect (often by benefiting the religious leaders at the time). These sects can be as small as one family and as large as Catholicism, but sects continually evolve and spin off one another, vary wildly from one another, and impact their followers to varying degrees.

We are not born with clean slates, but rather with genetic leanings to be more or less religious,[16] and these are nurtured or squelched to some degree by our religious surroundings. People with logical inclinations are more able to see through the religion into which they were born, but whether they will fully succeed depends on a number of circumstances, including the degree of the brainwashing. For the most part, people are born into religion, absorb it, protect it (even if it is to their own detriment), and breed. Bad sects make more bad people—that is, they turn people who might have been good into bad people—because the brainwashing is so thick that most skeptical tendencies are squelched.

At the same time, the local sects themselves evolve (if permitted to do so by their surroundings) as the religious leaders further enhance the religion's ability to grow and thrive (and benefit the religious leaders). All of this cycles back on the individuals living in a local cyclical evolution, passing along to the next generation adapted rules and memes, which further increase the likelihood of adherence. Individuals make choices and are rightly held responsible for their actions, but the religion cycle is a heavy influence on the way humans think and the choices they make.

So when we talk about religion and how to defeat it, we must remember the *cycle* of indoctrination, which leads to brainwashed people who breed children who are also indoctrinated, all while their religious sect continues to try to increase its power over the minds of the followers. When I refer to the *religion cycle,* I include these broad, long-term societal pressures religion creates, and which created it.

I am a *conclusionary* atheist (some use the term *hard atheist* or *strong atheist*). That is, I have read, thought, and studied enough to satisfy myself that there is no god, all gods are imaginary, and actively believing in a god is silly. I have concluded all religion is a scam. If a god shows itself, or if Santa Claus lands on my roof, I will rethink my worldview, but until then, fiction is fiction.

Nonconclusionary atheists are *still* atheists, but for some reason have not yet concluded gods are false with enough conviction to say so. Some use the term *weak atheists,* but I think that's a terrible term, as *weak* has obvious negative connotations and therefore incites those in this category to choose euphemisms. There is nothing inherently weak or soft in nonconclusionism, just lack of conviction, for any number of reasons. Nonconclusionary atheists have no active belief in a god, so they are atheists, but they are not quite of the same definitive mind-set as the conclusionists, and some try to avoid being called *atheists* even though it is still an accurate descriptor. As a result, atheism is often incorrectly defined as conclusionary by default, when, again, in reality it is far broader a term (see Fig. 4).

Despite their personal convictions, even some conclusionary atheists avoid using the A-word because they are conciliatory (often referred to as *diplomats*)—they find it confrontational just to use the word. They have been convinced by society that using the word, however accurate, is offensive to theists or somehow bad—so they deny what their intellect tells them in order to avoid confrontation or stigma. They need to cut that out.

Figure 4
Types of Atheists

Words Atheists Use

	Nonconclusionary	Conclusionary
Confrontational (Firebrands)	Has no belief in a god and will often emphatically call themselves agnostic or skeptic, and often get angry when confronted with the fact that they too are atheists (too bad). Look for phrases like "We are all agnostic."	Knows there is no god, knows "hedging" is unnecessary and counterproductive. Knows the truth can hurt as it helps. Uses the word *atheist*, damnit!
Conciliatory (Diplomats)	Has no belief in a god but often uses the religion in which they were raised to self-identify, possibly with modifiers (Recovering Catholic, etc). I suspect these are most likely to be closeted.	Knows there is no god, but believes in going along to get along. Uses any theist-approved euphemism for *atheist* and has excuses for using those other words (e.g., "I am more than just an atheist, I'm a naturalistic rationalist!").

All this not-an-atheist crap is designed to deliver false information—to soften the blow and make us look weaker and smaller.

Think about it: we enable bigotry by declining to face it head-on, instead feeding the bigotry against us by using confusing words that misrepresent ourselves—all to make those who are bigoted *against* us feel better.

Atheists avoiding the word *atheist* strengthen theism and weaken atheism. There's no way around that fact.

Calling yourself an atheist is activism. Calling yourself an atheist is humanistic. And, if you don't have an active belief in a god, regardless of reason or circumstance, calling yourself an atheist is truthful. *Atheist* is also, by far, the most understood term, making it the most efficient and strategic word to use as a tool against bigotry. People know what it means, so ignorance is challenged immediately by your smiling face.

Atheist. It's a good word. Embrace it.

Chapter 2

THE WAR HAS ALREADY BEGUN, AND WE ARE ETHICALLY OBLIGATED TO FIGHT

"I am driven with a mission from God. God would tell me, 'George go and fight these terrorists in Afghanistan.' And I did. And then God would tell me 'George, go and end the tyranny in Iraq.' And I did."
                                            —PRESIDENT GEORGE W BUSH[1]

"Does faith matter? Absolutely. . . . How can you have judgment if you have no faith? How can I trust you with power if you don't pray? . . . [T]he notion that you are endowed by your creator sets a certain boundary of what we mean by America."
                                            —NEWT GINGRICH[2]

Edwin Kagin, my late friend and former legal director of American Atheists, wrote in his book, *Baubles of Blasphemy,*[3] about what he called "the American Religious Civil War." He opined that the Religious Right has started a war we must fight in order to retain our religious freedom. Edwin was often right and this case is no exception. We are in a war right now, but like many religious wars, it's really a war against religious leaders and their followers, all of whom are either liars or victims.

Not all religious folk are involved, nor do they all support what the religious leaders are doing (*leaders* being a relative term). Many religious people understand the basics of the separation of religion and government, why that is imperative for freedom to exist, and why the attempt to destroy it is destined to fail in the long term, despite short-term successes by the Religious Right (as in the 2014 midterm election). Such people are typically nice, common, and way too quiet (and brainwashed into being so).

Atheists are way too quiet as well. Throughout the country, the vast majority of atheists are either closeted or silent, waiting for this thing, this seemingly inevitable conflict between the followers of Fox News and the haters of Fox News (many of whom also watch Fox News just to have something to hate), to happen *around* them. However, by remaining on the sidelines, they are helping to extend the war or even lose it. If you're one of those too-quiet atheists, I hope this book motivates you to make some noise.

Such motivation might come by way of some facts. I like facts. So please consider the following:

- In November of 2014, the Texas State Board of Education made changes to its curriculum and, in a brazen act of dishonesty, changed its textbooks to include statements that imply Moses, the fictional character from the Bible, was instrumental in the founding of America, influencing the writing of the Constitution, and providing the foundation for democracy.[4] These textbooks are used nationwide in public schools, so it's a good possibility that your public school system will soon be teaching our children revisionist, pro-religion lies in an attempt to legitimize religion and Christian privilege on a massive scale.

- President George W. Bush stopped stem-cell research almost entirely by placing heavy restrictions on the use of stem cells,[5] until a new, more enlightened president took over and fixed it. (Thanks, Obama.) This delayed the most promising research on Parkinson's disease, Alzheimer's disease, and many kinds of cancer. In one fell swoop, Bush prolonged delayed treatments for these ailments, reducing the life expectancy and the quality of life for all Americans, while giving a great competitive opportunity to scientists in other countries to catch up and possibly surpass America in its research (and jeopardizing our patent domination). Why? The pope said so, preachers joined in, and so President Bush jumped and obeyed. If you or someone you love has one of those diseases, someone else's religion has reduced their chance of being helped before it's too late. You, as a citizen of the planet, have suffered a Dark Ages–style delay on treatments that may have significantly increased your life span and its quality. Nobody called the president on it, and people *still* think Christianity is "pro-life."

- Abortion, Marriage Equality, and Death with Dignity are great examples of issues where religious laws invade our everyday lives. These attacks against our very ownership of and authority over our bodies are almost entirely religiously motivated, yet these laws are secular, affecting all of us. Some old man in a collar says his god wants you to obey his laws, and we as a country acquiesce (*theocracy:* "government ruled by or subject to religious authority"[6]).

I'm not writing a whole book on this, but I could. There are many more instances in which other people's religions affect your life with the help of our government, all while claiming it's about secular morality. It's not. It's about religion using the force of law to make nonadherents obey its preachers. It's been going on since the Dark Ages globally, and in America since it was founded, and it's the essence of the war we are fighting.

Many times I am asked why I do what I do with such fervency. Here's why:

- Because religion invades our lives, our wallets, our schools, and our government.
- Because we elect leaders who talk to their gods and, as a result of this "guidance," enact unjust policies at best and, at worst, send this country to war.
- Because even though we atheists are more populous in America than Jews, Hindus, Buddhists, and Muslims combined, we have no representation in Congress due to deeply held bigotry, and because this bigotry is promoted by our government via religious politicians.
- Because every penny we spend lies about us, insulting us (you bet it's an insult) with the accusation that we believe and, indeed, *trust in God.*
- Because our taxes are higher while the churches and synagogues and mosques pay far less than they should, sometimes nothing at all, just because "it's always been that way." We private citizens and small businesses have to pony up extra to compensate for these institutions, even if these same institutions preach lies and spread false information about *us.*
- Because *every* child of *every* religious background in *every* public school in America is reminded *every* day that their country voluntarily subordinates itself to the same god referenced on the money, and if they don't agree, they are a minority. *Every day.* And then, religion tells us that it's above criticism. It says it's offensive for us to claim our equality. Sure, religion sometimes allows debate within certain limits—but it always demands respect, claiming to deserve respect by default.

I do not respect religion. I abhor it. It does nobody any favors to treat the unrespectable with respect. Refusing to respect religion shocks the religious into realizing that serious criticism is allowed and can indeed be beneficial to everyone. Hearing someone call religion a myth, or addressing a preacher by his first name, or asserting that Jesus is an obvious rip-off of earlier gods, may even get some in the flock to think about their religion critically for the first time. We as atheists do no good for ourselves or for others by hiding in the closet.

I'm reminded of a Muslim friend of mine who once told me he respected my position on religion because it made sense and relied on logic. He admired my leadership in my cause. I thanked him. But then, he asked me to say I respected his religious beliefs in kind, in an obvious attempt to get an "I respect your religion too" statement from his atheist friend. He didn't get what he wanted—I said no. I told him that while I thought *he* was a nice guy and I respected *him* as a person, his religious beliefs were ridiculous and I did not respect *them*. He frowned and walked away.

Did I do right? I could easily have said, "Yes, I respect your beliefs," and we would have had a mutual love-in, and my friend would have left the conversation happier. But I would have been lying. Worse yet, I would have been hurting him by reinforcing his poison—religion ("Even the atheists respect my religion"). Even worse yet, I would have done it for selfish reasons—escaping a mildly uncomfortable situation in favor of a happier one (going along to get along).

But theists need and deserve conflict. They need to hear that their religion is not equal to atheism, *it is far beneath it.* They need to hear that they are *not* their religion (which is the opposite of what so many are taught as a child), and that their religion is crap. Lying to theists about the relevance and legitimacy of their religion does them no favors—it hurts them in subtle but profound ways, and it is our moral obligation not to do it. Firebrand atheism is harder on us and better for them—*that is what makes it humanistic.*

Others might assert that some religious people *need* their religion, that without the Lie of God some theists would collapse and be somehow unable to function. To this I have two responses:

1. Nobody *needs* religion. We know this because the country has many millions of atheists, and we have no need for religion. Atheists are human beings living perfectly fine lives without religion, so there's solid evidence humanity can survive (and thrive) without religion. It's fair to say those who assert they need religion don't really *need* it, they just *think* they need it, or *want to need it*—sometimes very badly. Religionists have a perceived need, planted there as a part of the brainwashing they've received. They need no religion, but they think they do, because religion has convinced them of it.

2. What would you say to your mom if she said she'd collapse and be somehow unable to function if not for her psychic, tarot-card reader, or astrologer? Would you take that seriously? If not, why exactly not? Many atheists still place religion on a pedestal by asserting that religion is somehow more important or serves a need greater than other "woo." Don't do that. You know religion is equal to other myths and scams, and you'd likely object if Mom was being scammed by an psychic, even if she said she *needed* the psychic, but you're okay with her thinking she needs religion and pays dearly for it? Is that a symptom of your own indoctrination?

I know this tastes bad. I get that it feels "religiony" to vocally support or preach atheism. Religion pushes itself for its own good. I'm saying we need to push atheism—to at least some extent—for the good of the theists. They need and deserve our help to be free of the bullshit that clouds their judgment. I'm not saying we need to go knocking on doors, but I am saying that preaching atheism has an unmistakable ethical component that we cannot simply ignore because we don't like how it tastes.

In the stereotypical example, if I knocked on my neighbor's door on Sunday morning, got invited in to talk about atheism, and then systematically led that family away from religion, you couldn't deny that good had been done. We need to own that. We need to own that preaching atheism has at least some component of good. We need to admit to ourselves that "live and let live" might not be a perfect solution, or at least not a perfectly ethical one.

Whether it's macro-level activism or one-on-one deconversion, I find it disturbing when people tell me we atheists are acting as if atheism were a religion. Religion preaches, but not all that preaches is religion. Politicians, unions, civil rights advocates, tax-reform advocates, pro- and anti-gun-rights advocates, and promoters of every kind also preach their agendas with fervency. That person knocking on your door Sunday morning may be a Jehovah's Witness or Greenpeace volunteer. However, it is unavoidable, and perhaps understandable, that when we talk about atheists pushing atheism, we get comparisons to religion—a phenomenon that does not occur in any of the other instances where positions are pushed.

It's total bullshit. Raising a fist and a voice, taking a firm stance for honesty, and pressing hard for equality is *not* religion any more than helping to free someone from the scam of astrology makes you an astrologer. The difference between what we are pushing and what they are pushing is stark—everything we say is consistent with everything we know; and everything the theists push goes *against* everything we know. That's how we know we are right and they are wrong. To attempt to equate the two reveals the pedestal on which religion sits, as this lame excuse for opposing activism only occurs when such activism opposes religion (nobody ever says, "Gee, you look like a religion when you promote the environment—you shouldn't do that"). And what it accomplishes—atheists protecting religion from criticism by telling other atheists not to be active because atheism looks too much like religion when we do—is exactly what religion wants, because it is only religion that benefits from bullshit like this.

Religion does not own activism. If atheists remain passive, religion will win because its members will be the only ones who are active.

While demanding respect, religion also demands privilege it does not deserve. Religion has a lot of privilege in America, while ironically claiming to be the victim of persecution. But striving for religious equality isn't persecution, it's the American Way. Consider the following objectives:

- An America where the government does not actually help religion, or atheism, at all.
- An America where politicians don't preach and neither does the money.
- An America where doctors and patients make medical decisions all by themselves.
- A larger tax refund and a smaller national debt, because every church pays its fair share in taxes.
- An America where real scientists practice real science without regard for the opinions of people who actively want the unknown to remain unknown.
- History books clear of revisionist history, science books without warning stickers, and all students feeling like an equal, no matter what their religious views might be.
- Loving adults adopting kids without hardship or hard times because of the sex or gender expression of the people they love.
- Atheists being elected to office, and theistic politicians courting our vote, because we are an accepted, normal part of society.
- *E pluribus unum,* One Nation Indivisible, and United We Stand.
- Everyone being equal—*really* equal—even those who don't believe in gods.

That's what a separation of religion and government means, and *that is our big-picture goal—the removal of unearned, unwarranted, and un-American religious privilege from our society, starting with our government.*

If religion has its way, we will never have a true separation of religion and government because in that situation religion would be relegated to *just* being religion. The religious would gather, sing, pray, and have all the rights they should have. However, without the perks and legitimization from the government, religion would dramatically shrink because its message alone is so weak.

Religions know this—it's not news, and this is why it would be near suicide for religion to stay out of politics. To abandon politics is to abandon the protectors of its huge tax advantages, so it behooves religion to stay in politics, and it does that by staying influential, pushing theocratic bills, and wielding its flocks to support them and the politicians who work with it. This is why we can't just fight specific issues, legal battle after battle—they will never cease because religion cannot *ever* cease. For us to protect our own rights as atheists, we must take aim at the source. We must fight religion, and we must win.

Now, I am talking here about fighting *religion*, not *religious people*. Remember, our main adversary is not the believers, but the cycle of religious indoctrination that, for lack of a better word, infects them. The believers are mostly nice people who are just victims of the cold and calculated brainwashing they've received since birth (as my own mother unwittingly and unsuccessfully attempted to do to me).

There are two kinds of preachers: victims and liars. The victims have been indoctrinated into religion, and though they may be intelligent, they truly believe the man in the sky personally wants them to preach whatever word they're preaching. I pity the believing preacher, as I pity all believers. The liars aren't really theists at all— they are just atheists faking their way through their jobs for money or power (the whole point of religion in the first place) or because they once were victims of indoctrination and now, after realizing their gods are false, are trapped in a job in which they lie for a living. I pity them more.

Many atheists count themselves as believers, attend services, and say the words they know are lies, for a variety of reasons—family pressure, societal oppression, politics, etc. They, like their preacher counterparts, are trapped in the church.

One wonders how many atheists are preaching religion to atheists.

All believers are victims, having been brainwashed during their lifetime via a process perfected over generations into believing things that break all known laws of physics (gods, angels, demons, etc.) are real, that believing without (or despite) evidence is a virtue, and of course, that (some) things are better, and (some) people are greater, than they appear.

The most important lie that religion tells is that there is no such thing as human death. All other animals die, and your body dies, but your "soul" goes somewhere to live for eternity. Whether it's Heaven, Hell, some other place, or reincarnation, religion allows people to escape believing in the one thing we as a species fear most: our own mortality. Religion allows people not to believe in death, literally— it's the world's most powerful empty promise, and a major hurdle to overcome. In fact, research (April 2015) suggests atheists remind theists of their own mortality, which leads to negative associations with atheism.[7] The brainwashing is solidified by promises of what we all want most—immortality.

Most religionists are subjected to brainwashing/indoctrination (same thing) from infancy, as was attempted on me. I was circumcised (branded as a Jew) at eight days old, began Hebrew school in kindergarten, and was constantly reminded that the Jewish version of the deity was the One True God. This was my personal religion cycle. Most people born to religionists have similar stories—the gods and teachings may differ but the indoctrination always starts at an early age—which is why most people stay in the religion into which they were born, without giving alternatives serious consideration. Nowhere can the effects of large-scale, long-term brainwashing from infancy be more clearly seen than in the fact that most believers believe in the god of their parents.

Brainwashing is a broad word, encompassing many methods, which can take place at any time in a person's life. Those who find religion as adults are also victims of the Lie of God. The reason churches preach to the imprisoned and the downtrodden is because these adults are presumably beaten down, with weakened mental resistance to religious infection. Religion is Machiavellian in its methods.

The good news is that brainwashing isn't always permanent.

It's not always about brainwashing. Some people are just flat-out liars.

Sometimes it's easy to spot someone who lies about his piety. Consider Bill Clinton, who allegedly had many affairs. Every time he committed adultery, he broke one of his religion's major commandments and entered further into a state of sin, according to what he claimed to be his beliefs. Here's a question: If you believed dying in a state of sin meant you would go to literal Hell, and that such death could happen at any time without warning, would you *ever* have a long-term adulterous affair? Would you *ever* risk an eternal hell for a blow job? You'd have to be really stupid to do so—like blazingly stupid. (Clinton was a Rhodes Scholar.) Maybe you'd screw up a time or three, and that is where Grace, Confession, and Forgiveness come in, as parceled out in the name of God by the preachers (before they ask for money). But that requires repentance, and repentance requires you to, well, not have long-term affairs (you're not repenting if you keep sinning).

It's plain to me that it never occurred to Clinton that an all-powerful, mind-reading god knew what he was doing when he was playing with cigars in the Oval Office over an extended time. He apparently had no fear of the god to whom he was supposedly praying or of the damnation about which his Bible warned him.

Here's another example: Mark Sanford, while governor of South Carolina, resigned in disgrace as chairman of the Republican Governors Association after being caught lying about his whereabouts while cheating on his wife with a long-term lover. A huge web of lies collapsed on Sanford, who had told everyone he was hiking the Appalachian Trail when he was actually in Argentina with his mistress.[8] So that's lying, coveting, and adultery—all commandments being broken over and over. Do you think he was worried about hell?

Sanford then successfully ran for Congress on the "God has forgiven me" platform. Of course, nothing in the Bible says God gives second chances for such transgressions (1 Corinthians 6:9: "Or do you not know that the unrighteous will not inherit the kingdom of God? Do not be deceived: neither the sexually immoral, nor idolaters, nor adulterers, nor men who practice homosexuality"), but that's not the point. Did God tell him he was forgiven, or did he just make that up? I don't think he was having a long-term affair and flying to Argentina behind a web of long-term lies *while* believing in eternal damnation for those very actions! In my opinion, he's like Clinton—either stupid (which I don't believe), insane, or lying about his beliefs.

It may be distasteful, but we must admit it—*these pandering hypocrites in Congress (and in churches) who talk as if they believe in a god but act as if they don't are probably atheists, lying about their beliefs for their personal benefit.* In this world, there are good theists and bad theists, and there are good atheists and bad atheists, but some of the worst atheists, the ones who feign piety for personal gain, are running religion and politics.

I seethe with hatred for religion, but I hate no human. Hitchens anthropomorphized religion and treated it like a consciousness ("religion poisons everything"), as I do in this book, because, as Richard Dawkins taught us, ideas spread from person to person in a fashion that seems deliberate (memes). So when I use phrases such as *religion wants* and *Islam tries,* I'm not referring to people, but to the ideas themselves. Nothing I write in this book should be construed as *all religious people are bad/stupid.* Religious people are *victims* of a bad thing and often do bad things because they believe they are being good, without seriously pondering their own positions.

For instance, let's take a look at stereotypical Christians who oppose gay adoption. These people will immediately and ardently vote against gay-adoption legislation because they believe that's what God wants them to do (as cherry-picked and dictated from their holy books by their preachers). However, take it a level deeper and things change. If you ask them whether, after a tragic accident that killed all adults in their family, they would want their *own* children to spend the rest of their childhoods in an orphanage or in a loving, secure gay household, you will be able to watch the turmoil in their eyes. They will readily sentence other people's children to orphanages, but would they sentence *their* babies to the same fate so that they aren't exposed to homosexuality? If they are truthful, they will admit they'd rather have their kids in a stable, loving, gay home, yet they oppose gay adoption for other kids. They don't think about the harm this does. They don't think about the whole "Do unto others as you would have them do unto you" thing. They follow their leaders and do bad in the name of good. They hold back love in the name of love. They hurt children so they don't have to oppose their preachers.

It's easy to get mad at these people, but they deserve more pity than anger. There, but for the grace of dumb luck, go us. None of us can be sure how we'd be today had we been born to other parents in another part of the world, subjected to different brainwashing and a different, perhaps more oppressive, religion cycle (I do look like a rabbi with a full beard). Religion is a mental injury, a result of indoctrination, and must be recognized as such, even in the most extreme cases of ISIS or the Southern Baptist Convention. Religious people aren't evil. They are damaged.

Like the Borg of *Star Trek,* religion makes a person a part of its collective. When we fight religion, we fight against humans who seek to protect and expand the collective because they are victims of said collective. We'd prefer, if possible, to free the victims from their affliction, and as nice people, we want to do so, but failing that, we have to fight against victims. Theists must be fought even as they are pitied.

Understand religion is weak—not in terms of power in America, but rather in argument. As loud as they shout, and as hard as they try, preachers keep bumping into the Great Wall of Logic and Knowledge. They are, in all their huffing and crying, talking about an invisible man in the sky, and theirs is no different from any of the others: Yahweh, Allah, Vishnu, Quetzalcoatl . . . all of them, myths. This is religion's Achilles' heel. The preachers are hawking mythology, and mythology is weak. That's why they need to indoctrinate— religion isn't learned, it's inflicted.

If you're a preacher, you make your living telling lies. I'm not saying all preachers are knowingly liars. I am saying they are *telling* lies, whether they believe them (victims) or not (liars).[9] I make this statement not to concentrate on the lies themselves but rather on the *making a living* aspect of preaching.

The stereotypical used-car salesmen know they are conning unsuspecting people into buying junk for good, hard-earned cash, but they have to make a living, and they probably didn't end up where they are because they attained their ideal career goal. Somewhere along the line, they found themselves in this job, they have families, and this is what they know. I would hazard a guess that most such people feel guilty for doing their job, yet are trapped into doing so. This is analogous to preachers who become atheists and yet still preach.

This is a different kind of victim of religion—someone stuck in a job telling lies with no way out. Many such preachers went straight to seminary without a decent secular education (or even reading their Bible first), only to learn their Bible is fiction *after* they became preachers. The more you learn about religion, the likelier it is you will figure out it's all a scam. Similarly, the more you learn about atheism, the likelier it is you will figure out *all* religion is a scam, mainly because *learning about atheism* includes *learning about religion*.

Some are so vested in the community they would lose their social status, friends, and perhaps even family if they changed career. So, with a heavy heart, these people who only intended to help others but ended up realizing they were doing the opposite are forced to continue lying professionally.

This broad scenario is faced by all the preachers of the world. Some always wanted to be preachers, while others chose the profession later, but all are making a living and have a self-serving interest in protecting their income. Those who are successful may think of their success as a sign from their god that they are doing the right thing, or they might know their job is a total scam, but in either case they have a monumental self-interest in keeping their job, their lifestyle, and their flock. Religion is a giant used car, and preachers have proverbial quotas.

Then there's that problem of weakness again. How do you protect your livelihood of preaching about a man in the sky in the twenty-first century when facing a seemingly endless barrage of attacks from science, logic, and perhaps your own conscience?

This is where government comes in.

Government has been used for centuries to promote and protect religion. The true root of all evil is power, and both government and religion are effective tools for massing and maintaining power. When used in conjunction with one another, both religion and government thrive, albeit at the expense of freedom. This is why throughout human history we can see government and religion working together to subjugate the population, and this is why religion is constantly trying to get itself official legitimization in any way possible.

The problem is that America, as everyone *should* know, is a secular nation, and that means no single religion can attain any status not enjoyed by all the others. This is horrible if you're a preacher, as it hobbles your ability to use the power of the government to keep your religion elevated above the rest. Where would Christianity be today if not for the constant droning of "one nation under God" by every child or IN GOD WE TRUST on every penny? Without the National Day of Prayer or the singing of "God Bless America" on the Fourth of July? How would Christianity look to Americans if Christianity had not successfully inserted itself into American society via government intervention?

This, again, is pure Christian privilege. We all know that America is supposed to be a free nation of equals, but straight out of *Animal Farm,* Christians are used to being *more equal than others*. Every lawsuit we file at American Atheists, every complaint we make, is about Christian (or religious) privilege, as opposed to Christianity or religion itself. Crosses on public land, school prayer, voucher schemes, fair church taxation—all are battles against inequality, not Christianity.

Some religions, Christianity in particular, have "witnessing" as a part of their mission, so Christians feel it is their duty to preach to non-adherents any way they can. The most obvious example is Christian clubs set up in public schools, used to lure in other people's children with cookies and pizza so they can be preached to. This is illegal (unless other religious positions are allowed the same opportunity), but Christians do it anyway.

Their mission does not give them the right to break the law, nor does it justify special privilege. That they *want* to break the law and their *religion tells them* to break the law doesn't *allow* them to break the law. Laws that mandate equality (or the judges that enforce the law) aren't antireligion just because religion craves superiority. If their religion is incompatible with the law, they, not we, have to suck it up and work *within* the law of the land. Pro-equality laws are only "anti-Christian" because Christianity is anti-equality, and this is *their* problem, not ours.

When we fight for equality, we become the "bad guys" in the eyes of those who currently enjoy superiority. In 2013 American Atheists settled yet another "Ten Commandments on public land" lawsuit, this time in Bradford County, Florida. In brief, we won the right to put an atheist-sponsored monument next to the Ten Com- mandments. (I will talk more about the monument in chapter 8.) The Christian monument stood alone, illegally. But when we complained in the name of equality, we were "bashing Christianity," "holding back their free speech," and "persecuting" the poor Christian people. Our monument, when installed, was "mocking Christianity," "aggressive," and "right in America's face."

These complaints and accusations came from people who did not lose anything from the placement of our monument—except a mo- nopoly position. They complained anyway because this was never about the freedom of Christians to place a monument. It was about inequality in their favor, and they are willing to do whatever they can—including lying about the motives of those championing equality—to preserve their superiority.

Another example of privilege-influenced behavior is when the attempted removal of *under God* from the Pledge of Allegiance is called an attempt to make the pledge atheistic. Removing the phrase would not make the pledge atheistic; it would make it religion-neutral (secular). Adding the phrase *under no god* would make it atheistic. It would be the same with money—removing In God We Trust would make it neutral. That's the way it was originally, yet the idea of removing this phrase was seen as an attack against Christianity when American Atheists challenged it in 1978. If atheists actually intended to attack Christianity, we would have demanded our money include the phrase *in NO god we trust*. In truth, the real attacks have already been made, by Christian politicians, against us, when they inserted these religious declarations into the lives of all Americans (in the 1950s) in the first place—we just seek a *return* to religious neutrality.

They attack or break the law. We stop them, and we are considered the bad guys. They dismiss our demand for their adherence to the Golden Rule, "do unto others," and ignore that this rule can only lead to the elimination of privilege. If everyone treats others as they would like to be treated, the inevitable result is equality. We, the atheists, by demanding equality and nothing more, are doing unto others as we would have done unto us. The Christian Right is not and does not care. Why? Because they are not thinking straight— they are victims of that which poisons good people and makes them hypocritical assholes.

So often we hear lame "we are a Christian nation" arguments, but one argument we never hear is probably the best (albeit still inaccurate):

"The 'Christian' Golden Rule is imbued in our Constitution in the form of equal rights, because doing unto others as you would have done to you can only yield equality across the citizenry when applied to a nation."

This is an easy one, but we never hear it from talking heads because it means Christian privilege is both unchristian and un-American, and preachers and talking heads would rather preserve privilege, thank you very much.

The other side of Christian privilege, the tax exemption, is even more insidious. All these other efforts, as well as the new efforts to insert mythology into science classes in the guise of "intelligent design" or revisionist history books, all serve (at least in part) as giant distractions. Religious organizations want us to spend our time and resources fighting those battles. Don't get me wrong, they want to win, but they *really* don't want us looking at fair taxation.

Why don't churches report their earnings or pay the same taxes as other nonprofit organizations? Why won't any politicians bring this up, even while we as a country suffer through such hard economic times? Fair treatment of churches would mean billions of dollars in tax revenue for the country, but no politician dares suggest it.

This is partly our fault because we are not screaming about it. Even today, facing record deficits, crumbling economies, and defaulting local governments, few are suggesting the churches step up, either by paying taxes or providing real community service.

I'll get into all this later, but I wanted to show you the larger picture. Religion is too weak in premise to live and thrive without government intervention, so it has entwined itself in government, engaging in a constant barrage of offensive moves as a defensive strategy to protect its already ill-gotten gains—tax breaks without oversight—from the wallets of the American public.

Then religion uses the legitimacy it gains from the government to preach to the flock with authority about these secondary issues. Religious leaders go on about such things as abortion and stem-cell research, not because of such requirements in the Bible (how could they be?), but because they want to mobilize their forces to fight the secondary battles, partly as an offensive move to gain power over the masses and to enforce theocratic rules, partly to stay politically engaged, but also as a distraction from their primary concern—keeping more of their money without oversight of any kind.

Religious leaders talk about God's wishes, which they apparently know far better than those followers who don't read their Bibles. By placing their own words in the mouths of their god, they can justify urging people to harm themselves (give to the church even if it is beyond your means) and their society (support politicians who support tax breaks for the church) for the benefit of the preachers and their religions.

The greatest enemy of religious tyranny is the separation of religion and government. Find the politicians who are endorsed or advanced by preachers, and you'll see a politician using religion for political advantage—aka the "vote for me because God is on my side" ploy. Some are guiltier than others, but unfortunately, most politicians from both parties fall somewhere along this scale. The preachers bring the votes in exchange for this legitimacy, and the politician will support the religion's privileges. Hence there are no attempts to tax the church fairly from Washington, DC.

Separation of religion and government protects everyone equally and indeed is a synonym for "freedom of religion" and "religious equality." The more religion and government are merged, the less freedom of religion is enjoyed by the citizenry. If the government favors one religion over others, or religion over atheism, people have fewer choices in their everyday lives—even for those members of the preferred religion. In such a situation, where people are members of the ruling religion in a theocracy, consider what happens when they doubt or contradict the word of whatever preacher is in power. Suddenly the individual who was once in the majority is in the minority, and the government has the opposing preacher's back. Where is the freedom there? Any deviation from the official preacher's word in a theocratic regime places the individual immediately in the second class. With just a little thought you can see how even the most ardent believer in the majority official religion can, and will, lose freedom in a theocracy. This is why preachers and politicians don't talk about benefiting the flock and instead talk about God's will and *pretend* that it benefits the flock.

Theocracy is relative, and therefore every step away from total separation of religion and government is a step toward theocracy, and away from religious freedom.

Atheism is perfect. Yes, I know every religion says the same thing about itself, but religions are wrong. (Yes, I know they all say that about atheism too.) What I mean by this is atheism is so simple that it cannot have any flaws. It is simply a lack of a belief in gods, so unless there is a reason to believe in gods, it is a logically perfect position. Once a single piece of scientifically valid evidence for the existence of any deity is unearthed, this will change, and atheism, being the single condition of the absence of a belief in a god, will have a flaw, but as this has never happened, I'm not nervous.

Everything that happens within a universe is completely bound by the laws of that universe—a perfectly logical conclusion based on all the facts currently available to humanity. Now granted, we don't know everything, so atheism provides "I don't know" as a truthful, logical, and meaningful answer to those questions that are still unanswerable by fact-based evidence. Saying "I don't know" is not a flaw. It is a true and valid statement that does not take the totally illogical leap of "I don't know . . . therefore a god did it." It communicates the simple and reasonable proposition that we need to learn more.

Atheism cannot and does not involve illogical leaps, and it has no exceptions. There is no "Problem of Evil" (the question of how to reconcile the existence of evil with that of a deity who is omnipotent, omniscient, and omnibenevolent,[10] which I and many others consider a logical disproof of Christianity), no circular reasoning, no mysterious ways, no "you have to have faith," and no self-hypnosis via repetition of mantras (prayer). Nobody is ever told, "If you don't understand Dawkins, repeat this phrase five times." We tell you to look it up and ask questions and be prepared for some *I don't knows* because saying so is part of telling the truth.

In the history of mankind, *atheism has never had a single moment of failure.* Never, not even once, has atheism been proven wrong, and once is all we'd need to drop it completely. If atheism had been proven wrong, if one god had been verified, if one supernatural event had been measured, if one ocean had really parted, or if one person ever really rose from the grave, I would quit my job because I'd be wrong.

Now compare this to the "perfect" word of the supposedly immortal superbeing in the sky, who says in Genesis 1 that Earth came before light ("In the beginning God created heaven and earth . . . and darkness was on the face of the deep . . . and God said, Let there be light").

Wrong. Earth is composed partially of carbon atoms that were formed inside other suns, and suns give off light, so Earth came *after* the first generation of light-emitting stars. Therefore, Genesis 1 is provably wrong (I'll get into religion's inability to admit it's wrong later on). Despite glaring flaws, many Christians and Jews still call their book perfect because they have been brainwashed to overlook glaring inconsistencies. Atheists seek truth; theists ignore it.

Have *I* been brainwashed? According to neuroscientist and author Sam Harris in his book *Free Will,* we are all essentially brainwashed by our surroundings and our upbringing, so I have to take this question seriously. We all should. For many years, I certainly was brainwashed into believing Judaism was more than a religion. But the extent to which Harris goes with this argument—saying we may indeed have no free will at all—makes me uncomfortable. My discomfort doesn't automatically make Harris wrong; it only encourages me to learn more and eventually come to an informed conclusion. I may conclude the thing I don't want to be true is actually true, and as a skeptic I need to be open to this possibility.

As to my being brainwashed into atheism, I've read the books from the other (religious) side, done my studying, even given my daughter a King James Bible and told her to read it (she has, and it comforts me that she has). I would *love* to be proven wrong! As I mentioned earlier, I want, as much as any theist, to be immortal. I want my daughter to live forever, and I want to see my parents in a beautiful, happy heaven after I die. I wish there were some reason to believe it is true, but there isn't. When someone shows me real evidence, I will gleefully join whatever the true religion is. But in all of human history, this has never happened—because it's all a farce.

Prove me wrong, even once, and I'll convert. Now, does that sound brainwashed?

> No one is ever going to convince me that the word of God is not true.   —KEN HAM, PRESIDENT OF ANSWERS IN GENESIS
> AND YOUNG-EARTH CREATIONIST

> We would need just one piece of evidence . . . and you would change me immediately.   —BILL NYE THE SCIENCE GUY

If this war is to be won, it must be fought on many battlegrounds all at once. It is not enough, nor will it ever be, to take a singular approach. Some atheists who choose to fight believe quite adamantly that the way to win the war against bigotry toward atheists is to be outwardly nice to theists and never ruffle their feathers. They want to help theists understand the atheist point of view, hoping to recruit the more moderate among them as allies against those who would rather live in a theocracy. Others, such as me, choose to fight with words, raising awareness of our movement while attacking the assumption of respect behind which religion hides. Still others take a "separate but equal" approach, insisting that simply living their lives as open atheists in society will allow them to lead by example.

They are all correct.

All battles *must* be fought simultaneously for us to succeed, and this means we have to understand and appreciate the breadth of the movement. Even though atheists are numerous in this country, few are active in the national, organized atheist movement, which consists of about ten large organizations across several movement segments and hundreds of smaller regional, specialty, or local groups. American Atheists, the hard-core "marines of the movement," has over 160 affiliates nationwide. In other words, we are spread thin as a movement, and some segments are poorly represented, even though each segment is necessary for our ultimate success. Every segment serves as a magnet for atheists who agree with that segment, which will therefore lead to movement growth.

Those who join us will be as diverse as the movement itself, ranging from the softest diplomat to the most fervent firebrand. They all must have a place to go. "Touchy-feely" atheists who come to American Atheists will most likely not stay long, and they might leave the movement as a whole if they believe we're their only option. However, if those same atheists find like-minded friends over at the American Humanist Association (AHA) or the Center for Inquiry (CFI), they might stay longer, maybe even permanently. The opposite is also obviously true, as firebrands like me would likely encounter resistance and frustration with the diplomat wing.

All kinds of atheists help the movement and are vital to its success. We cannot and must not waste any time trying to trip each other up. Yes, criticism is valid, but it must end there, and it must have the primary purpose of advertising the differences between the segments, not to try to change the other segments—such efforts would likely fail. This way, our internal criticisms will be used as a building tool for the movement as a whole and not generate infighting.

The world has been in a constant religious civil war since humanity invented religion, and the United States is only one of many battlegrounds. We must keep in mind that our war is global, and even when we win the battle in America (which we will), we will still be under attack from other countries. This war will not end in our lifetime, but I am confident the battle for America will essentially be won before 2040 *if* we work together. I'll get into that soon.

We fight a defensive war against an intruder into our lives. If there were no intrusion, if there were no clear intent from religion to spread into and dominate our lives, then we would have no fight and I would have no passion. We fight for equality for everyone and freedom for all, even those who disagree with us. That's what makes us the good guys.

Chapter 3

TELLING THE TRUTH ABOUT THE LIE OF GOD

Just wanted to let you know that you people are scum you are the bacteria that grows under a pile of shit. And david silverman that unamerican piece of shit faggot loving son of a rotten cunt. Needs to move to another country he obviously has no love for america and its values. Im gonna continue to tell you people what parasitic garbage you are. Have a merry CHRISTmas. Buncha douchebags.

—An e-mail to American Atheists in December 2012

So when I meet somebody who claims to be religious, my first impulse is: "I don't believe you. I don't believe you until you tell me do you really believe—for example, if they say they are Catholic—do you really believe that when a priest blesses a wafer it turns into the body of Christ? Are you seriously telling me you believe that? Are you seriously saying that wine turns into blood?" Mock them! Ridicule them! In public! Don't fall for the convention that we're all too polite to talk about religion. Religion is not off the table. Religion is not off-limits.
—Richard Dawkins

The sum total of all scientifically valid proof supporting the existence of all of world's gods, combined, is zero.

Beyond the rhetoric, beyond the lies, and beyond the marketing, never *once* in the history of our species has any religion found, offered, or shown any verifiable and testable proof based on scientifi-cally valid evidence and the scientific method (you know, the way we would *prove* anything else) of any supernatural being or phenomena. Ever. As I said before, if I am ever proven wrong on this point, I will quit my job and donate the proceeds of this book to that specific god's religion, and I shall do so in a tremendous hail of publicity so that everyone will know. Indeed, if you believe in a god, I double-dog dare you to find even the smallest fallacy-free, scientifically valid proof of anything supernatural or any miracle anywhere, ever. Go. Have fun with that.

I begin this chapter with this specific bet in order to exert a little firebrand atheism. The theists who read this will be motivated to prove me wrong. They will say, "Hey! My religion has proof," and then rush off in vain to find it, just so they can eliminate my job and be the hero for their god. They will ask for help from their friends and pastors. They will have Facebook discussions that will include phrases like "proof doesn't have to be scientifically valid" (yes, it damn well does, or it's not *proof*) or "I just know in my heart" or "how else can we explain something we don't understand" or "God is love and love is real, so God is real," but none that will include the phrase "Here! I found scientifically valid, testable proof" and be true. If they are honest with themselves when they fail, they will be half-way to freedom, for they will know that religion is made up of lots of things, but facts aren't among them.

What will that do? Will it get theists angry at me for saying some-thing against their religion? Probably. Maybe the challenge will get them really pissed off—it's meant to, because if it were mild, they wouldn't take it to heart. I'm saying *no religion has ever had scientifically valid proof of its god, in even the smallest quantity, ever.* That's a bold state-ment, dismissing all religions as ancient mythologies and fairy tales—which they are. Christianity, Judaism, Islam, Hinduism, and all the rest have no more proof for any supernatural phenomena than "Han-sel and Gretel" and "Little Bo Peep"—zero. With my blunt challenge

I dare their adherents to prove me wrong. I challenge their sensibilities and I tilt their religion's pedestal. If believers choose to ignore this challenge, they do so knowing they cowered away from finding proof for the god to which they swear and donate. I hope that gnaws at them.

But those theists who want to learn, who have the courage to confront their upbringing, might take me up on this challenge and try to find their proof. It might lead to discussion, and perhaps the discovery that all religion, even theirs, is a lie and a scam. It may be discussed around large circles of theists trying to prove me wrong and failing, and then ideally they all get the message and escape religion, leaving them free to live happier and healthier lives.

Hopefully, they will bring their friends, their families, and their kids. How much better would those kids' lives be? Yes, some of my readers already don't like me, but in the end I'm only trying to help injured people recover, and in doing so to dramatically improve their lives. To me, that's totally worth a little dislike.

Christians who don't read the Bible aren't real Christians. Yes, I am fully aware of the No True Scotsman fallacy (Angus puts sugar on his porridge; no (true) Scotsman puts sugar on his porridge; therefore Angus is not a (true) Scotsman),[1] but let's be honest—literate but non-Bible-reading believers are just poseurs. If they really thought they possessed the perfect word of God, they'd read it (*I* certainly would—in fact, I'd memorize it). They don't read it because they fear finding exactly what they will find—it's boring, primitive, and ridiculous, far from being perfect or even good literature. So they don't read it, lie about having done so, and listen to what their preachers say without even considering that preachers pick and choose their passages to speak about, tailoring their message to grow their flock and line their pockets. The conflict of interest astounds.

Am I a dick because I encourage—*dare*—supposed theists to read their own holy books, knowing they will see the truth of their poor quality by doing so? Is this a firebrand move—or a diplomatic one?

On the "War on Christmas"

Religion demands a pedestal—in the case of the United States, Christianity demands a pedestal higher than every other religion based solely on privilege and tradition. The so-called "war" on Christmas is a great example of how Christianity demands respect it doesn't deserve. Christmas was made a national holiday in 1870 in an act that merged religion and government with serious ramifications—the destruction of Christmas as a Christian holiday.

Surely, when the law passed that made Christmas a national holiday, some felt it would benefit the church, just as it has, by legitimizing Christianity using the force of government. But the legitimacy conferred has not been able to keep up with the nation's growing diversity. What's an atheist to do? What's a Hindu to do, for that matter? Or a Jew? A Muslim? Non-adherents are not converting to Christianity because of the forced observance and celebration of the birth of Jesus. Rather, they are celebrating the more secular aspects of the holiday (primarily the parts stolen from other religions and practices). In turn, the non-Christian aspects of the holiday have evolved to be more and more important. This is the reason Christmas is becoming increasingly secular, to the annoyance of every Christian preacher. We saw this happen with Thanksgiving, which is now religious only in name. In the not-too-distant future Christmas will become equally secular.

This has never happened to a religious holiday that was not made into a national observance. There is no campaign to keep Moses in Passover.

Christian ideologues know this and hate it because they are losing their privilege as Christmas becomes secular. They complain about stores saying "Happy holidays" instead of "Merry Christmas" because the more inclusive statement doesn't grant Christianity any special privilege. Christmas goes from being presumed to be *singularly important* to simply one of many holidays. Stores do it because they know 30 percent of the population isn't Christian, but some Christians hate it because "Happy holidays" acknowledges that 30 percent, so they complain that Christianity is under attack. Again, equality is an attack.

Every American understands the basic concept of equality, or at least they should, but we are simply not used to it when it comes to Christianity. Realize that the idea of equality to women is threatening to some men, just as the idea of racial equality is threatening to some white people, because they perceive becoming equal as a *loss of privilege*. This is also the case for some Christians who fear losing privilege and becoming *only equal* to other religious and atheistic positions. They are correct; they *are* losing privilege as we gain equality, but it's an unearned and undeserved privilege, and it's right that they should lose it.

Christians know, deep down, they have no reason to oppose equality except their own greed for privilege (which comes from Christian hegemony). Equality is the American Way, and it should not be considered a *punishment* or a *loss* when people of privilege lose their privilege in favor of equality; and if it *is* viewed as such, too bad.

"Equalophobic Christians" must be called just that and called out for it. They care when a politician says "Happy holidays" instead of "Merry Christmas"—it's all about demanding inequality, singling out one holiday as special over the others. A *holiday* tree. *Season's greetings.* Some Christians freak out if they don't get preferential treatment. Soon, as Dennis Miller has said, "I won't be able to sing 'White Christmas' without being called a racist!"

Or not. The endgame is Christians *will* be treated equally. No one is calling for restrictions on what's done on private land or in churches, but we all own the government and the public square. Equalophobic Christians will have to get used to the lowly position of equality with the rest of us.

In the meantime, we need to call the War on Christmas what it is: another reason for anti-equality Christians to whine about being *only equal*. If someone claims to be offended by our assertions that we deserve equal treatment, it's because they are used to privilege and social superiority and actually fear *just* being equal. I call them equalophobes because they fear what we as a nation should be striving for. Equalophobes fear the American Way.

This de-religionizing of Christmas is inevitable—as long as non-Christians are forced to take December 25 off, the process will continue. It is also inevitable that the Christian Right will continue to blame atheists for the decline of Christmas into secular observance, even though the fault rests with them. If they could separate religion and government, and Christmas reverted to being a religious holiday only, then it would once again be all about Jesus. But it's way too late for that. Our entire economy spins on the season, so I believe the point of no return has long passed. Christmas's religious meaning is destined to continue to decline.

We can help the process along by chipping away at the legitimacy granted to Christianity by the government. By protesting the government's (illegal) favoring of the Christian-only aspects of this national holiday, we force the government to highlight only the secular aspects. Ironically, the act that sought to legitimize Christianity by nationalizing its biggest holiday will yield the *elimination of religion* from the holiday, not the "religionizing" of America.

Of course the equalophobia goes far broader than just Christmas. Equalophobia is why they fight against our monuments next to their Decalogues, why they push their Bibles in public schools but fight it when we distribute atheist literature, and why they care so much about *under God* and *In God We Trust*. Their loss of any of those issues is a win for equality, which chips away at their religion's pedestal and implied government endorsement. Christianity has good reason to fear equality.

It's coming anyway.

Part of the danger we face from religion arises because anyone, regardless of religious affiliation, or lack thereof, can be elected to political office in the United States. I think that's a problem.

I don't think we should have a religious test per se, but I do think we should have a religious *priority* test. Specifically, politicians should be asked which is more important—your religion or your country, and what happens if the interests of the two conflict? We need to make sure anyone who takes public office will place the law of the land and the well-being of *all* citizens above his or her religion's demands. We need every politician everywhere to state unequivocally that the *US Constitution outranks everything, including religious texts,* as the US Constitution (article 6, second paragraph) specifies:

> *This Constitution, and the laws of the United States which shall be made in pursuance thereof; and all treaties made, or which shall be made, under the authority of the United States,* shall be the supreme law of the land; *and the judges in every state shall be bound thereby, anything in the Constitution or laws of any State to the contrary notwithstanding* [emphasis mine].

All citizens have the right to their own religious beliefs and practices, but once the people place you in power, your allegiance is to the *people,* even if that requires actions not supported by, or even contrary to, your religion's teachings or interests.

If a conflict arises, are religionists willing to put their religion aside in the name of the country they are swearing to uphold? If so, no problem! If not, the person is simply not qualified to take office. In a religion-versus-country debate, the country wins all the time. This is the only way a pluralistic society can enjoy religious freedom—the leaders must pledge to rule in a secular manner and follow through.

A small adaptation to official oaths would make it easy. For example, the current Presidential Oath of Office reads, "I do solemnly swear (or affirm) that I will faithfully execute the Office of President of the United States, and will to the best of my ability, preserve, protect and defend the Constitution of the United States." Simply append "as the supreme law of the land" to the end. There! That is *my* kind of religious test—say yes to the supremacy of the Constitution as the law of the land or go become a preacher instead.

That's a big step, and until we get there, asking your politicians if they agree with article 6 of the Constitution, which specifies that the Constitution is the supreme law of the land even above religious texts, is a great way to learn about their priorities and whether they place your rights above or below their religion.

On Jewish Atheism

I've said in the past that Judaism is both a religion and a culture. At various stages in my life I have been committed to this idea. For example, my wife, Hildy, and I sent our daughter to a Workmen's Circle Jewish school, which taught Jewish culture and the Jewish religion from a historical perspective. *Our ancestors believed in a god that did this, our ancestors believed in a god that said that, this is a latke, and this is how you dance the hora.* This all made sense to me at the time because I considered Judaism to be both a race *and* a religion, separable from each other.

I have since concluded I was wrong—when I tried to justify Jewish atheism, for this book, and failed.

During this period I discussed the issue with my friend Penn Jillette, who has long called Jewish atheism bullshit (he calls lots of things that), noting that any genetic bonds Jews have with each other are actually only ties to specific regions of descent, not a commonality called being Jewish. He opined that since you can't convert to being black or Italian, but you can convert to being Jewish, they can't be the same thing.

Penn is married to Emily, some of whose family members insist that not only is Emily Jewish, but so are her kids, due to Judaism's matrilineal-descent dogma, which states that all children of Jewish women are "Jewish by birth." They are all Jews *according to Judaism,* even though Emily herself rejects the term and the kids aren't being raised with any such concept or exposure. Penn wrote to me, "They try to claim my children are Jewish by 'Jewish law.' They say I have no choice."

I became more and more confused about the whole Jewish atheism thing as I thought and wrote about it. My words were inconsistent, and when I took what I wrote and changed the word *Jewish* to *Muslim* or any other religion, I found myself unable to reconcile what defines Jewish identity without the religious aspects.

One event in particular helped further clarify my views. During my first Passover after my mom died, I watched my wife perform the seder (ritual service and meal), and I realized that Passover in my mind had nothing to do with my ancestors whatsoever. They celebrated the holiday in a quite different manner from us. My mother's seders when I was growing up were lax religiously (as opposed to the ones apparently led by my Orthodox great-grandmother). Indeed, my family's Passover wasn't ancient at all—with its recently established family traditions it bore little resemblance to its predecessors. It was a lot less religious, and a lot more Mom-, food-, and family-centric. Picture Thanksgiving with different food, a ten-minute "service" led by my Uncle Harvey (who didn't have a yarmulke so he wore a napkin on his head), and five cups of wine (making that napkin-yarmulke the funniest thing ever). As I sat there, now motherless and uncleless, watching my wife lead the seder, I realized how different it was from that of my upbringing, just because my family had evolved. Both were celebrations of the same Jewish holiday, but what exactly did that mean? What *is* Jewish, and how different was my family's Jewishness to my great-grandparents', and how can such blatant differences be so profoundly ignored? Where does Judaism start and family tradition end? Where is the *Jew* in secular Jew?

A second clarifying experience happened at a science museum, where I observed an Islamic display. Curious, I wandered into the display, only to see the same theme over and over: here's a person, this person invented a thing, this person was a Muslim, and therefore Islam gave the world this invented thing. As I went from person to person in the display, I became bitter at Islam for taking credit for the accomplishments of its adherents. I realized it is similar to Jews proudly crowing about all the Jewish Nobel Prize winners, as if Judaism, and not a whole slew of other factors, was somehow uniquely responsible. This is just religion trying to make itself look more relevant and important by claiming credit where credit is not due.

Then I realized that Judaism is simply doing the same thing with regard to Jewish culture and ethnicity—taking credit where it is simply not due in an effort to make itself look more important.

For example, there is no such thing as Jewish food or dance. For the most part these traditions are all based on national or local traditions that have nothing to do with religion. They don't make bagels "Jewish" any more than falafel is Muslim or chow mein is Buddhist. Almost everything nonreligious commonly known to be "Jewish" is actually specific to only one sect of Jews from the Eastern European nations called the Ashkenazim. If the culture were Jewish, it would include the large number of non-Ashkenazi Jews as well. But this is not the case. Whole sects of Jews have no association at all with "Jewish culture" (nobody associates bagels and lox with Ethiopian Jews, because it is not a part of *their* culture), so it's not *Jewish* culture (by definition), but rather Eastern European culture, with Judaism simply taking the credit.

And then there's the issue of matrilineal descent, which determines who is a part of the Jewish "race" in the most nonscientific way possible—someone decided it should be that way and declared it true.

Matrilineal descent claims any child of a Jewish mother is a Jew by blood. The father is not considered in this determination, which invalidates any claims to a race, because we all know genes from both parents make up the genetic inheritance of offspring. For example, when a person of Asian descent has a child with a person of African descent you don't get a "pure" Asian or African child. You get a mixed-race child. Matrilineal descent implies racial purity despite the reality of dilution.

Despite this, if your mother is Jewish and your father is not, you're considered Jewish by most Jews, not a half Jew. As my daughter Winter puts it, that's "not a thing." Genes don't follow human dogma. That it's matrilineal and not patrilineal itself is simply a *choice* someone once made and codified into Jewish law. This rule isn't divine, nor is it scientific; it's imagined. So this means in this world some people are Jewish who would not be Jewish if whoever decided on matrilineal-versus-patrilineal descent had made the opposite choice (and all the same breeding had occurred). Similarly, some non-Jews today would be Jews if their father's "blood" had been the determining factor. So, some people are only Jewish or non-Jewish because of the choice some people made a long time ago. There is nothing— *nothing*—uniquely and universally physical about Jewishness, so it's not "in the blood" at all.

And to complicate matters, certain segments of Judaism changed their minds in modern times and began recognizing matrilineal or patrilineal descent as equally valid for claiming a child is Jewish. Now it is possible for people who consider themselves to have been born and raised Jewish, to be Jewish in every single way including religious practice, to be told they aren't Jewish by members of another segment of Jews—that in fact I, the atheist who has denounced

Judaism, am a "real" Jew by virtue of my mother's having been Jewish and my believing, practicing counterparts are not because their mother was a non-Jew.

That's ridiculous.

In fact, these Eastern European Jews, according to Eran Elhaik, a geneticist at the Johns Hopkins School of Public Health, are mostly the descendants of converts with no genetic linkage to ancient Judea. No link, genetic or otherwise, exists with other sects of Judaism—all genetic similarities between Eastern European Jews are native to Eastern Europe. Indeed, according to Elhaik, "There is no Jewish genome and certainly no Jewish gene."[2]

My thoughts, as they stand now, are that my link to Judaism is just a result of my immediate family's upbringing, and the religion of Judaism is taking credit. The Jewish race is looking a lot more like a tradition, and nothing more, among some Jews to call Judaism a race. Once again, religion is taking the credit for something it does not deserve so as to benefit itself by inflating its membership.

This whole Jewish atheism concept seems merely a defense mechanism for Judaism to protect itself against atheism or conversion, much as circumcising a boy at eight days of age brands the child so he will always be marked as a member of the Jewish "people." If your atheist kids were told they were "Jewish by birth," and then got older and went through a religious phase, they'd likely turn to Judaism, as opposed to whatever other faith they might have chosen. It's like an insurance policy: "Come on in, there's no conversion needed for you, you're already one of us. If you're going to try out a religion, start with your roots!"

Moreover, the false notion of a race keeps people self-identifying as Jews despite a total abandonment of the religion. It works. Approximately half of the people who call themselves Jews are atheists, hiding the truth about their atheism.[3]

Additionally, these atheists who buy into the secular-Jew concept still give allegiance and financial support to Jewish and Zionist organizations, bolstering theistic Judaism with money via guilt and misinformation. Israel is a huge benefactor of the lie of the Jewish race, inciting passionate support globally from people who think their "people" are in danger, and that a country with a state church of Judaism is vitally important to their preservation. It's a fantastic scam that leads to huge amounts of money flooding into Israel, including from America, all made possible by the lie that Judaism is more than just another religion.

Softer, less tangible terms such as *culture* and *ethnicity* and the idea that all Jews today are connected through the Holocaust are just further attempts to justify clinging to the idea that Judaism is something more than it is. It's almost ex-parrot-esque[4] in its attempt to justify grouping all descendants of Jews as Jews even after they dump the religion. Cultures can be abandoned, but when you try to leave Judaism, you are told you can't because it's in your blood, which is a lie.

Ethnicities are location-centric, but since Judaism has strains from many different areas of the globe, and the different strains share no commonalities except the religion, "ethnicity" is the wrong word too.

Those who call Judaism a culture, ethnicity, or nationality are ignoring that some Jews have no ties to this culture, ethnicity, or nationality. Jews from different regions (Ashkenazim, Sephardim, Ethiopian, etc.) have very different cultures and continue to separate themselves from each other. Are they all Jews? Yes, because they all have the Torah in common—until they drop the Torah and become atheists (who happen to be children of Jews).

As to the guilt-laden, "we are all linked by the Holocaust, so don't denounce Judaism because that is what Hitler would want" routine, the truth is neither the Holocaust, the Spanish Inquisition, nor all of the other attempts at eliminating Jews combined make Judaism "more than a religion," nor does it give me the responsibility to pretend I'm something I'm not. I am not morally obligated to continue the race, tradition, or whatever just because it's "what Hitler would have hated." The Holocaust should not be a tool to spread the lie Hitler wrongly used to his advantage. Reality, and being honest about it, cannot be a betrayal.

The truly broadest definition I've ever heard for "What is a Jew?" is that Jews are the people anti-Semites (and Hitler) hate. In other words these people are defining themselves as Jews because ignorant bigots call them Jews and hate them for it, thereby allowing themselves to be defined by the people who hate them, rather than by what evidence shows us. When I hear this, I hear a person desperately reaching to find a way to make Judaism more than a religion.

What's more, most non-Jews don't understand the concepts of "secular Judaism" or "Humanistic Judaism" (as I showed earlier, 70 percent of Americans don't understand the term "secular," and nearly 90 percent don't understand "Humanist") so when they hear it, they assume the norm—theism—the exact opposite of the truth! In this very real way, atheists who call themselves Jews (of *any* kind) are calling themselves *theists* as far as most listeners are concerned.

So I am reminded that we are all victims of indoctrination, and I am no different. I was taught a lie—that Judaism is more than it is—and I stuck by it without examining its veracity because I was taught not to. There is no way around it—I was suckered into defending a false idea in the same way theists are suckered into their false ideas. It took this book, in which I originally attempted to justify Jewish atheism on paper, to conquer my cognitive dissonance on the subject.

I don't call myself Jewish anymore. I've realized that when someone asks me if I'm Jewish, saying anything but "No, I'm an atheist" will yield misleading information and derail the conversation from where I want it to go. So call me an atheist—the Jewish thing just seems like, as Penn would say, bullshit.

If you're an atheist and still call yourself a Jew, please reconsider what's important—and what's true.

On Islam and Religion-Inspired Terrorism

Fight and kill the disbelievers wherever you find them, take them captive, harass them, lie in wait and ambush them using every stratagem of war. —QUR'AN 9:5

Bring forth him that hath cursed without the camp; and let all that heard him lay their hands upon his head, and let all the congregation stone him. —LEVITICUS 24:14

I'm sometimes called Islamophobic. And while I do admit to fearing some major factions of Islam, I don't like the connotation or the politically correct assertion that such fear is irrational. Concerns about Islam are very different from, for example, concerns about Judaism because Islam is unique among religions today in posing a real threat to the human condition. I would go so far as to say an educated fear is a completely rational position. It's not about race (Islam is not a race), and it's not about people (victims)—it's about an ancient and particularly violent desert religious sect, separated from society and honed over generations by a destructive religious cycle into a barbaric nightmare that, unlike Christianity and Judaism, has yet to be tempered by modern values (due to that very separation).

Islam was born in the desert, where food and water were scarce and life was cutthroat. According to Dr. Wafa Sultan, psychiatrist, author, and critic of Islam, "Raiding . . . was the only means of survival. The tribes fought one another in their quest for water and food. . . . Then Islam came and tried to regularize raiding operations, justifying raids by its Prophet and followers, but proscribing raids by others. . . . Islam tried to justify these raids by regarding them as death in God's cause."[5]

According to Dr. Sultan, Islam is a religion founded in justifying violence in the name of its god. One can easily imagine how such a beginning might yield a religion with a very different character from a religion formed in agrarian or fishing societies, where gods provided ample food and water. Since then, like other religions, it has splintered, fractured, and evolved into many sects of varying beliefs, each of which calls itself "true Islam," but all stemming from the same basic beliefs and lore, which, according to Sultan, yields a commonality of thinking among Muslims: "Muslims eat raiding, dress raiding, talk raiding, and drive their cars like raiders."[6]

That last sentence is too broad a generalization for my taste, but I can see the point—a religion formed in a brutal environment, where whole communities lived and died by stealing from one another, glorified raiding and conquest as central in its teachings, which makes it different (yes, more barbaric) from other religions at its core.

According to the popular version of Islam, you may not draw the Prophet Muhammad's face or representation, and you may not portray him onstage. In September of 2005, when Danish cartoonists dared to disobey this command, riots or protests occurred in nearly every country with a Muslim majority, and the brainwashed followers of this barbaric religion killed more than a hundred people over comics of their prophet.[7]

The world gasped, and then caved, en masse. The ability we once had to draw Muhammad, see his picture, or poke fun at him in any way evaporated, and the world started obeying Islamic law, just a little. Suddenly, most people viewed depicting Muhammad as an act of provocation, not expression.

American Atheists embraced "Draw Muhammad Day," where, again, all we did was disobey someone else's demands to follow their religion's primitive tenets, and we were called "instigators." I disagree. *Islam* was the instigator by telling *me* that I have to follow *its* arbitrary rule in the first place. I have the right to draw anything I want, and I'm defending it by doing it in defiance.

We were not alone in our opposition to this prohibition. Nationwide and worldwide, other atheist and free-speech organizations opposed this PC-cloaked censorship and continued to draw Muhammad and criticize Islam.

Then, on January 7, 2015, Islamic militants launched another attack on our right to express ourselves, storming the headquarters of the French satirical newspaper *Charlie Hebdo,* murdering twelve people. With shouts of "We have avenged the prophet," these religion-made murderers killed people as a punishment for printing cartoons of Muhammad.[8]

The world mourned. In huge demonstrations of solidarity, people who finally began to understand that their rights were being threatened stood together screaming, *"Je suis Charlie!"* But the US press still caved and would not do what it needed to do—show the cartoons that the shooters used to justify their murders. "Defy their demands!" we complained, and the social media shares of the comics were indeed huge, but the mainstream press acquiesced, again, largely refusing to show the cartoons out of fear cloaked as "respect."[9]

Most recently, on May 3, 2015, two Islamic militants opened fire on unarmed civilians inside the US, in Garland, Texas, where a group was hosting a "Draw Muhammad" contest. Yes, the people who were holding the event knew they were being provocative, but no, that does not make the shooting their fault in any way.

Americans see attacks and riots over such depictions of Muhammad and fear for their fellow humans. In response, citizens of the United States, the country that defined freedom of speech, obey these repressive demands—and criticize those who do not! They may not fear for their own lives, but they fear for others, globally, and their empathy makes them respond by obeying and pressuring others to obey. The anticipated guilt they would feel if they were to break the code of the "all-peaceful" Prophet Muhammad and "terror riots" or shootings were to erupt where innocent people could die because of their actions makes them comply. That's yielding to terrorism.

But let's be clear: the people depicting or drawing Muhammad are not responsible in any way, shape, or form for any riots or deaths that might occur—the rioters and killers are. Willingly submitting to this religious proscription amounts to yielding to terrorism, and recoiling in the face of this violence only teaches the terrorists that they have an effective tool to curtail our most basic rights. In short, obeying in the face of violence begets more rules to obey under more threats of more violence!

If a mob of atheists went on a killing spree every time someone burned a picture of Charles Darwin, who would deserve blame for the deaths? The picture burners? No. The people to blame for killing sprees are the killers. Just as Theo van Gogh (assassinated for making a film with Ayaan Hirsi Ali that was critical of Islam) was not to blame for his own murder, neither are the Danish cartoonists, nor the newspaper that printed the cartoons, even remotely. The rioters were the killers and bear all the blame.

Can we all agree on that? If you say something to offend me, I mean *really* offend me, so I take out a gun and shoot you, is your death your own fault? Did you deserve it? No. The people expressing their opinions, like the organizers of the Draw Muhammad contest, hold *zero* responsibility over the actions of those who disagree.

When fanatics say, "Obey our religious laws even if you're not a believer," the immediate response must be to break whatever religious laws they are talking about. Don't draw Muhammad? Here's a picture. Don't criticize Islam? Hell, yes, I will say what I think. If militant Muslims riot and kill people, they are to blame. We are not to blame for exercising our rights. That can simply never be the case.

It's pretty sad that Islamic fanatics think we would give up any portion of our right to freedom of expression, press, and speech, but that's exactly what they are demanding. It's sadder still that in many cases they are right—nobody seems to be complaining except atheists (and only the firebrands at that), while the politically correct crowd chastises us for being too in-your-face and calls us names. Meanwhile, people relinquish their rights readily and eagerly in a quest for peace with religious fanatics that will never be realized.

Case in point: let's look at Bill Donohue, president of the almost-always-wrong Catholic League, blaming the victims for the *Charlie Hebdo* shooting in a manner that I can only describe as pandering to fanatics (in this case, it's a rather obvious attempt to leverage the shooting to quell criticism of his own failing faith):

- "Killing in response to insult, no matter how gross, must be unequivocally condemned. That is why what happened in Paris cannot be tolerated. But neither should we tolerate the kind of intolerance that provoked this violent reaction."
- "Those who work at this newspaper have a long and disgusting record of going way beyond the mere lampooning of figures and this is especially of their depictions of religious figures."
- "Stéphane Charbonnier, the paper's publisher, was killed today in the slaughter. It is too bad that he didn't understand the role he played in his tragic death."

Indeed, it seems a majority of Americans are eager to give up rights in exchange for peace with radical Islamists. They don't even consider that rights are lost in increments, and if we allow our country to obey some part of Islamic law, the same militants will use these successful tactics to force obeisance of their next law, and then the next, and so on. Notice how the 2005 demands of "do not *draw* Muhammad" have now broadened to become "do not *insult* Islam"—restrictions grow in baby steps.

Giving in to terrorism will yield more terrorism, because it works. The way to defeat terrorism of this nature is to show that it doesn't work. The way you show it doesn't work is to continue to break as many of Islam's laws as possible, and even more so after terror riots and murders occur.

Figure 5: NOT the Prophet Muhammad.

NOT Muhammad,
Profit of Islam

See that word *not* next to that smiley face's title in Figure 5? That wasn't there at first; security and business concerns made its addition compulsory. Terrorism, as we all know, is real, and the damage caused by it is real, and while I am happy and eager to defend my right to draw Muhammad, I would place bookstore owners and people who work for my publisher in jeopardy without that *not*. Ridiculous, isn't it? A smiley face labeled *Muhammad* may conceivably be used to excuse murders (note how I didn't say *cause* murders).

In short, I had to yield to terrorism to publish this book, and I'm angry about it.

For the record, I openly and wholeheartedly endorse people drawing Muhammad. I admit to doing it myself and state definitively that I will do it again. And if anyone kills me because I do it, I hope that you, dear readers, will pick up the slack and continue the tradition. Indeed, my safety depends on the terrorists' knowing that such is exactly what will happen.

Rights are lost if not protected, and drawing Muhammad is *not* the last step in radical Islam's terror campaign to place its laws above our rights as Americans. Yesterday we couldn't draw Muhammad; today we can't criticize (or "insult") Islam at all. What's next? The next step is forced, feigned respect. My answer is always no, and I hope you stand with me on this important issue.

Some will counter my drawing of Muhammad with an assertion that I am offending a billion people. To this I reply with two points:

1. We didn't start drawing Muhammad until we were told we could not. This is not about offending Muslims—otherwise we would have been doing it all along. This is about protecting our rights, and *it is* they *who are insulting and offending* me *(and us) when they insist we obey their ridiculous religious laws.*

2. I would gladly offend a billion people in exchange for protecting a single right. People get offended all the time and they get over it. However, rights once lost are usually gone for good and, again, are rarely the last rights you lose. Having rights is more important than not offending people, and protecting rights is far more important than being nice or "respectful" to those who wish to take even the least of our rights away.

Jews, as a counterexample, don't like it when we spell out the name of their god in Hebrew. I was reminded of this when I did just that for the Hebrew billboard American Atheists put up in Brooklyn (more about this in chapter 9 on the Reason Rally). I received a call from a synagogue requesting to take ownership of the vinyl after the billboard came down so it could be disposed of in their "preferred method." However, not once was I told not to dispose of the billboard myself or that *I* needed to obey Jewish law—the synagogue just wanted to dispose of the imprint of their holy name in its own way (not enough though, because I offered to sell the vinyl for what I paid and the synagogue passed, so I just threw it away). No harm, no foul.

Of course, if the Jewish population were trying to prevent us from writing something through laws (or terror rioting), I would be writing whatever they proscribed because that, like the proscription against the drawing of Muhammad, would be an attempt to reduce our freedom and lead us further into theocracy. The answer would be no.

In summary, I draw Muhammad, I spell the name of the Jewish god, and I otherwise do as I see fit without regard to other people's religious laws. Political correctness and religion's archaic and arbitrary rules don't stop me, and neither should they stop you. When religion demands you refrain from doing something otherwise benign, that's just a provocation to do it more.

There is no argument that Islam creates many terrorists, subjugates women, and brainwashes children. But while Islam may present the biggest and most obvious threat, Christianity and Judaism are not innocent. Sure, Christianity isn't breeding too many terrorists today—unless you actually count:

- Anders Breivik, who murdered seventy-seven people in July of 2011, including children, in Norway after creating a fifteen-hundred-page Christian manifesto and identifying himself as a Christian Crusader.[10] (Whom Bill O'Reilly quickly proclaimed was "not a Christian.")[11]
- Eric Rudolph, Christian American terrorist and Olympic Park Bomber.[12]
- Timothy McVeigh, the Christian Oklahoma City bomber.[13]

Globally, Christianity spurs hate, division, and murder, as it has throughout history. Consider the establishment of the death penalty for private homosexual acts in Uganda,[14] the promotion of the spread of AIDS due to the Catholic prohibition against condoms, particularly in Africa,[15] and let's not forget that political war between the Catholics and the Protestants that killed thousands in Northern Ireland.

And then there's Judaism, which, apart from participating in a never-ending war over the tiny piece of land it (and Christianity and Islam) calls holy, also hosts among its orthodox the barbaric practice of some mohels (ritual circumcisers) of sucking the blood from a baby's penis following circumcision—a different kind of "oral tradition," called *metzitzah b'peh,* that can spread deadly herpes to newborns! In 2013, Rabbi David Niederman, executive director of the Hasidic United Jewish Organizations of Williamsburg, told ABC News, "If, God forbid, there was a danger, we would be the first to stop the practice."[16] Of course, now that thirteen children have been infected with herpes, some of whom died while others have suffered brain damage,[17] the rabbis are still defending this horrific practice.[18]

Additionally, in 2011, in response to the brutal murder of an eight-year-old child, Ben Hirsch, president of Survivors for Justice, reported, "For decades, our community's [Brooklyn Hasidic] leadership has been protecting pedophiles. This is going to sound shocking, but the safest place for a sex offender to reside is within the Hasidic and strictly Orthodox community, employed as a teacher."[19]

As for Catholicism—do I have to even mention the pedophile-priest scandals spanning decades? Or the genocidal history of the Inquisitions, support of the Nazi extermination of the Jews by the ironically named Pope Pius XII, and so on from the moment the so-called Holy See was established?

Religion breeds extremism by its very nature. Every spin-off, every cult, every zealot, has the potential to do evil in the name of their gods, and we all must recognize that. Yes, Islam is a problem, but Jews and Christians have nothing about which to crow and are in no position to judge, because they all have histories of barbaric acts done in the name of their religion. Yes, atheist dictators such as Stalin have done horrible things, as have Christian dictators such as Charles Taylor[20] and Mobuto Seko,[21] but this isn't about bad people doing bad things. It's about evil deeds committed *in the name of religion,* it's rampant and widespread, and *every* major religion has blood on its hands.

Hinduism: Classism and Fatalism Run Amok

I would be remiss if I didn't also talk about the horrible classism incarnate that is Hinduism. While not nearly as prevalent in America as the Abrahamic religions, Hinduism is the oldest religion in the world, with estimates of its age exceeding six thousand years.[22] According to Zeenews India, there are over a billion Hindu people; "Hinduism is the third largest religion of the world after Christianity and Islam and 97 percent of all Hindus live in three Hindu-majority countries—India, Nepal and Mauritius."[23]

Here in America, our sheltered view of Hinduism usually conjures up images of vegetarianism, yoga, and tantric sex, but these niceties hide an undercurrent of rampant intolerance and stifled, primitive behavior.

Hinduism has several main gods and millions of smaller ones (which some say are all manifestations of one primary deity).[24] Like so many other religions, Hinduism has deeply ingrained misogyny and gender bias.[25] Like so many other religions, Hinduism has a long history of violence against other religions and between its sects.[26] However, none of this is what makes Hinduism so unusually abhorrent. That honor comes from the concepts of fatalism and reincarnation.

Hinduism asserts that a person is reincarnated after death and born into a new life that reflects how good a Hindu the person was in the past life. If you are a good Hindu in this life, your reward in the next is a richer and happier life. If you are bad, you can be born a poorer, lower-caste person or, worse, an animal. The caste system is a manifestation of this sentiment—upper-caste members have better jobs and more money, lower-caste members are the community's impoverished and uneducated. Whatever your situation is, whether it's a position of wealth or poverty, health or illness, it is what the gods have determined you deserve.

Think about how this affects adherents—it obliterates compassion for the poor, empathy for the underprivileged, and responsibility to help the needy! After all, they deserve what the gods have bestowed on them. The rich have no responsibility to help out because they also deserve their good fortune, and they wouldn't want to displease the gods that punished the poor, lest they be downgraded in the next life!

The division is stark and permanent. If you are in a lower caste, an upper-caste person might think nothing of kicking you in the street if you are in the way. Lower-caste members are sometimes referred to as "untouchables" because upper-casters find them so vile they will not even cross shadows with them for fear of defilement.[27] As a result, untouchables might not even be able to find jobs as maids and servants of the rich because the rich won't permit them in their homes. (I've heard a story of rich people with dirty toilets because the rich are too pompous to clean their own, but they will not allow members of lower castes in their homes to do the work either.)

Moreover, a person's place in the caste system is permanent, again because the gods have determined that people are in the right places. This eliminates striving for betterment. It stifles attempts, or even dreams, of improving your lifestyle. If you are lower caste, you will stay there, as will *all* of your descendants. There is no way up. Lower-caste members need to obey the rules and maintain the status quo for their whole lives, in the hopes of moving up in caste in the next life. There is no mixed-caste marriage, and on the off chance one occurs, the couple is sometimes exiled or executed.[28]

In his book *Culture Can Kill,* Subodh Shah describes how Hinduism's fatalism has stifled Indian society:

Fatalism is worse than laziness. It provides us with philosophical foundations to justify our laziness and failures; imparts an aura of respectability to our inactivity and passivity; and shuts out hard work as a possible choice. If my life is beyond my purview, why bother being industrious or ambitious? Even if I bother, will it help? Do we have the power to shape our destiny? The regular answer from our populist culture of fatalism is a resounding No. How can this culture ever have a motivation to strive, struggle, win or advance?[29]

Moreover, and an obvious part of the scam, Hindus place the concept of faith above intelligence. Indeed, the religion of Hinduism looks down on intelligence as an evil force to be avoided! Shah continues:

Hindu theosophy assigns intelligence a much lower place than faith even when it pays lip-service to intelligence. Unquestionable faith in gurus, scriptures, saints and mythology is routinely advocated, emphasized and assumed. Absurd myths are preached, defended and believed under various pretexts. These encourage irrationality that becomes a habit of the mind in the populace. Irrational attitudes imparted to children become entrenched through life. Popular culture makes non-reason legitimate and acceptable. . . . Pious people in India believe that intelligence is a hindrance in matters of religion. To them reason or even skepticism is not only undesirable, it is an unmitigated evil.[30]

Finally, as one might predict, the pedestal on which the Hindu leaders (swamis and gurus) sit enables rampant abuse, much of it sexual. A simple Google search yields instance after instance of gurus, being gods to their followers (remember, Hinduism has millions of gods, some of which are self-deified gurus), using their position to have sex with followers.[31,32]

I added this section to illustrate the breadth of the problem of religion, even among those many people wrongly believe to be benign. One can easily see how the six-thousand-year religion cycle has evolved an ancient myth into a powerful force for classism. Hinduism, like other religions, seeks expansion and government protection and demands respect, but deserves none. The Lie of God goes way beyond Abraham.

The Bad Atheists

I've spent most of this chapter talking about religion, and over and over I've restated that when I do I am not calling out individual people. Now I must take a break from beating that drum to talk about some people who, as individuals, deserve to be held in low regard because they are not the victims, they are the liars—and they are atheists. I wish we could look at the broad spectrum of atheists and say we are all on the same side pushing for our own equality, but this is not the case. Many atheists are simply working against us, usually for their personal gain.

The most obvious of these are the atheist televangelists and other preachers who spread lies for money without regard for truth, fairness, or justice. They are the true stereotype—immoral liars who convince the uneducated victims in their flocks to donate their hard-earned money in the name of a god the preacher knows very well does not exist.

Now, I'm not talking about those preachers trapped in their jobs who can't get out. I'm talking about the ones who make money in the names of their gods, fooling their flocks, often teaching that atheists are bad, damned, and worthy of contempt. Imagine the immorality of being an atheist pretending to be pious, and teaching people to hate honest atheists, for personal gain!

Remember the reasoning I used for our friends in Washington: if they believe in hell and an all-seeing judging God, and if they speak to/with/through this god, they'd be pretty stupid (or insane) to risk repeated affairs or other wrongdoings. So let's expose some preachers to the same logic:

- George Rekers. A vocal antigay activist in the name of God before he was caught taking a trip to Europe with a man he allegedly "rented" from a Web site in May of 2010.[33]
- Ted Haggard. Another antigay pastor who (allegedly) paid for gay sex over three years with a man from whom he admittedly bought methamphetamine in 2006.[34]
- Jim Bakker. In 1980 he was involved in a sex scandal with Jessica Hahn, and he was convicted in 1989 of bilking followers out of over $158 million.[35]
- Harold Camping. He was *sure* the world was going to end in May of 2011. He might have been insane, but given that he never apologized for being wrong, and 2011 was his third such prediction,[36] I think he was probably a liar.[37] A liar worth $75 million.
- Peter Popoff. Claimed to be getting signals from heaven about the pain people in his audience were experiencing. How did he know? He was getting a signal from his wife, with a radio transmitter, through a hidden earpiece. He was exposed in 1986, with recordings and all, on national TV by James Randi.[38] (Popoff still preaches though, and he still has followers.)[39] But you tell me—is this the mind of a true believer, an insane person, or a liar who has no fear of lying in the name of God?

Whoever says "I know him" but does not keep his commandments is a liar, and the truth is not in him. —JOHN 2:4

It is repugnant to accept, but we must. Some of the worst people in religion are atheists, and we have to own that to keep our perspective. Just like religion, atheism does not innately yield integrity.

On the subject of integrity, our final adversary is the least palatable, but still useful—the apologetic atheist. These are the atheists who apologize to the theists for being atheists or for other atheists' behavior. These are people like S. E. Cupp, who has gone on record as saying she would never vote for an atheist like herself and she wishes she were a theist: "I envy religious people. . . . I envy the faithful. I would like to be a person of faith, but I'm not there yet."[40]

Malcolm X seethed with anger at what he called "Uncle Thomas blacks" who reinforced white supremacy for their own selfish betterment by working within the white establishment (having achieved an elevated status due to their acquiescence) without trying to change it. They vocally approved of segregation and other poor treatment of blacks by whites by agreeing with and repeating the twisted logic that white people used to support it. Here we see Cupp doing the same thing, sitting among the religionists claiming she is an atheist while saying it's okay to be bigoted against atheists. To wit:

> *And you know what? I would never vote for an atheist president. Ever . . . because I do not think that someone who represents five to ten percent of the population should be representing and thinking that everyone else in the world is crazy, but me.*
>
> *I like that there is a check, okay? That there's a person in the office that doesn't think he's bigger than the state. . . . I like religion being a check and knowing that my president goes home every night addressing someone above him and not thinking all the power resides right here. . . . Atheists don't have that.*"[41]

Whether Cupp is actually an atheist remains to be seen. Note that "I'm not there yet" comment—what does that say to you? My (fake) psychic powers tell me she is planning to convert to Christianity and write a book sometime in the near future, which will spread bigotry against atheists, increase the level of ignorance about us, and make her a megaton of money. If I were an immoral Christian posing as an atheist to help Christianity, or an immoral atheist looking to make a ton of cash, that is what I'd do. The payday would be huge.

Another side to Ms. Cupp's position is in the no-such-thing-as-bad-press category: she certainly does get the word *atheist* out to one of our target markets. She doesn't set a good example, but she does put atheism and the reality of our existence in front of people, and much to our own chagrin, we must admit this has value. When Christian S. E. Cupp fans meet another atheist, there will likely be less of an anti-atheist knee-jerk reaction because they know of at least one atheist they like.

In-groups are powerful things. They allow good people who are Christians to protect bad people who are Christians. They allow good people who are Jews to defend bad people who are Jews. We must not be like that if we are to be ethical and logical people. Bad atheists exist, and they deserve no special treatment or regard just because they are atheists. If we are to be the good guys, we must begin by demanding good behavior even from within atheism. Atheism is broad, and our ranks span the gamut of politics and ethical positions. I'm all for that breadth, but let's not allow our in-group to be about atheists that hurt people or hurt our country and our cause via deceit and lies.

We must internalize that atheists can be assholes just like religionists, and all are responsible for their own actions. None get a free ride because they are on our side of the religion fence. Criminals need to go to jail, and liars need to get called out.

Ethics first.

The reason there are good Muslims who credit their goodness to their religion *and* bad Muslims who credit their evil (which they think is good) to the same religion is the same reason why both good and bad Christians, good and bad Jews, and the rest all push their holy book as the source of their good or bad activity.

They are all wrong.

If the Bible and other holy books were at all reliable sources of morality, good and bad religious people wouldn't *both* be able to point to their holy books as guidance and inspiration to support their positions. If morality is completely separable from religion, we would expect to see exactly what we do—people making their own moral decisions and then ascribing that morality to their particular holy book. They use their scripture as a shield to both defend their actions and to insulate themselves from criticism.

Bottom line: You don't need anybody telling you what is good. You are probably already good. You are definitely already godless— because there are no gods.

Chapter 4

FIGHTING THE GOOD FIGHT

you people really disgust me, freedom of religion, or is that not in our con-
stitution, i am not a zealot, but people like you make me want to throw
up. you guya and the aclu are the ones destroying the moral fabric of this
country and the holes are showing. after your deayhs we will see who was
right. ill bet it will be hot where you guys will end up.

—AN E-MAIL TO AMERICAN ATHEISTS

They knew that to put god in the Constitution was to put man out. They
knew that the recognition of a Deity would be seized upon by fanatics and
zealots as a pretext for destroying the liberty of thought. They knew the
terrible history of the church too well to place in her keeping or in the keep-
ing of her god the sacred rights of man. They intended that all should have
the right to worship or not to worship, that our laws should make no dis-
tinction on account of creed. They intended to found and frame a govern-
ment for man and for man alone. They wished to preserve the individuality
of all to prevent the few from governing the many and the many from per-
secuting and destroying the few. —ROBERT G. INGERSOLL

I'm sick of being told not to be a dick, and not just because I dislike
gender-specific insults (which I only use in this case because it's what
some people call me).

It's sometimes important to do things that make people call you a dick. I'm going to spend some time talking about why acting in a manner that some people regard as dickish is not only appropriate, but also necessary to the movement and the country, and, in an important way, downright nice.

So, what's a dick? The definition varies from person to person, but to many I'm a dick whenever I say something that makes theists angry or even mildly puts them out. If I call a religion a myth, I'm a dick. What I say may be true, but I'm still a dick. If I say theists are brainwashed from an early age to believe a myth, or to pretend to believe if they don't, I'm a dick. What I'm saying is true, but I'm a dick for saying it. I am accused of saying things that incite hate and anger, but it is not as if I begin my sentences with "Yesterday, when I was skull-fucking your savior . . ." I simply tell the truth and use labels that are accurate, if not politically correct.

The people who get angry at me when hearing the truth do so because the truth hurts. Just for example, look at the multiple hadith (sayings of the prophet, which many Muslims regard as holy scripture)[1] that state that Muhammad married a little girl ("Aisha reported: Allah's Apostle married me when I was six years old, and I was admitted to his house when I was nine years old").[2] That Muhammad consummated his marriage with Aisha when she was nine ("The Prophet wrote the [marriage contract] with Aisha while she was six years old and consummated his marriage with her while she was nine years old and she remained with him for nine years")[3] is important because it calls into question the so-called perfect morality of Muhammad. It also calls direct attention to the plight many young girls continue to face because Muhammad's rape of Aisha is cited in certain parts of the Muslim world as sufficient justification today for little girls to be married off and raped.[4]

See how I used the word *rape* there to talk about sex between an old man and a little girl? That's me being a dick again by telling the truth.

In the US justice system, such horrible behavior would justifiably lead to long prison sentences (and in prison, such a rapist would be low on the social totem pole—below murderers[5]). Nobody whose morality is perfect can hurt a child, at least in the opinion of most good people, and this means Muslims need to deal with this fact about their prophet.

If I say, "Muhammad raped fifty children," most followers of Islam would laugh because it is not a true statement, but if I mention the rape of Aisha, those same Muslims get angry because it's true (according to their own texts). Truth hurts, and they must deal with truth—unless nobody mentions any of this for fear of being labeled a dick.

I may be called a dick for speaking the truth, but some of the real dicks are the atheists who tell me not to be one. Some verbally attack me with a holier-than-thou attitude usually reserved for the most pompous of preachers, laced with bile and vulgarity reminiscent of the crap we get from the Religious Right. They don't wonder about whether there is room for breadth in the movement, or even if there would *be* a movement without "dicks" like me. They see their way as the only way, from which any deviation warrants an in-your-face confrontation with allies, all to protect the wrong people from hearing something true. They are abrasive to us, their brothers- and sisters-in-arms, because we are slightly different from them. I am not saying all "nice guy" atheists are assholes, just those who are so shortsighted they can't see how quickly and by how much this movement would lose its steam without firebrands to blaze the way for discussion by breaking the barriers of political correctness.

Not calling bullshit on bullshit is *bullshit*.

———

Allow me to illustrate my point about the need for breadth with a brief detour to the 2013 Boston Marathon bombings. Boston has a strong and thriving atheist community, led in part by Greg Epstein, humanist chaplain at Harvard. As a popular, friendly leader in a city with a large population (and high tolerance) of the nonreligious, Greg was perfectly positioned as a nice-guy atheist to get support and inclusion from the religious community.

And then the Boston Marathon bombing occurred.

Suddenly, President Obama is heading to Boston for an "interfaith vigil" with the local faith leaders. Greg, along with other secular representatives, knew and contacted the right people about getting involved, but they turned him (and us) away from the vigil. We represent nearly 40 percent of the Boston community,[6] but were excluded from a "communitywide" mourning event, just as we were after the Newtown massacre and from every single 9/11 memorial, because of bigotry. The nice-guy approach didn't work.

I have two problems with accommodationism, one of which, as I already explained, is the legitimization of religion in the eyes of the theists, the pedestal on which religion sits, and the bigotry that pedestal enables. The other issue is that accommodationism addresses the wrong target—individuals.

"Diplomats" envision changing religion from within, de-demonizing atheists in the eyes of one theist at a time (the method of catching more flies with honey, not vinegar). This is analogous to how the churches have changed over history. Society evolves sufficiently beyond the church's teachings until the church is forced to change to keep parishioners—which it does to the smallest degree possible to avoid looking as if it's admitting it was wrong. For example, the recent changes in the Vatican and major churches toward the LGBTQ and atheist communities are a direct result of activism on those issues pulling society toward tolerance, and society dragging religion along with it. The broad secular community is partly responsible for the pressure that is modernizing the Vatican. This kind of change happens slowly, in baby steps, because religion loathes change, which disproves its claim to objective truth based on infallible texts.

Diplomats seek to emulate this evolution by changing the minds of the believers—not about God, but about atheists (usually using more theist-approved euphemisms such as *unbelievers* or *humanists*), thereby forcing religion to become more pluralistic. It's easy and pleasant and seems polite.

What many accommodating atheists don't understand is that all religions have one thing in common—they are anti-atheist. We are the last out-group on which all religions can agree. If they support equal treatment for atheists, they in effect advocate stepping off their pedestals (if atheism is equal to religions, religions have no advantages or pedestals over anyone at all), and so *our equality endangers their legitimacy*. So, yes, representatives of religions can smile at us and shake our hands, but religions will *not* back us, help us, or support us when it counts. To do so threatens their existence.

Diplomacy alone cannot trump greed, money, and power. That's why diplomacy alone will always ultimately fail to produce the results all atheists seek in a timely manner. That's why diplomacy alone failed in Boston.

Enter the firebrands.

We chip away at privilege, disrespect the unrespectable, and refuse to obey someone else's religious rules. We laugh at threats of hell, literally and loudly, while demanding total equality. We attract everyone's attention to atheists' existence and issues. Firebrands are the movement's awareness generator. Firebrands go on TV complaining and shouting and demanding, and then the diplomats come out to soften our statements—sometimes emphatically so. In the end, the firebrands look like the "bad atheists," the diplomats look like "good atheists," and guess what that means to believers? Good atheists *do* exist!

This is called "shifting the Overton window" (a new name for an old strategy), and it is well described by Josh Bolotsky at beautiful trouble.org as follows:[7]

> *The Overton window . . . designates the range of points on the spectrum that are considered part of a "sensible" conversation within public opinion and/or traditional mass media.*
>
> *The most important thing about the Overton window, however, is that it can be shifted to the left or the right, with the once merely "acceptable" becoming "popular" or even imminent policy, and formerly "unthinkable" positions becoming the open position of a partisan base. The challenge for activists and advocates is to move the window in the direction of their preferred outcomes, so their desired outcome moves closer and closer to "common sense."*
>
> *There are two ways to do this: the long, hard way and the short, easy way. The long, hard way is to continue making your actual case persistently and persuasively until your position becomes more politically mainstream, whether it be due to the strength of your rhetoric or a long-term shift in societal values. By contrast, the short, easy way is to amplify and echo the voices of those who take a position a few notches more radical than what you really want.*

I wonder what would have happened if a few hundred firebrand atheists had protested our exclusion from the Boston Marathon memorial service. Would it have brought more attention to our cause? Would it have gotten us included? I cannot say for sure; I just know that the nice-guy approach fell short, again, and nobody heard from atheists, cared about our inclusion, or considered us a part of the severely injured Boston community.

Because of the firebrands, change is happening not on an individual level, but rather on a national level. Our lawsuits force a change in religion from *without*—humbling it by demanding enforcement of legal equality—while our honesty chips away at the pedestal on which theists place their religion. It is the firebrand who primes the theist for the diplomat. I wonder if the Obama administration and Boston-area clergy would have seen the Harvard Humanists in a different light if American Atheists had been the "bad guys" in Boston.

Criticism against what we do focuses only on the idea of respect, not on the truth. This only plays into the hands of the people who run religion. Religionists want religion's placement on the pedestal of re-spect preserved by any means. But religion deserves no respect. Rather, it has earned scorn, ridicule, and in-your-face opposition, as have its trappings. Exhibiting disrespect toward religion in public chips away at its hold on the listening population. Men wearing funny hats (with rare exception, it's always men) need to be addressed by their first name because calling them Father or Your Eminence places them undeservedly on a higher tier than everybody else—a privilege that should be reserved for people who actually accomplish something noteworthy or worthwhile and deserve the titles they've earned (e.g., Doctor, General, or Governor).

I find it disturbing that religious folk are always suggesting or even demanding we be respectful of religion. Even if we disagree, we are told we must be nice and respect religion's place as equal or superior to the secular, rational position. But giving reverence to religion gives it strength and protects it from the criticism it deserves.

Would you say it was okay for a major corporate executive to shuf-fle around pedophile employees and withhold information about them from the police? How about if the executives got caught and, instead of admitting guilt, chided the *victims* for making their abuse public? Yet worldwide this is what we do for religions because fire-brands are too few and far between, and everyone is giving rever-ence to religion because religion demands it. As a result religion gets a bye on heinous crime after heinous crime, and its only defense is that religion gets to do what it wants because its god says so. The fictional executive of this paragraph would get life in prison, hated by all. The real Pope Benedict retired in luxury and honor.

Remember, placing someone on a pedestal means the person is constantly looking down on you. I think religion deserves to look up to atheism. If anyone deserves a pedestal, it is those who revere and live by logic and reason.

Recently, a priest against whom I was debating asserted I should call him Father. What a repugnant idea. *My* father is dead, and he hated religion to boot (Dad called preachers and rabbis "whores"). No priest comes close to deserving the same title as the man who helped rear me.

This priest then asked if I would use his professional title, Reverend, which I said was a reasonable request—if he did the same for me and used my title, President. He didn't like that, oh, no. He wanted to call me Mr. Silverman, using the standard honorific, while I used his professional title and called him Reverend.

I gave him the choice: each uses a standard honorific (Mr.) to address the other, or we each use professional titles (Reverend and President), or first names (which I preferred), because we are equals. He got angry and walked away.

When you put preachers on your level, they get offended. They resist being treated as equals because they aren't accustomed to it. Well, too bad. We get that a lot. So much of what we do is demanding equality, and then being attacked because religions—mostly Christianity in America—don't want equality. They want—no, *demand*—favoritism because they are used to it. They call equality "offensive."

If I called you ugly, you'd legitimately be offended. Any personal insult directed at you, an individual, would be reasonable cause for taking offense. Insulting religion is *not* offensive, at least not in the same way. Religion is not a person and has no opinions or feelings, but the masses assign a personification (god) to their religion and then decide if your words or statements offend this fictional character. Just as gods can endorse candidates, so too can gods be offended if you insult their mythology. The followers simply feel insulted *on behalf of* their god, assuming they know their god well enough to decide what he/she/it would or would not find offensive.

Let's say you thought I'd insulted your friend. You would feel angry your friend was insulted and would therefore be offended by proxy, unless your friend said, "No, wait, it's okay, I'm not offended for X reason," in which case you would feel better. Insulting a god is different because all of the decision making occurs in the mind of the believers. They hear something, then decide whether their god is offended and become offended or angry on behalf of that god. Since none of the gods seem to be capable of telling believers, "It's okay, I'm not offended" (gods only tell believers they are right), people often take action to defend their god's honor in accordance with their individual opinions of what the god might want. Just as some pick and choose their morals and life lessons from their particular holy book, so too do they cherry-pick that which offends their god.

You might be thinking, *So shouldn't we do the very best not to offend them?*

Let's examine that logic.

In American Atheists' advertising and public statements the objective is to further the cause of atheism, get more atheists out of the closet, and increase knowledge about and tolerance for atheists. That's it, by the way. Nothing in American Atheists' charter seeks to force religious TV shows off the air or force all mention of religion out of the lives of Americans who believe, although that's what we are regularly accused of.

For instance, though she's been dead for nearly two decades,

Madalyn O'Hair is still being accused of trying to take off the air all shows that mention God.[8] The most famous "victim" was *Touched by an Angel,* which she successfully ripped from the airwaves after nine successful seasons,[9] *just a few years after she died!* All this stems from a rumor that she once started a petition to remove all mention of God from the airwaves, which never happened, as explained by TruthOrFiction: "No such petition has ever been presented to the FCC by Madalyn Murray O'Hair or her organization of American Atheists. In fact, this eRumor is more than 20 years old and has produced more mail response to the FCC than anything in its history."[10]

I wonder what Madalyn's ghost will do next!

Our mission is not to stop private citizens or TV or radio stations from using or promoting religion. Tons of religious shows, songs, and stations are out there, and they are all legal (unless they appear on a government-run channel). Perform a Google search, look at all the accusations against us for doing such things, and look for proof.

We seek to bring atheism into the realm of the regular, because *it is regular.* We seek to make people think, convert closeted atheists into outed atheists, and increase acceptance of atheists by theists. We seek the total and absolute separation of religion and government because that's how you achieve religious freedom for *everyone.*

Some fervent believers are not going to convert no matter what we do, but they *can* become more tolerant. The past few years are full of stories about benign atheist billboards panned or banned by believers. The United Coalition of Reason's "Good Without God" (2009) and the Freethought Action Project's "One Nation Indivisible" (2010) billboard campaigns were nice and completely inoffensive, yet they were hated by Christian believers and defaced.[11]

These people weren't placated by the positive content of the billboards. They didn't care what they said—only that they *existed.* Their god, they determined, was insulted at the presence of *any* expression that atheists are extant, let alone relevant, and they complained loudly and emphatically.

This is analogous to how atheists all face bigotry in our lives, not because we are hateful or rude, but because we are atheists. Have you ever lost friends because they found out you were an atheist? Did you have to offend them first? Not likely. Your experiences have probably mirrored mine—someone finds out I am an atheist, and then suddenly that person is no longer my friend (this has happened only a few times, fortunately, and to my surprise, it didn't bother me *at all* because I knew I was better off without these so-called friends).

That's theists being rude. That's theists being bigoted assholes as a result of serious brainwashing by a poisonous religion cycle.

They're not going to change their minds because of what we say or do. They want silence from us, and anything else will be taken as an attack on their god.

So why should we be nice in our advertisements or speeches? Why are we pussyfooting around the truth to placate those who will only be truly placated by our silence? Why not concentrate on the segments of our market that might actually bring about the evolution we seek? We don't need to worry about offending those who are offended because we have the gall to exist, or those who will lie about us to make us seem less reasonable. We need to shout from the rooftops that which we know is true: religion is a lie (yes, all of it), gods are myths (yes, all of them), and most people already know it (yes, they do).

This is why, as president of American Atheists, I've taken a harder line with the organization's advertising policy. Other organizations can put up smiling faces and appeals to religious folk to like us. It's a part of the movement's overall strategy, but it won't work alone, and it doesn't work for me. We need not beg for affirmation from those with unrespectable positions.

Rather, we who know the difference between fantasy and reality need to claim that position proudly. We, who are right, need to *say* that we are right, so doubters can explore their doubts, knowing there is a place to land when they come to a conclusion. We have the responsibility to make fair and verifiable information available to them to perform that exploration.

Yes, we need to reach out to the doubters, even if the theists hate us for it. Yes, we need to use the press to the best of our ability, even if that press is Fox News.

Now, many atheists believe the best way to promote these ideas we all share is by leading with an outstretched arm, extending olive branch after olive branch, hoping that the nice-guy approach will get us to equality. But frankly I tend to doubt that will work because it never has in the past. Remember, our adversaries are *not* the believers, our opponents are the string pullers—the professional liars and victims who wear robes and pronounce themselves holy, and the politicians in their pockets. Being nice may change the perception of atheists to some followers, but true believers follow their leaders, and their leaders aren't likely to walk away from power and money just to be nice. We are their last great Bad Guy. Accepting atheists dooms religion to the equality preachers fear so much.

Now, to be sure, some friendly theists out there won't like their religion being called a myth, or their belief being called silly or backward. This does not detract from its being true—these nice, well-meaning people pray to an imaginary deity because they are victims of the religion that promotes it. They don't just "think differently"; they are *incorrect* and they stick to their guns despite evidence to the contrary. It is not a respectable opinion, yet they, the moderate friendly theists, demand respect for it and get offended when it is not granted. But again, religion is on a pedestal because we allow it to be, and my answer to their demands for respect for their religion is no.

Smart people can and do believe stupid things (that's what brainwashing is for), and it's important to internalize this fact. So many times I've heard atheists call religious people stupid, but these people aren't stupid, they're injured. They are force-fed from their earliest memories the idea that they *are* Christians or Jews or Muslims. They had no choice—the religion was drilled into them as a part of their core identity. As a result, even when you correctly criticize the religion, they will take it as if you've attacked them personally. This is where I step in and make sure I am being clear in my criticism of the religion, as I respect the human who, like the vast majority of the world's population, believes what the person's parents and religious leaders said about the man in the sky.

We must remember our targets. Change is not going to come from the theist, but rather from the atheist. Being nice might make us more likable to small numbers of individual theists, but in the end theists take cues from preachers, who make money and earn a living by tearing atheism down. We need to concentrate on the atheists coming out and taking their rightful place in society, and this is done by motivating them to make the change. This is done with frank, honest talk without regard to political correctness, combined with compassion for the individuals afflicted with theism.

All Religion Is Cafeteria Religion

> *If a man has sexual relations with a man as one does with a woman, both of them have done what is detestable. They are to be put to death; their blood will be on their own heads.*
>
> —LEVITICUS 20:13

Orthodox believers often criticize less strict members of their faith for practicing "cafeteria (insert name of religion here)," meaning they aren't observing every chapter and verse of the faith and are therefore not as "good" a Christian, Jew, what have you as those who do.

Here's the truth: *every religionist is a cafeteria religionist.* Every time Christians and Jews meet an atheist and don't kill the person,[12] they are committing *cafeterianism*. Every time a woman teaches a class,[13] every time a man holds an old-fashioned football,[14] every time anyone wears a blended fabric,[15] the person ignores and breaks a biblical law.

Why? Because these laws are stupid.

That's really it, isn't it? Nobody worries about the biblical laws we all as a society collectively dismiss out of hand because they're stupid, outdated, or just plain inconvenient. Not only are these laws imperfect, they are not even worthy of a second thought, yet these laws stem from the supposed perfect word of God, or so Bibles are marketed. I am reminded of the man on the Internet who tattooed *Leviticus 20:13* on his arm, in a clear statement against LGBTQ equality, while he totally ignored that just a few paragraphs away, in the same context, is a commandment against tattoos.[16]

This à la carte approach is especially apparent among the mainstream religionists. A 2003 *Washington Post* poll found that 88 percent of Catholics believed using a birth control pill or condoms was morally acceptable, which is the exact opposite of what Catholicism preaches.[17] It's all—*all*—subjective.

Since it's all subjective, it's all up to the individual (as influenced to some degree by the person's religion cycle). On the granular level that means all religionists are unique in their beliefs. So while some claim Christians are a majority, the truth is that when it comes to specific beliefs, *everyone* is in the minority because everyone is making conclusions about their god and morality individually.

Please let this soak in.

This means all good (and bad) morality is the result of your unique combination of genetic tendencies interacting with your moral upbringing, including your personal religion cycle, if any. As I've mentioned, religious people might think they *are* (for example) Christians, but in fact religion is only a part of who they are. To varying degrees, the meme of religion invades our natural selves and imprints itself on our personalities, affecting people differently, depending on all the other factors that make us *us*. Religion doesn't make people, but it changes them and shapes their morality, sometimes convincing otherwise nice people to make immoral judgments—essentially making nice people act like assholes.

Holy books are broadly interpretable, with many examples of good and bad morality presented in a positive manner, as approved by God. Those passages people dismiss as immoral are judgment calls they all make, individually, *irrespective of whether God says it's moral*.

In other words, terrorism is just as much a part of Islam as brotherhood. Killing gays and blasphemers is just as much a part of Christianity as loving thy neighbor. It's all individual—people make their own determination, pick out the parts of their holy scriptures with which they agree and call their morality *objective and perfect*, whether it supports flying planes into buildings or helping a stranger in distress. The stuff in religion that you hate has no less of a basis in the source material than the stuff in religion you love.

Morality is fluid. What was once moral is immoral today, which includes rape,[18] slavery,[19] and infanticide.[20] We simply cannot rely on the texts that promote such horrible ideals as sources for morality, because deciding whether a particular passage is moral or not is subject to the whim of the reader.

Again, religion hates to admit it's wrong because it insists its tenets are divine and therefore perfect, but morality is fluid and ever evolving as we as a species learn and grow. As a result, religion will continue to espouse yesterday's values long after society has moved away from them. This can be seen today when preachers preach against LGBTQ equality or even women's equality. Because of its resistance to change, which is the result of its reliance on a supposedly divine (and therefore perfect) source, religion will constantly espouse things that are immoral by today's standards. This cannot change because religion cannot admit it is wrong without sacrificing its

perceived moral perfection as a result of divine intervention/inspi-
ration/dictation. Ironically, the moral pedestal on which religion
places itself keeps religion immoral.

By its very nature, religion will remain defined by yesteryear's
morality, always and forever. Thus, there will always be sects of religion that are immoral to the modern mind.

Invariably, moderate religionists will accuse radicals of not "really" being a member of that religion. They defend their religion by
not admitting it is so broad as to support bad behavior, so they try
hard to disassociate their religion from the people who, in the name
of that same religion, do bad things. For example, Bill O'Reilly
argued that Anders Breivik (who murdered scores of people, including children, in a 2011 Norway attack) was "not a real Christian,"
even though Breivik stated outright that he did what he had done in
the name of God, calling himself the "savior of Christianity."[21] Who
was right? Both O'Reilly and Breivik supported their arguments with
the same Bible, so how do we know who is correct? Similarly, many
Muslims decry the acts of terrorism committed in the name of their
god, saying the terrorists aren't following Islam at all and are "per-
verting the Qur'an,"[22] but as you would expect, supporters of the
Taliban have some very different opinions on what makes a "true
Muslim."[23] Both sides use their holy books to defend their positions,
so who is right?

Religious moderates are also doing what American Atheists is doing, but in the wrong direction—they are normalizing the extremists
of religion by increasing their religion's perceived penetration into
American society, while protecting that same religion from criticism
when people do bad things in its name. They are making religion
look better than it is by openly giving credit for their goodness to
their religion, while downplaying, ignoring, or actively denying the
religion's immoral teachings. This is obviously the result of the indoctrination they received that taught them propping up their reli-

gion is a good thing, even when they know religion is flawed or wrong.

If religion includes everything from heroism to genocide, and the believer picks which parts to observe, where is its utility? If it gives no more guidance than real life, where are the lessons and why would its instructions be more relevant than any other teachings, especially those based on today's morality, knowledge, and society? Isn't real life the actual teacher here? If involvement strengthens religion, aren't all adherents (and atheists claiming to be adherents) really strengthening yesteryear's morality (modern immorality)?

People need to realize that all the god-supported immorality in holy books is simply a relic of yesteryear's morality that serves as indisputable evidence religion is never perfect, objective, or even remotely dependable as a source of moral guidance.

Good religious people are not good *because* of the moral teachings in their holy books—they are good *despite* the immoral teachings— that is, their genetics and other factors, which would make them good people, outweigh their indoctrination. By the same token, bad religious people are bad despite the good teachings in their holy books. Both are victims of the indoctrination they've received as a part of their religion cycle. It's all picking and choosing from the religious cafeteria. It's all individual. It's all relative.

I'll Pray for You

Prayer is useful to everyone except the person praying. It is used to reinforce submission and reassert the power of religion over the life of the believer. If a preacher can get people on their knees begging for something, and the preacher controls what those people think about the god to whom they are praying, that preacher has a lot of power. And if the believer has a lot of power in the real world? Well, that's why I cringe when I see any world leader paying pious homage to a religious leader. Who is in charge then?

Prayer is also used by believers to pretend they are doing something good. If they are powerless to do anything tangible, they beg their god to bend his will to theirs, then stand up feeling as if they've helped in some way. The old atheist axiom "two hands that help are better than a thousand lips that pray" comes to mind.

Most often I hear the standard "I'll pray for you" by some believer (usually Christian) who thinks it is an escape mechanism—a witty closing line to give just before leaving the scene, a religious version of "Yeah, whatever." To be clear, I'm not talking about those instances when theists know they can't help you with a particular problem or bad situation, so they tell you they're praying for you in an attempt to show support. I don't mind this because they are doing something they think will help by praying for my health or well-being. It's useless (and, if they know I'm an atheist, insensitive), but not malevolent. What I'm talking about is the "I'll pray for you" I get while debating or discussing religion, said by someone hoping for divine intervention to "help me see the light"—usually served with an extra helping of smugness.

Some atheists respond with something witty like "I'll think for you," but given the opportunity, I would rather educate than insult, and this situation *is* an opportunity. The better way is to inform the people they are acting in a hostile manner.

The believers who say they are praying for me are victims of a lie and think they are doing something good; I let them know they are not. I tell them to imagine I had a newfangled gun that forcibly turned religious people into atheists. I tell them the gun didn't really work, but I thought it did. Let's say I decided to force them to be atheists, so I pointed the atheist gun at them and pulled the trigger. Would they think that was a nice thing to do? Would they appreciate my effort, or would they feel assaulted?

When you pray for me, you are asking your god to change me.

You are asking your god to forcibly enter my life and my brain and change my way of thinking (using euphemisms such as asking God to "open my heart to Jesus" is evidence of the intent of the assault). Like my fictional gun, the prayer won't work, but believers think it will and deploy a weapon that they believe I cannot defeat—a god— to make me just like them. It's not a nice thing to do, and it's not a minor thing to do. Rather, it is religious intolerance incarnate and demonstrates religion's unwillingness to peacefully coexist. "Don't pray for me," I tell them, "accept me as I am instead."

That usually gets the message across.

On "Proofs"

Possibly the lamest excuse to believe in God is Pascal's Wager. Even "I dreamed about God" is better than this pale attempt to justify belief. Pascal posited that your belief should be measured on the downsides of the alternatives. Since the downside of being an atheist is bad (hell for eternity) if you're wrong, and the downside of being a wrong Christian (you just die) is not as bad, you should be a Christian. So pick the side with the worst downside for not believing and follow that just in case it's right (and for no other reason).

Many have written of the flaws of Pascal's Wager (God can read minds and knows you're just hedging your bets, for one), so I won't go into them here except to say people who use this argument are simply not thinking. They are thinking with their heart, not with their head, which is another way of saying "pretending to think" but actually not thinking at all. I am reminded of a time when Richard Dawkins appeared on *The O'Reilly Factor* and backed Bill O'Reilly into a corner with the following simple observation:

> **RD:** "But you know that if you'd been born to another religion, if you'd been born to a Muslim family, you'd be

a Muslim with every bit as much fervency as you are a Christian now."

BO: "Yes, but I choose to believe that my religion is correct."

This is totally bogus. Belief is involuntary, you can't "choose to believe" something you really don't. You can choose tuna for lunch, but even if I held a gun to your head, you could not choose to believe that the world is flat. You believe the world is (essentially) round, and nothing can change that but a substantial amount of evidence to the contrary. Therefore, you cannot choose to believe, you can only *choose to pretend to believe* in God. You believe what you believe, without regard to the ramifications thereof, and when people use the euphemisms of "choosing to believe" (or "thinking with my heart"), what they are usually saying is that they don't believe it at all, but are faking it and don't want to admit it. This usually stems from the societal and familial pressures to conform to the religion in which they were raised. True believers do not *choose* to believe in their god—they just believe—but many self-proclaimed true believers may be choosing to pretend they believe what they are saying for all sorts of reasons, none of which are "it makes sense to me." As Yoda might say, "Believe, or believe not, there is no choose."

> *The interest I have in believing a thing is not a proof of the existence of that thing.* —VOLTAIRE

But this brings me to the worst part of Christianity—the punishment for thought. Their Bible says thoughts are enough to send a person to hell, even though they are involuntary (e.g., Mark 16, below). What kind of god would do that? It's like punishing you for other involuntary things such as breathing or having a wet dream. True belief cannot be controlled. You can pray, dance, sing, and prostrate yourself, but none of that can allow you to control your knowledge-based doubts.

Those doubts are often begun and fostered by other people, and the church does not want you to doubt. So the church added in one more major sin that is always going to lead to hell. Again, not murder. Not rape. Not theft. No, the one "big bad" that trumps all these crimes is the victimless act of blasphemy.

Blasphemy is an immediate go-to-hell penalty. It says in Matthew 12:31, "Blasphemy against the Holy Spirit shall not be forgiven." Deny the ghost and you're toast! This means if someone says something to you that sounds blasphemous, you'd better not agree (even in your mind, even a little), and again, since hearing the words might *cause* a lack of faith, you'd better avoid anyone who blasphemes. This is how cults work around the globe—segregation and brainwashing, all to keep believers away from the Forbidden Zone of Religion—doubt. This is how you make a flock of terrorized, obedient sheep.

And in Christianity, for the crime of not believing, you are punished forever in the lake of fire. In Mark 16:16, Jesus says, "He that believes and is baptized shall be saved, but he that believes not shall be damned." Can't get much clearer than that! If it doesn't make sense to you as a Christian that babies should go to hell for not having been baptized—something the baby had no control or say over—you're going to hell. If it doesn't make sense that Eve was conned, or that God could have just forgiven people without the whole murder-my-son-the-savior exercise, you will spend eternity in hell, burning forever, while the true believers rejoice above you in heaven.

And so Christians fear. They fear because parts of the Bible make no sense at all, no matter how hard you pretend. They fear because they are brainwashed from childhood into thinking they are sinners who will go to hell for these involuntary thoughts, and their only way to salvation is confession, obedience, and the self-loathing practice known as prayer, which, again, is just begging. They fear because God will send them to hell for something they cannot control, any more than a baby can control being baptized.

And here it is—the reason the New Testament is not only evil, but also evil genius: *Christianity feeds off the fact that thoughts can be involuntary.* In Matthew, Jesus says, "If you lust after a woman, you've committed adultery against your wife." Time to go to church and beg forgiveness for this involuntary and victimless crime! If you think God is a bit less about love and more of a tyrant, go to church or go to hell. It may occur to you that in Mark 13:30, Jesus said, "I tell you the truth, this generation will certainly not pass away until all these things have happened," referring to the second coming. This time has long passed, yet for two thousand years Christians have been saying, "The second coming is coming any day now." If you even think it may be all a lie, you have sinned by thinking too much and you need to (say it with me) repent and go to church.

And what does the church tell you? Obey the church, work hard, donate, and avoid outsiders and doubters. Remember, thought is not linear—you can have doubts and still fear the consequences of doubt, especially if you're raised that way. It's another part of being human. You can be taught to fear what you don't think exists, which is why people fear the dark, the bogeyman, and, yes, gods. And the religious-but-doubting Christians fear God, so they comply. And the church grows, and the churchgoers defend it, because if you don't, the church won't help you navigate the haunting knowledge in the back of your mind that God is *exactly like every other myth you dismiss.*

And if you don't lose that knowledge, if you don't suppress it completely and utterly, you risk eternity in hell, where nobody will ever save you. It's up to God to decide if your thoughts are pure enough, and you won't find out if they were until after you die.

Eternity in hell for involuntary thoughts *and* you go through your entire life wondering if you've had too many such thoughts to be admitted into heaven.

This is not love. This is terrorism.

All true believers in Christianity are afraid. They are all hoping, with every bit of hope they have, that the all-powerful mind reader will decide they have enough faith to get into heaven. Any degree of doubt equates to a degree of fear (unless their doubt is so severe they finally realize there is nothing real to fear). Those who doubt wish their belief were stronger and often try to make themselves believe more to convince themselves their own skepticism is wrong. This can be very frustrating because the facts are 100 percent on our side. Their religion is the most important thing in their lives, or at least it's supposed to be. More important than love, family, even their own children, religion needs to be number one. Whether you are good is not as important as whether you are (overtly) faithful.

Faithfulness gets you into a heaven, but being obedient, productive, and generous makes you a good Christian. When you add faithfulness, obedience, productivity, charity, and poverty mixed together with a whole bunch of fear that can only be alleviated by the church, guess who benefits from that combo platter?

God? No.

You? Certainly not.

Conveniently, the church gives you someone to obey who will tell you to be generous and give your money, which you earned through your productivity, to a charity . . . like that very church (hmm). You're welcome, here's the collection plate.

You can taste the scam.

To take it one level deeper, parents are told they are bad Christians if they don't brainwash their children into the same church, inflicting the same cycle of doubt and fear on their kids. Parents of atheists are (to a degree) failed Christians, so parents inflict religion on their kids to be good *Christians,* without realizing it's the exact opposite of what a good *parent* would do. Religion has once again convinced good people (parents) to do bad things (inflict religion on children) in the name of good (while actually just benefiting the church).

Our ancestors were wrong. Our parents were wrong. We do them no service by pretending they were right. We are under no obligation to pretend to believe the lies our parents believed, but we are certainly under an obligation to tell our children the truth.

There is an easier answer to Pascal's Wager, however. Since Pascal posited following the religion with the worst penalty for not believing (I feel dirty just typing that), simply create a religion that has a worse penalty than Christianity's hell and apply.

So, I propose a new religion: Silvermanity. If you don't do exactly as I command, you will spend eternity in Superworsehell, and all your ancestors in Heaven will also go to Superworsehell, as will all of your descendants. That's worse than plain old Christian Hell! *And* there is precedent—just as Adam's sin washes over all his descendants, so will your sin of not following Silvermanity retroactively and in the future wash over your entire bloodline. Your parents, your children, all will pay for your sin against me for all eternity in an ocean of fire (much bigger than that tiny lake in regular Hell).

There, a worse penalty. Believe it or face the horrible guilt and consequences. If you believe in Silvermanity and it's wrong, you lose nothing (except the money you give me and the control over your life you yield to me, which is nothing compared to the bliss of Superawesomeheaven, where all good Silvermanites go after they die). But if you disbelieve and it's right, the penalty is far worse than not believing in Christianity. So use Pascal's Wager and follow my new religion—because even if I say, right here, that I just made it up, you can't prove it's not true with 100 percent certainty (after all, you don't know everything in the Universe, and I might just be testing your faith) so you must give it relevance and respect it as you would any religion. I'm either right or wrong, so that is a fifty-fifty chance, so you better err on the side of caution, believe (or at least pretend to), and obey.

Forever.

See how easy it is to create a religion based on fear, and to use double-talk to make it sound reasonable? Try it yourself. It's fun *and* potentially ridiculously profitable—just Google *L. Ron Hubbard*.

For other "proofs of the existence of God," numerous other books and online resources give excellent refutations of all of them (without exception—none of the proofs hold water). But I want to take a moment to point out the same fraud in the most common proofs.

Evidence suggests that Neanderthals invented the Lie of God[24] to explain the things they didn't understand. Why does it rain? Why does the sun move? Where did we come from? I don't know, so it *must* have been God. God made the rain, God made the sun move, God made us. Of course it was a very different god (or gods) from the ones over which we fight and die today, but they were based on the same concept—*I don't know, therefore God did it*. I can't imagine that the first argument for the existence of a god between those early Neanderthals didn't include this line of thinking.

Then we found out how the rain was really made, and why the sun traversed the sky, so the number of things we don't know (and therefore the number of things attributed to a god) shrank. God no longer made the rain, but we as a species didn't understand lots of other things, so God did all those things. Then we learned more and God did less. Now, the set of what we don't know is much smaller than it used to be, and so the number of things attributed to God has shrunk. This is called the Shrinking God of the Gaps Argument, because as the gaps in our knowledge are reduced by scientific learning, the God who supposedly did all the stuff we still don't understand becomes smaller and less important.

The arguments have not improved over time, but they have been disguised to cloud the issue. Many of today's popular "scientific proofs" of God are only the same Neanderthal-era thoughts, dressed differently in an effort to make them look more logical, or more based on reason. Following are some good examples.

The teleological argument—what a great name! I love it when apologists think up complex names to hide the total scam they're peddling. This is also known as the "argument from design" and it goes like this:

> *The name* the teleological argument *is derived from the Greek word* telos, *meaning "end" or "purpose." When such arguments speak of the universe being ordered, they mean that it is ordered towards some end or purpose. The suggestion is that it is more plausible to suppose that the universe is so because it was created by an intelligent being in order to accomplish that purpose than it is to suppose that it is this way by chance.*[25]

In other words, we start from the *assumption* that the universe is *deliberately ordered* and was made for a *purpose* or according to a "design" (note that no specific purpose/design is posited, just that one *must* exist because it *appears so* to the observer, with no factual support given for this blatant assumption). Whose purpose is it? *Nobody knows, therefore it must be (my) God.* The argument presupposes a thing, asks who (not what) created the thing, and since there is no obvious rational answer currently available for this presumed thing, answers with "God did it" and calls itself science.

Let's try another one.

The cosmological argument (another great name) is an even more blatant rip-off of its Neanderthal roots:

> *The cosmological argument is the argument that the existence of the world or universe is strong evidence for the existence of a God who*

created it. The existence of the universe, the argument claims, stands in need of explanation, and the only adequate explanation of its existence is that it was created by God.[26]

At least we can save a step this time. We don't have to invent a "purpose" or "design" about which to ask the question, we can just ask the exact same question about the universe itself that the Neanderthals asked about the rain: Where did it come from? *Nobody knows, therefore God did it.* Just like the Neanderthals' rain, God is the "only adequate explanation" (because for some reason "we don't know" is not an option). There. Science.

Pay no attention to the man behind the curtain.

The third copy of the same argument is the **argument from morality:**

Moral arguments take either the existence of morality or some specific feature of morality to imply the existence of God.[27]

I'm sure you can see where I am going. This is analagous to the cosmological argument, asking the same question about a different thing and getting the same answer: Where did the universe/design/morality/rain come from? *Nobody knows, therefore God did it.*

In my experience, these three arguments are the most commonly used. and they are the *same argument* that has been used since the Ice Age! There are no new proofs of gods. There are only new ways to dress up the old ones.

The ridiculousness of these arguments becomes even clearer when you realize they could be (and have been) used to "prove" other gods. "I don't know, therefore God" is exactly the same as "I don't know, therefore Zeus" or "I don't know, therefore the Flying Spaghetti Monster." How can a single proof prove multiple mutually exclusive solutions?

They can't. The God of the Gaps argument, no matter how it's dressed up, fails for this very reason: it's not proof at all; it just posits that what we don't know or understand *must* be supernatural *because* we don't know the answer, and claims credit for whatever god is espoused by the speaker. The fundamental argument is based on ignorance and bad skepticism. The dressed-up versions are cons.

I think it's about time we stop thinking like Neanderthals.

> *I'll tell you why [religion]'s not a scam, in my opinion, all right?*
> *Tide goes in, tide goes out, never a miscommunication. You can't*
> *explain that.* —BILL O'REILLY

Of all the so-called proofs of a god's existence, none is given more unearned credit than the **ontological argument**. It's a clever word game used by preachers to convince doubters within their flocks that their god is real. Notice how I never said it was used for conversion, because I know of no one who was ever changed in any way by this migraine-inducing mess.

While all of the thinkers in the atheist movement dismiss the argument as the game it is, none that I've read have hit on the central point of why this argument doesn't work.

Here's the argument, in a nutshell: Imagine a "most perfect" being. Either this perfect being exists or he doesn't. However, existence is greater than nonexistence, so a perfect being that does not exist would not be a "most perfect being." A perfect being must therefore exist as a simple facet of being perfect.[28]

I know. I shouldn't have inflicted this on you. Feel free to put this book down and go get some Motrin. I'll wait.

Here's how I disprove the ontological argument: Imagine two identical people, Person A and Person B. They are exactly alike except Person A is an unrepentant axe murderer and Person B is not. Given only that information, which person is more perfect? As a decent human, you obviously said B is more perfect than A, because B doesn't kill people.

This is because responsibility matters. People who kill must be judged by that action, and in almost every society on earth, they are. This must be factored into the idea of perfection for this argument.

Imagine now God A and God B. They are all-powerful (perfect), omniscient gods, and the only difference is that God A exists, and God B does not. God A, then, is singularly responsible for all the suffering on earth, ever. He is responsible for every hungry child, every hurricane, every disease, and every ounce of suffering endured by every living thing, ever, because being omniscient and all-powerful, he could have prevented it all but chose not to (the Problem of Evil).

This is not canceled out by the good of our existence in the first place. Since God A could have created all of us without any pain or suffering (all-powerful means he can do anything), it must be assumed that he gave us suffering for some less than perfect reason. Creating a being that suffers its whole life is not a good thing—it's horrible—and it's far worse when you consider it's not necessary. It's an optional net-negative, and the responsibility would sit squarely in the lap of the all-powerful deity who made it happen.

God B, on the other hand, does not, and never did, exist. As such, he bears no responsibility for anything in the universe. Nobody can point to God B and accuse him of anything, as he didn't do anything!

Now imagine a perfect being. This perfect being either exists or not. However, a perfect being would not be responsible for all the death and suffering in the world, but a god that exists, assuming he were all-powerful and omniscient (as this argument is positing, since that is part of perfection), would definitely be large-and-in-charge and bear 100 percent of the responsibility. Therefore, a more perfect god would not exist, bearing no responsibility at all.

The ontological argument fails because *perfection* is subjective. My perfect god includes responsibility for evil. Others may differ, but in either case it's a subjective definition of an objective-sounding word. That's the trick—there can't be a most perfect being, any more than there can be a most beautiful person. Perfection is in the eye of the debater, and in my opinion, any being that willfully causes *all* the pain and suffering on this planet for all living beings throughout history is far from perfect.

Every proof of every god has something in common—none of them are actually proofs of any gods at all. They are all word games and logical fallacies. As I mentioned earlier, we, as a species, have a set of information we call facts. These are things we know. While we don't know everything, it would take real, solid evidence to change our minds because we are extremely confident in what we *know* (as opposed to what we *suspect* or *think*).

For instance, we know people cannot fly based on all available evidence. We don't know everything, but we can state "people can't fly" with confidence because we know it. If you come to me and say you know someone who can fly, I'm not going to seriously consider the possibility that you're telling the truth—unless you can prove it.

If some flying person then swoops in and is proven to fly by scientists (who perform a few tests to make sure it's not some kind of trickery), or if you find remains of people with wings or some other convincing evidence that proves the existence of flying people, I'm right there. I'll accept I was wrong.

However, if instead you support your assertion with "You don't know everything—you can't *prove* no human can fly" or "I like to believe we can fly, the world would be much better if humans could fly" or "How did this person get from point A to point B? You don't know, therefore he flew," I'll know you're insane, brainwashed, or have an agenda.

So now let's look again at God's supposed attributes:

- God is immortal.
- He was never born—he has no parents.
- He is everywhere at the same time.
- He has power to create matter and energy with his will.
- He knows everything and can read minds.
- He can control people's thoughts if he wants to.

That's far less believable than a flying person! *All* of these attributes break the known laws of physics and therefore go against what we know as a society. To posit a being with *one* of these attributes would require solid proof—but *all of them*? And this is just a short list!

For anyone to propose a being that has so many impossible attributes exists, the person has to have real, positive proof for it, at least as much as we would demand for the far-less-implausible flying human. I don't need "How else can you explain . . . ," I need "Here is scientifically valid support that an eternal being can exist, and here is scientifically valid support for a being that can create and destroy matter and energy, etc."

If you're going to tell me that everything we've learned is wrong, about *anything,* you're going to need to actively prove it with testable, peer-reviewed results.

Anything less than proof is no proof at all. To date, 100 percent of the proof offered for any god's existence has been no proof at all.

On the Defense of the Indefensible

Recently I had a discussion with a minister's wife who proposed a Stockholm syndrome–like defense of God's outrageously hateful behavior. God's seemingly immoral actions were moral, according to her, because God can do all the things he does. His *ability* to create hell and send billions of souls there for eternity made it *moral* for him to do so. Just as victims of Stockholm syndrome defend their captors, so too did this believer defend what she admitted to be horrific behavior. She further opined that since God created us, he could do whatever he wanted to do to us (much like an owner would treat a slave), all under the aegis of morality. I could hear the religion destroying her brain right in front of me.

If I had the power to create a human, knowing in advance that the person would be tortured forever, it would not give me the moral right to do so (and if I did, most would call me a monster). But God of the Bible does just that, and religion poisons brains into thinking that it's okay.

No matter the motivation, defending the indefensible in this manner is par for the course. Indeed, the entire business of religion hinges on its ability to dodge criticism.

> *One cannot insult other people's faith, one cannot make fun of faith. . . . There is a limit. Every religion has its dignity. . . . In freedom of expression, there are limits.*
> —POPE FRANCIS, JANUARY 2015

Religion *must* be correct and it must convince believers it is correct, all the time. The problem is that religion is wrong so often, and on so many levels, that even basic knowledge can be inconvenient, to say the least.

Let's take another look at Genesis 1, which reads as follows:

> *In the beginning God created heaven and earth. And the earth was waste and lifeless, and darkness was on the face of the deep. . . . And God said, Let there be light. . . . And God called the light day, and the darkness he called night, and there was evening and there was morning, the first day.*

Science proves religion wrong all the time, and religion hates science as a result (remember, science is just another term for *learning,* as opposed to *believing what preachers tell you*). Since the advent of science (about 350 BC)[29] apologists have been trained and recruited in an attempt to explain why science isn't actually proving religion (in this example Judaism and Christianity) wrong, but rather right. Genesis 1 is a perfect place to demonstrate their dishonest tactics.

In the beginning, God created the heavens and the earth. In 1978, astronomers Arno Penzias and Robert Wilson were awarded the Nobel Prize in Physics for their discovery of cosmic microwave background radiation, which provided important corroboration of the big bang theory of the universe's beginnings 13.8 billion years ago. However, Christian apologists simply read what they wanted and tacked it on their religion. "God said it and *bang*—it happened." This shows a common theme. Apologists basically retrofit their holy text to mean something it didn't originally, after science fills in a gap of knowledge. Hence, the big bang is just the "echoes of the Great Creation by God." One can see how easily this same argument can be applied to any god (including the Flying Spaghetti Monster). But moreover, there is a huge difference between *God created heaven and the earth* and what actually happened during the big bang, as explained for this book by Dr. Lawrence Krauss[30] (author of *A Universe from Nothing,* which you should read):

> *Heaven and Earth were created anything but together. . . . Our Earth is only 4.5 billion years old, whereas the observable universe is 13.8 billion years old. Literally billions of stars have emerged and died before our own Sun and Earth arose from a dense gas cloud in the Milky Way. Indeed, there is nothing about Genesis that gets the Big Bang right, in order or detail, except for the trivial fact that both imply our Universe had a beginning. Perhaps the most important difference is that our Earth resides in a random place at the outskirts of an average galaxy in the middle of nowhere. There is nothing special about*

its location or the time in which it arose. Moreover, over 95 percent of
the Universe is composed of something other than that which makes up
our Earth. We are a bit of cosmic pollution in a sea of dark matter and
dark energy.

So herein lies one of the common tactics of apologists—taking their wrong information and calling it right. Science proves "what the Bible clearly states," even when it doesn't. The problem is that believers, already desperate to hold on to their beliefs, will nod in frantic agreement when this lie is told because they want their bible to be right—even when it's way off.

And there was evening and there was morning, the first day. Here's a great place where we often hear, "Oh, that's a metaphor for billions of years." If I walked up to you and said, "There was an evening and a morning, the first day," you'd probably assume I was talking about a day. You certainly wouldn't think I was talking about a billion years, yet that's what old-earth creationists will tell you, with a straight face.[31]

Remember, religion hates to admit its bible is wrong. To admit it *is* wrong is to admit the words of its god are imperfect, and therefore nondivine in origin (the alternative is to have an imperfect or deceitful divine author, to whom nobody would pray). To admit it is human-made is to place it on the same level as all the other books written by humans, removing its pedestal. A bible with errors written by humans—why do we care again? Without perfection and objectivity, religion is totally unnecessary and preachers know it, so they forever push the lie of perfection to protect the Lie of God.

This is why religion will never admits its errors, but instead uses shtick like this, again reminiscent of Monty Python's ex-parrot sketch, to deny all wrongness ever, regardless of the facts. So when scientists proved, beyond any reasonable doubt, that the universe is billions of years old, these creationists lied—to themselves and to others—that *day* no longer meant "day" but actually "ages." That wouldn't be so outrageous a claim if the word *day* wasn't modified by *and there was evening and there was morning,* which kind of takes away all doubt that the writers were talking about days as we know them and not about a magical day lasting a billion years. This is where it all becomes a "metaphor." This is where you wonder how a perfect god could create a book that could be so misleading as to use the word *day* to mean "a billion years." This is where you wonder how wrong that other stuff could be.

This is where religion becomes the ex-parrot.

And God said, Let there be light—after he created earth. Again, wrong, because carbon. To date, I've not heard the apologetic response to this proven incorrect statement from Genesis 1. Even the most religious scientists, the most brainwashed victims who can't get past their wall of indoctrination with their own knowledge, will tell you carbon is a major element of this planet (and all life thereon). They will also tell you that carbon was not formed in the big bang, but rather in the bellies of stars, all of which produce light at some point.[32] Given everything we know, see, and can measure, the earth did *not* precede the existence of light, as Genesis clearly states. It's not even a "day equals ages" thing—it's completely the opposite of what has been proven true (see Krauss).

Pastors like to say a god is the author of their bibles. If that's true, then their god was wrong. Once again, with this kind of provably incorrect information in the Bible, one wonders how sane people could look at anything therein and be sure they are reading the truth. But again—brainwashing.

Another place where denial of reality is rampant is in the creation and evolution debate. This is where it gets more fun.

The evidence in support of evolution leaves no room for doubt.

Any theist reading this should, if he or she doubts, read any of the wonderful books on the subject, including Richard Dawkins's *The Greatest Show on Earth: The Evidence for Evolution*, or just go to any natural-history museum or fossil shop. There is so little doubt that the Vatican[33] and even Pat Robertson[34] have admitted evolution is true.

But there's a problem with this admission. If you grant evolution, you acknowledge the Garden of Eden didn't happen. You acknowledge Adam and Eve both had parents, and those parents seemed every bit as human as did their children. You admit no man from dirt, no woman from a rib, no Garden of Eden, no talking snake, no original sin, no need for redemption or a savior.

In this way, evolution disproves the entire basis for Christianity (as well as Judaism and Islam), but of course the theists can never admit it. Those who have chosen to embrace young-earth creationism are never going to be respected because most high school kids can prove their ideas wrong. Those who embrace old-earth creationism embrace one of their major weaknesses—everything in Genesis is wrong, including original sin, so there is no need for a savior, so Jesus had no purpose and died for no reason. Without Adam and Eve the core of Christianity falls away.

Evolution is proven, sure stuff, and it proves all creation myths, including the Old Testament, wrong. Religion hates to be proven wrong, so it will pull out all the stops to deny it, including dumbing down our science classes with mythology cloaked in the euphemism of *intelligent design*. This is done in an attempt to elevate myth to the level of science and discredit that which we know is true in order to allow religion to avoid admitting it is wrong.

That's why we have "creation museums" where cavemen ride dinosaurs and Noah's Ark is totally feasible, because theists want the public ignorant. It's dishonest, immoral, and directly hurts every child who is never taught how to determine fact from fantasy. It is one of the worst sides of religion.

Some preachers attack the scientific method, instead of addressing their own arguments, which is ridiculous, because in a nutshell, science is a form of learning.

Let's say you were trying to solve a maze, and you were at a point where you had three paths from which to choose. You choose Path A (you hypothesize that Path A is correct). You take that path (testing Hypothesis A) and find a wall, so Path A fails and is not the correct answer. Then you try Path B, but it also fails because you hit another wall. Finally, you try Path C, and you succeed, so Path (Hypothesis) C is the answer. If you describe your efforts to your friends, some may try out the same puzzle, and if they take the same steps as you, they will get the same results (peer review).

Congratulations, you've used the scientific method to learn the answer, *as we all do in everyday life.* Trying on clothes, finding a new way to the store, eating a new food—it's all learning via a form of the scientific method. It's all hypothesis/test/revise. It's how we learn.

Then your friend, who is stubborn and refuses to admit they are wrong, insists Path A is correct because it was what they were taught. You show them the path and the wall to which the path leads, but your friend insists you're still wrong. You argue, and your clearly wrong friend insists, despite being pummeled with undeniable evidence they are wrong, that it's just best to say both A and C are equally possible. Path A is correct to *them,* and Path C is correct to *you.* They then say that your method is an assault on their belief.

Hating the scientific method is hating learning. Those who oppose learning via the scientific method seek not to find the answer, but to find a way to justify their incorrectness. Failing that (as they will every single time), they demonize science itself, choosing to label science *antireligion,* which betrays a complete ignorance of a basic fact—science is not atheistic by choice or practice.

Science is only in line with atheism because science has never found any proof of a god. If science ever finds proof of a god, it will immediately become the antithesis of atheism. Science is antireligion in the same way it is anti–flat earth and anti-geocentrism—those things are wrong. Should atheism ever be proven wrong, it will be proven so by science.

I'm not holding my breath.

Chapter 5

USE, OR AT LEAST UNDERSTAND, FIREBRAND TACTICS

I want Dr. King to know that I didn't come to Selma to make his job difficult. I really did come thinking I could make it easier. If the white people realize what the alternative is, perhaps they will be more willing to hear Dr. King.   —MALCOLM X

Human decency is not derived from religion. It precedes it.
                        —CHRISTOPHER HITCHENS, *GOD IS NOT GREAT:*
                              HOW RELIGION POISONS EVERYTHING

If you think I'm a dick because of what I say or do (or more likely, what other people say I say or do), then you probably don't understand what I'm doing or why. If you think I'm rude for the sake of being rude, or if you think firebrands such as me are just trying to get attention for the sake of getting attention, or for those of you who think I'm angry at your god, you need to take some time and get a better perspective. This chapter should help.

Firebrand activism works. I'll show you the proof behind that statement soon. But that's not the reason I became a firebrand. The mentality came first; the proof of efficacy is just encouragement.

Everything I say about religion comes from my core and is based on a deep anger at how people have used the Lie of God to hurt others for millennia. Religion has no positive value. Yes, some people claim to do good in the name of religion, but this is just good people using religion as an excuse to do good, giving credit to the religion instead of the people (again), and without religion these good people would still do good, but under a different name, as witnessed by the atheists performing charity all over the world. Religion serves no purpose except to funnel money and power away from those who need it and leaves in its wake nothing but broken promises and damaged families. Religion sucks, so I fight it with my greatest weapon—words (never violence, because violence is the weapon of the weak and the wrong).

This chapter is about those words and how and why I use them to (metaphorically) punch religion in the face.

In My Beginning . . .

I had to think long and hard to remember when my firebrand style of atheism was born, and why. It could have been in those early lunchroom discussions with my then-future wife and all her Orthodox Jewish friends in college. It could have been at my first job in Harrisburg, where I was the first atheist *anyone* in my office had ever met. Or it could have been when a Christian "friend" invited me over for dinner, only to secretly invite her church pastor and a bunch of friends to try to convert me (newsflash—it didn't work). But while these were formative, no single incident was the trigger that made me the firebrand I am today. They did not teach me the effectiveness of proud truth.

One source of kindling for my internal fire is a rage against the harm religion does to society. I suppose anger is not a necessary component of being a firebrand, but it helps a lot.

My first time feeling this kind anger came from my first activist action—marching for choice, safety, and bodily autonomy of women.

Activism for choice first showed me how deeply religion cuts into the lives of non-adherents, and the hypocritical arguments theists use to justify clear religious oppression. I first felt then the bile bubble up from my stomach fighting for this cause for which I first raised a voice, a fist, and a picket sign. Religion's intrusion into the lives of half the population in the name of "love" (obviously bullshit) kindled my curiosity into the many other places religion infects our lives and led me to atheist activism.

I put my righteous anger to good use for atheism for the first time several years later, fighting against an obscure bill called the Religious Freedom Restoration Act, or RFRA. The year was 1998, and I was angry at all of my allies.

The prior year, the Supreme Court had overturned the national RFRA as unconstitutional, and rightly so (but for the wrong reason). Simply put, the RFRA was about changing the burden of scrutiny when it comes to religion, and *only* when it comes to religion. Basically, the RFRA dictates that a person has to obey the law *unless* the reason for breaking the law is religious, in which case the government has to prove why it needs the culprit to obey it. This version of religious exceptionalism was bound to create a second set of laws, giving a specific and legal advantage to religion while making the government bear the burden of proof, even if the church broke the law. This idea was bad to the core.

The RFRA wasn't overturned because it was clearly intended to advance religion; it was overturned on a technicality, and the wonderful New Jersey legislature was now considering a New Jersey version of the RFRA, which would do the same thing on a state level. It was coming to *my* state. I had to fight it.

Fortunately, I'd already made a great set of allies. As the New Jersey State Director for American Atheists, I met regularly with fellow activists from the ACLU, People for the American Way, the NJ Education Association, and other liberalish organizations to keep each other informed and organize mutually beneficial activities. We'd been working with each other for some time by then, and I was ready for a united, concerted effort against this clear injustice.

I didn't get that.

What I got from my "liberal" friends was acquiescence. I hadn't expected the teachers' unions to take up arms for this fight, but the others caved as well, seemingly resigned to let it pass. I urged, challenged, and pleaded with them, but in the end I could not get them to join me. What I got instead was among the most distasteful responses I ever received: "Well, the truth is we have a lot of religious members who support this bill."

I remember who said those words to me, but I won't reveal the person's name—it would be too embarrassing for the person and the person's organization, the latter of which is still a strong ally. My point is that yielding to religious members silenced my allies. We could have won together, but because my allies didn't want to cause heartache to religious members, I was left to fight this major battle solo. I was alone and angry, and the fire in my belly energized me as never before.

I organized a group of volunteers to canvass the state capitol with flyers opposing the RFRA. I loved my team, which was mostly made up of elderly women who were eager to stir up trouble, and in this case that meant handing out flyers until we all got thrown out of the building. We called every representative in Trenton and met with those who would meet with us. We wrote to every paper in New Jersey. I even recorded a PSA for a local television station, WWOR-TV, in which I stated:

While right-wing conservatives hail the Religious Freedom Restoration Act, or RFRA, as benevolent, the bill will actually create a privileged

class by allowing religious people and organizations special rights to cir-
cumvent laws on discrimination, zoning, health codes, and child abuse.

People should not be subject to different laws based on their religion,
and the enforcement of laws should not depend on the religion of the
perpetrator. American Atheists urges everyone to fight all attacks on
equality, especially those dishonestly cloaked in buzzwords like religious
freedom. *Defeat the RFRA.*

We pushed hard, even going to Trenton to protest against the bill.
Our last effort was made at a public hearing about the RFRA, during
which I was expected to testify. American Atheists was the *only* organization that opposed the bill, and I was the only speaker slated to
speak against it. As my volunteers and I sat in attendance, waiting
for me to be called, one of our few allies in Trenton moved to table
the bill—and succeeded! Since this was the last session when it could
be raised, this effectively killed the New Jersey RFRA. Just like that,
we'd won! We cheered, knowing all the ruckus we'd raised must
have made a difference. Sure, we pissed off the religious people who
had heard our shouts and seen our writings and watched my PSA.
But for at least the time being the laws of New Jersey would remain
fair—until the new national RFRA was passed a few years later, usher-
ing in the era of faith-based initiatives and corporatized religious
bigotry (e.g., the Hobby Lobby decision of 2014).

Below is the text of what was distributed to everyone at the hearing, the day the original New Jersey RFRA died:

To: Members of the State House and Senate
All Members of American Atheists in New Jersey
American Atheists NJ Affiliated Organizations
New Jersey Church/State Separation Supporters and Organizations
Members of the Press
Governor Christie Whitman

From: David Silverman, New Jersey State Director, American Atheists

Date: March 7, 1998

Ladies and Gentlemen,
*Members of the New Jersey legislature have introduced bills A.903 (State Assembly) and S.321 (State Senate) which, if enacted, would give **special rights to the religious** at the expense of the non-believers. These bills, which are local versions of another bill **already rejected by the Supreme Court as unconstitutional,** are worded in such a way as to appear harmless, while threatening the core of church/state separation.*

*In order to fully understand the nature and intent of this "special rights" bill, we must first understand what religious freedoms and restrictions are currently in place. Surely, no legislator would draft a bill granting rights that already exist. **Today, in this country, individuals can:***

- *Practice whatever religion they prefer, or none at all*
- *Wear religious jewelry in public and on the job, barring uniform standards*
- *Display religious icons (nativity scenes, etc.) on their own property any time*
- *Pray/proselytize in public, including handing out propaganda*
- *Pray in schools during non-class time (in student-led groups or alone)*
- *Pray to themselves anytime, anywhere, including in school during class*
- *Sue under special laws if they are not treated equally for religious reasons*

In fact, the only religious restrictions, aside from breaking the law in the name of religion (e.g., bombing abortion clinics), in place today are:

- *Interfering with another person's right to believe (or not believe) as they so choose*
- *School-sponsored prayer*
- *Giving preferential "special rights" to believers on the basis of their belief*

The only purpose of these restrictions is to **protect minorities and individuals** from incursions on their freedoms as citizens. If passed, this new "freedom" law would eliminate that protection, allowing minorities and individuals little protection against forced, state-funded, or "official" religion.

The bills state:

New Jersey also recognizes the right of religious freedom and affirms "the inestimable privilege of worshiping Almighty God" in accord with the dictates of one's conscience and provides that "no person shall be deprived" of that right.

This passage is designed to allow religious proselytizing anytime, anywhere, and by anybody whose "conscience" so dictates, without restriction or regard for the rights of others. This is designed for and will yield:

- *Open school-led prayer to the deity chosen by the teacher, be it Christianity, Islam, Scientology, or Branch Davidianism (remember, cults are religions too), regardless of the wishes and beliefs of the family. This passage will open the door to pushing little-known rituals and procedures by cults and "non-traditional" religious groups on our children. The teacher may do as s/he pleases, with full legal protection (atheism, since it is not a religion, is not protected—religion is therefore officially favored).*
- *Similarly, schools can invite evangelists (from any religion or cult) to preach to children during school time, without regard for non-religious beliefs or views of parents or children.*
- *Employers will be forced to give unlimited breaks to workers who*

"need" to pray. In the event the employer in any way pressures a person to work instead of praying, the worker has the right to **sue the employer for damages.** *In this way, this passage opens the door to countless lawsuits to be filed by anyone who feels their employer did not give them enough "special rights" to satisfy their religious needs.*

- *Again, it will be the non-religious workers who will be forced to take up the slack for these workers' breaks, without the ability to get the same breaks for themselves. In effect,* **this law legalizes making non-believers work more than believers.**

Another passage in these bills read:

"Actions of any governmental entity which are facially neutral towards religion may nonetheless burden religious exercise" and that "Government should not substantially burden religious exercise without compelling justification."

- *This means no governmental entity can be secular in nature, because this law makes secular neutrality "anti-religious" by definition. Absurd, isn't it? Neutrality is not anti-religious; it is exactly where the government should be on this issue.*
- *This passage essentially places religion in every state and local government office and action, leaving the non-religious relegated to second-class citizenry. No consideration is given to the fact that actively* **promoting religion of any kind encroaches on the rights of the nonbeliever.**

On the surface, this law is deliberately designed to look harmless. You may think some of my views are worst-case scenarios, but these are the exact situations for which this law is designed. The Christian Right would not push a law that gave them nothing.

We already have freedom of religion, as guaranteed in the Constitution by the First Amendment. This new law would only serve to

limit the freedoms of individuals, minorities, and especially nonbe-
lievers.

   Some may suggest that the Constitution will protect us from state
laws which restrict atheism or give "special rights" to believers. How-
ever, we need only look at the "In God We Trust" on the coins, or listen
to our children pledge their allegiance to "one nation under God" to
know that we can't depend on that, especially with the RFA poised to
gut the First Amendment. All attacks on individual rights, especially
those cloaked in buzzwords like "religion" or "freedom," must be coun-
tered not only by every nonbeliever, but by every US citizen who cares
about freedom and America.

   Dave Silverman, NJ State Director, American Atheists, Inc.

Speaking of Hobby Lobby (which is the result of the national
RFRA), Supreme Court justice Elena Kagan chided Antonin Scalia
about religious-based exemptions to the law, using warnings remark-
ably close to my language from several years earlier:

"Your understanding of this law, your interpretation of it, would es-
sentially subject the entire U.S. Code to the highest test in constitutional
law, to a compelling interest standard," she told Paul Clement, the law-
yer arguing against the mandate for Hobby Lobby and Conestoga
Wood. "So another employer comes in and that employer says, I have
a religious objection to sex discrimination laws; and then another em-
ployer comes in, I have a religious objection to minimum wage laws;
and then another, family leave; and then another, child labor laws. And
all of that is subject to the exact same test which you say is this unbe-
lievably high test, the compelling interest standard with the least re-
strictive alternative."[1]

She was right, but it wasn't the Hobby Lobby case that started this,
it was the RFRA that changed the law and allowed preferential

treatment for religion. I stand firm in my opinion that if the national organizations favoring separation of church and state had been willing to risk pissing off some religious supporters to protect everyone's rights, we would be a stronger and fairer country today, and Hobby Lobby would be just another store instead of a national symbol for religious privilege writ large.

In 2014, I was honored to speak in Washington, DC, at a pro-ERA rally on the lawn of the Capitol, sponsored by We Are Woman, at which I spoke about the RFRA and its effect on women's equality:

> *Good morning, allies! My name is David Silverman, president of American Atheists and proud feminist, and I am thrilled to be here to talk with you about our common enemy, the Religious Right.*
>
> *Now we are all angry about Hobby Lobby, but we must remember that they were just the plaintiff in the case, and if they weren't the plaintiff, some other company, perhaps Walmart or Chick-fil-A, would have taken their place. In truth, the Hobby Lobby decision wasn't about Hobby Lobby at all, but rather the law on which the decision was based, deceptively entitled the Religious Freedom Restoration Act, or RFRA.*
>
> *This law elevates religion above civil law. In other words, where religion clashes with secular civil law, the religion wins most of the time, because of the RFRA. And thanks to Citizens United, corporations are people, and when "corporate religious rights" conflict with civil rights of the employees, the elevated religious dogma wins, and shamefully, civil rights get trampled. Given the combination of the RFRA and Citizens united, a Hobby Lobby–type decision was inevitable, and mark my words, we will see more lawsuits like this, endangering more rights for more people in the name of corporate religious rights.*
>
> *Who made the RFRA and still defend it today? The politicians in the pockets of the Religious Right, who use God to defend inequality for atheists as they use God to defend inequality for women. The*

Bible preaches against gender equality just as it preaches against religious diversity, and when this mentality is elevated to a higher status than civil law, as the RFRA has done, people lose rights, and America becomes less free and more theocratic. The principal reason to oppose the ERA has nothing to do with public restrooms—that's a smoke screen. It's all about a legalized patriarchy bolstered by biblical sexism that says females are not equal to males, and that's what makes the ERA a separation-of-church-and-state issue, and that makes our movements allies against a common foe.

Bible-based bigotry against women, atheists, or anyone else has no place in Washington, or anywhere for that matter.

Our cause is equality, and religion is the enemy of equality. By attacking and defeating religion's influence in Washington, we will eliminate almost all of the opposition to equality and achieve our common goal: a free country of equal citizens, regardless of gender or religious expression.

I am honored to be working in conjunction with multiple organizations across multiple movements to preserve and promote equality for all Americans. This is a cause we can and will win, by booting the morality and mythology of yesteryear from American politics.

On behalf of American Atheists, I want to thank all of you for fighting this fight. Thank you for your attention, and most importantly, thank you for your activism for America's fair and free future.

Unfortunately, my prediction above was correct and the RFRA has taken another baby step toward establishing a special class for religious people. In Indiana, as of March of 2015, a newer version of this overtly unfair law was signed by Governor Mike Pence that allows *corporations* to preserve their *religious right to be bigots*, usurping civil antidiscrimination laws[2]. The law was clearly set up to allow bigots to discriminate against anyone they want, in defiance of antidiscrimination laws, in the name of their "corporate religion." The outcry over this blatant bigotry was thankfully fierce (and firebrand-y), and the law was soon changed,[3] but other states are currently considering similar measures. You can be sure we will continue to see more actions like this as a result of this unconstitutional and inherently un-American act.

Fighting the NJ RFRA was a huge learning experience for me, as this was when I discovered, firsthand, the efficacy of the firebrand mentality. I had always identified with the hard-line approach and was well aware of the firebrands from victorious movements of the past (Act Up, the Black Panthers, the "bra burners"), but this was the first time I implemented it and saw its effect for myself. My criticism was harsh, my words were blunt, and my accusations were direct—and the press loved it. They wrote about us. They put me on TV to show people the "mean" atheist fighting against religion, and all I had to do was make my case well in the time they allotted me, which I did. This brought attention to the issue far beyond what it would have been without my personal firebrand effort.

Whether our publicity and campaigning was the only reason the bill failed will never be known. My point is that the bill supported religion and failed, and the only negative voice being heard in the media was my harsh-but-true criticism. Did our efforts single-handedly generate enough awareness of the bill's downsides to kill the New Jersey RFRA? Unlikely, but not impossible. Were we part of the reason it died? Undoubtedly. Would we have gotten that much notice if I had acted in a more "congenial" manner? Well, nobody congenial got noticed at all.

Firebrand Atheism, Defined

American astronomer, writer, and skeptic Phil Plait, in a now-famous speech in 2010, complained about the atheist movement's "dicks," asking, "How many [of you] became a skeptic because someone got in your face, screaming, and called you an idiot, brain damaged, and a retard?" He subsequently made it clear that he was not talking about anyone in particular, but this is one of those quotes that, when heard, somehow draws glances my way.

To be clear, this is *not* what I am about. Yes, I am loud and proud, but I don't insult just to insult. I've been married to Hildy, a theist, for twenty-plus years now, largely *because* I've never called her names for believing in God.

Firebrand atheism is simply *telling the truth*, with the emphasis on *telling*. There is a difference between telling the truth only when cornered and *proactively* speaking what you know to be truthful, helpful, and healthy, and the latter is where I live. Silence often implies acquiescence or even agreement, and often that makes it a lie.

I tell the truth. People need and deserve to hear the truth, and the truth needs and deserves to be told. Indeed, it often needs to be shouted.

My five simple precepts of firebrand atheism rely on telling versus silence, honesty versus lies (including the lie one commits when remaining silent), and correctness versus political correctness:

1. *Tell the truth* as often as possible. Some examples of true statements are "religion is a lie" and "all gods are myths." These truths should be stated loudly and often, yet political correctness and religious privilege make telling these truths difficult. Tell the truth anyway.

2. Don't feign respect for the unrespectable—feigning is lying. If you say you have respect for beliefs you actually find silly, you are lying. See point 1 and tell the truth. If you do not respect the belief in an invisible man in the sky, say so.

3. Don't accept inequality (privilege) as acceptable even if it is the norm—accepting inequality is feigning respect (see point 2). It's not okay for some people to get something, obtain a privilege, or even be acknowledged over others by the government simply because they think a god exists. We are a nation of

equals, and we need to protect that or lose it. Nobody wants to be second-class, but sitting back and letting privilege run unchallenged is acquiescing to second-class citizenship, even if only to a small degree (as I mentioned before, small infringements serve as precedents for larger infringements). If you don't think that's fair, then you have every right and indeed the responsibility to challenge it loudly. Silence, again, implies acquiescence, which means silent atheists imply their consent to Christian privilege. Don't do that.

4. Do not let the words "I'm offended" silence you. As Richard Dawkins has said many times, there is no such thing as a Christian, Jewish, or Muslim baby,[4] but most theists are indoctrinated from birth into believing their religion is a core facet of their identity, every bit as much as genetic lineage. This does not negate the need to tell the truth (believers are wrong, and that's the truth), but it does open the door to theists taking it personally when you criticize religion. Always make it clear that you are criticizing the belief, not the believer. Say something like "You are many things—a father, a son, a professional—and one of those things is religious, and it is only that small portion of you that is wrong." In my experience, this works well most of the time. Remember, the truth sometimes hurts, and some believers' knee-jerk take-it-personal reaction is nothing more than a manifestation of the brainwashing they've received. It is certainly not a reason for you to stay silent (thereby implying agreement, which is lying) about your atheism. If they can talk about their myth, you can and should talk about reality. Anything else is unequal, and disingenuous acquiescence to inequality is dishonesty (see point 3).

5. If someone tries to limit freedom by using religion, follow points 1–4, only louder. This specifically refers to the defensive nature of our firebrand activism. For example, consider

again Draw Muhammad Day. We draw him not because we know it pisses off Muslim people, but rather because some Muslims are trying to make *us* obey *their* laws not to draw him. We are resisting an attempt to infringe on our rights to *draw what we want,* and that they are telling us not to draw him because it's against *their* religious views is the only reason we do it.

That's really all I do and all I ask of *you.* Tell the truth, be an honest person, and don't let the well-intentioned-but-wrong political correctness of today's society, which is (not coincidentally) heavily influenced by religion, squelch you. This is not an attack on religious people. This is not an insult to their god. This is the *truth*: we are right and they are wrong. If we never tell them that, who will?

This is why religion hates the firebrand atheist more than anyone else. We use words to shove religion off its pedestal, thereby stripping it of the privilege that insulates it from law, morality, and common sense. It's effective and it benefits the whole movement by highlighting our issues and our existence, and allowing the nice guys to garner publicity on their own as a by-product. We raise awareness of our existence and our issues on a national level, chipping away at the lie we are not a large enough segment of the population to be relevant, while demanding nothing more than equality. Add on that atheism is being de-demonized to the population at large by our work, and you can see the win-win-win of firebrand atheism.

Billboards and Methods

Press coverage is one of the main goals of the billboards we erect. It is an important part of our messaging plan.

Billboards have indeed influenced this movement, and American Atheists is far from the only organization posting them (indeed, I think almost all of the major atheist organizations are now doing so). However, the billboards I put up have a specific set of requirements and attributes that distinguish us from the herd.

The primary target market of American Atheists' billboards is, again, the press. For that reason every board is visually stimulating and, yes, intentionally edgy. The amount of exposure one gets in the press dwarfs the exposure one gets from a billboard, so our billboards are deliberately interesting enough to get shown on the news, *which requires the press to show our prominently displayed name and Web site.* In fact, we provide the graphics to the news sources, with the proviso that the images cannot be cropped or covered, ensuring the Web site's inclusion.

We also send out a press release that quickly and efficiently explains why this billboard is special enough to talk about. Observe the progression and how each board—though individually unique in message—is part of an overall narrative:

- "You KNOW It's a Myth." A billboard near the Lincoln Tunnel calling the nativity a myth. This is the first time any board "dared" to do so. The message quickly and efficiently explains why this billboard is special. This proof-of-concept board was on the national news in *nine different countries* and appeared on *The Colbert Report, The Daily Show,* and *Saturday Night Live.*
- "You KNOW They're All Scams." Accused religion of being inherently dishonest, and was the first to implicate Islam and Judaism. This board generated enough incremental publicity to get me on *The O'Reilly Factor,* where the WTF face (I'll get to that soon) was born.
- "You Know There Is No God, We Know You're Right." Five boards in the "Christian" city of Des Moines, Iowa. "Christian city" was a phrase used by one of the billboard companies that refused our ad, and we used it for a nice press release about

overcoming bigotry in Iowa, where our annual convention was being held in 2011. The press loved it.

- "You Know It's Nonsense." A good, old-fashioned billboard war on a national scale against the rapture scam of May 2011. Wouldn't you know, we were right—there was no rapture. Again. The press loved our caring press release to the victims of the scam after it didn't happen.

- "Tell Your Family You Don't Believe." The first billboard aimed at encouraging discussion and self-outing around the dinner table.

- The first boards in Arabic and Hebrew, erected in Muslim and Jewish communities, just in time for the Reason Rally. These billboards wrote their own press as I knew they would. Even though the boards never mentioned the Reason Rally, I cited "promotion of the Reason Rally (reasonrally.org) to the atheists in these religious communities" as the stated intent of the boards, so almost every news report on them mentioned the rally, while showing pictures of the billboards, with the Web address.

- "Atheism Is Patriotic" Independence Day flyovers. We wanted to have planes with this flyover banner crossing cities in all fifty states, but knew we might not succeed. The reason? In some states we couldn't find a single aerial-banner pilot willing to promote an atheist message. This was still a win-win—either we succeeded and got fifty flyovers, or we had a nice story about prejudice against atheists. We got the latter.

- "Keep the Merry, Dump the Myth." Inspired by the original Lincoln Tunnel billboard, but this one was in Times Square. Just a bit edgier, and actually called on people to dump their religion.

- The Austin "Quotes Campaign." Ridiculed and shamed politicians for what they've said. Six billboards in Austin and one

in Dallas, hitting right-wingers in Texas. Pastor Robert Jef-
fress and former US senator Rick Santorum actually thanked
us for using them, causing us to get several nice press hits (of
course, they used our boards to get press for themselves, but
this was predicted, because that's all a part of the game).

- In 2013, we placed a video billboard in Time Square that
literally included a hand crossing out the word *Christ,* declaring,
"Who needs Christ in Christmas? Nobody!" As a result of this
billboard, New York state senator Andrew Lanza compared us
to Nazis on his Web page, and in what I think (hope) was the
stupidest move in his life, called for a boycott of Times Square,
during the holiday season, in protest of our billboard. Yup.
He even threatened to take away our nonprofit status![5] Par-
alyzed with fear, I immediately put up the same billboard in
his district and launched a press release daring him to try to
revoke our 501(c)(3) status. He responded by calling and
apologizing.

  Are you counting? That's one press event for launching
the billboard, a second for Senator Lanza's attack, a third for
our response, and a fourth for his apology. Four press hits for
one billboard (each featuring a picture of the billboard, with
the Web site at the bottom), everyone knows our opponent is
an intolerant bigot, and we are the good guys. Swish.

- In 2014, we left our major cities and went to the Bible Belt. In
five cities, we erected boards that featured a little girl writing
to Santa: "All I want for Christmas is to skip church. I'm too
old for fairy tales." This was the first time we placed billboards
near schools and openly "targeted families," which sent the
press into high gear and prompted two rebuttal billboards from
our religious opponents and a petition, each of which resulted
in press attention for us. What I loved most about this campaign was the idea that the girl is too old for God, but not for
Santa. What kinds of discussions did that prompt?

- In preparation for our 2015 convention, we put up the same little girl on the same billboard in Memphis. After two weeks, we changed the language to Arabic, bringing a new wave of attention from the press just in time for the event. Most outlets showed both versions of the board.

Each advertising event is a press event, providing us a level of market penetration and saturation that no billboard alone can deliver or even approach. The billboards are designed that way and work just great. We tell reporters what's different, what angle the billboard promotes, provide some good quotes, and let 'er rip. The press get a great story that's easy to write and receive lots of social-media shares/ likes (which incites them to write the next story), and we get our message out via a far more effective medium.

As time progresses the efficacy of the billboards fades. We will have to get increasingly provocative until the press loses interest. But remember, the press is not proactive, it's reactive, so when the demand for stories about our billboards fades, it will be because we are succeeding and the shock of atheists speaking out is wearing off. Overton window: shifted.

The secondary target of our billboards is closeted atheists. Some 99.9 percent of atheists are *not* involved with the organized movement, a number that has to change for us to succeed, and using the press to carry our message—"we exist and are on your side"—is an efficient way of addressing this market. Admittedly, when I go on Fox News, I reach far more believers than atheists (closeted or not), but I do sometimes get additional press coverage after going on Fox News, and for this and other reasons I will explain below, I go. Incidentally, people often ask why I go on Fox News instead of CNN (for instance), as if I have a choice. I go where I'm invited, and since controversy gets ratings, I get invited on to Fox News more often.

The golden moments occur when liberal-leaning shows such as *The Daily Show* with Jon Stewart feature my Fox News appearances, as much of their audience is atheistic. (Stephen Colbert, while making fun of an appearance of mine on Fox News, gave me my Twitter handle by calling me "Mr. Atheist Pants.")

I have another goal when I go on conservative-leaning shows—to encourage atheists to watch. Most atheists don't watch Fox News, ever, and as a result they never actually hear what these folks are saying.

Sun Tzu wrote in *The Art of War,* "If you know your enemies and know yourself, you will not be imperiled in a hundred battles."[6] How else, had I not gone on O'Reilly, would atheists have known that he is willing to change the definition of his religion (Christianity is a "philosophy")[7] to maintain his privilege? We must watch these guys, at least occasionally, so we can better know how willing they are to cloak immorality in religion. This is where we reap a huge benefit from YouTube—it allows appearances to live forever, facilitates comments and discussion, and enables atheists everywhere to see for themselves what we fight without having to sit through an entire episode.

The tertiary target for our ads is the theists, but my intent is not to convert them. Atheists will never convert *anyone* with billboards. However, I will get them to talk or complain about us, and when they complain, they will often find themselves doing so *to* closeted atheists in their families and circles of friends. Their complaints are my sales pitches. The perfect situation is a preacher complaining about our billboards in a sermon—advertising the movement's existence to the closeted atheists in the pews, and arming and motivating believers to go home and complain about us (re: advertise us) to their friends. The theists are marketing tools and will be treated as such.

American Atheists (atheists.org) is a cause organization. If we were a for-profit corporation, our advertising would be all about showing us as above our competitors in the marketplace. But we are *not* competing with other organizations. As I've said before, and will continue to say, I'm not in this for American Atheists—I'm in it for America. American Atheists is a tool I am using for the benefit of the country as a whole. That means we have to thrive, but so do the other players in the movement, and it's my responsibility as president of American Atheists to help everyone in the movement.

Do I? Let's look.

We already know controversy sells, and we already know the press love to write about it. So as a quick example, let's look at the Christmas 2012 billboard, "Dump the Myth." This was a huge board with a picture of Santa and a crucified Jesus in Times Square. The Catholic League had a fit, and the press had a field day.

The CNN *Belief Blog* featured a great article[8] on the billboard (featuring the graphic, of course). The implied intent was to focus on the "controversy" of the "factions" of organized atheism. However, the piece actually communicated a story of diversity within the atheist movement, highlighting our breadth for all to see. In the article, CNN reporter Dan Merica talked about our billboard and compared our efforts to those of other atheist organizations, specifically the Harvard Humanists' interfaith efforts to raise money for charity, and the Secular Student Alliance's Xmas parties. In the end, everyone in the article looked good.

That's a positive story for the Harvard Humanists and the SSA on the front page of CNN.com that would not have happened without the "Dump the Myth" billboard in Times Square. Yes, we look harsh in that story compared to the nice-guy atheists, which again tells America . . . there *are* nice-guy atheists. American Atheists stands by what we do, and I mean every word I say, but I also know well that I highlight the nice side of the movement by being assertive. I may be called a dick, but I help nice guys succeed—our efforts give them attention they wouldn't otherwise have received. Another example of how the diplomats are the beneficiaries of the firebrand.

Data Proves Being a Firebrand *Works*

I am asked often, "What is the point?" Why do what I do, and why do it just the way I do it? My detractors in the movement, who sometimes seem a bit too anxious to throw stones, often throw out "What will that accomplish?" when I launch some campaign or initiative they don't like.

First of all, the big picture is atheist normalcy. We aren't looking to outlaw religion or even to shame believers into the closet (although the latter will probably happen over time, and I'm okay with that). The big picture is the normalcy of atheists, which includes the elimination of bigotry against us. I liken our big-picture ideal to where the Jews are now in the United States. Today, anti-Semitism is met with negative consequences, so most anti-Semites think twice about openly trumpeting their hatred of Jews. That's our endgame too—for atheism to be considered a normal part of America, and for open bigotry against us to be considered a negative in polite society.

So how do we get atheism normalized? Well, the best way to normalize it is to de-demonize *us,* and that means de-demonizing the word.

Again, that's why I am such a proponent of using the word *atheist*—that's why using the word in everyday conversation is important. The more the term is used, the more normal it becomes, the weaker it makes the bigotry against us. By using it, we de-demonize us and help to defeat bigotry against us in America. How openly and frequently the word *atheist* is used can be seen as a barometer of how we're doing.

But does firebrand atheism have an effect? If so, how can we tell?

It's a good thing we have data! Atheists *love* data. Let's look at Figure 6.

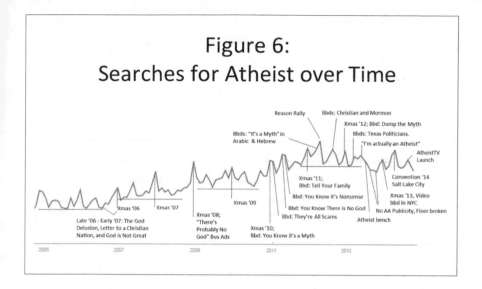

Figure 6:
Searches for Atheist over Time

This chart shows the use of the word *atheist* in search queries over about ten years. I annotated the chart to make a few observations. Note the horizontal "floor" lines. They show how low the search volume goes when no major news stories are happening, which I consider a barometer of atheist normalcy.

I've noted Christmas for every year because the Fox News "War on Christmas" always spikes searches for the term then (this is what I call "the O'Reilly factor").

You can see how the release of *The God Delusion, Letter to a Christian Nation,* and *God Is Not Great* seem to coincide with a rise in the floor, as one would expect. Several excellent books by the best authors in the industry, all going on book tours and TV interviews, should have had exactly such an effect.

Another advertising event, the major London bus ads exclaiming, "There's Probably No God," seemed to do quite well in contributing to a Christmastime spike in the US that raised the floor again, to a point at which it stayed until American Atheists put up its first billboard, "You KNOW It's a Myth." That coincided with the highest peak in the searches since the bus campaign two years earlier.

Note how Christmas '07, '08, '09, '11, '12, and '13 immediately precede a decline near the floor. Not so in 2010, due apparently to the "You KNOW They're All Scams" board and the infamous O'Reilly "tide goes in, tide goes out" (more on that soon) segment in January. This is a telling data point, as it's the only exception to the down-after-Christmas rule. Additionally, a Google search reveals that no other atheist-specific press event seems to have happened in that time frame. The billboard/O'Reilly event seems to be single-handedly responsible for this uptick. The same goes for the pre–Reason Rally Arabic/Hebrew billboards in 2012. This brings into question how ads by other atheist organizations have fared in this measurement. If the height of the peak for a month in which only American Atheists had activity is not different from the peaks for months in which efforts were also made by others, it suggests that activities by other organizations have a negligible effect. In other words, it seems the marginal increase of "nice-guy" activity is rather inconsequential for raising the atheist bar.

Many American Atheists billboards appeared in 2011, each one corresponding to an uptick in searches, leading to a new floor 33 percent higher after my first full year as president. You can almost see our activity pull up that floor—twice as large as the first two rises, and in a fraction of the time!

After the atheist bench was installed, American Atheists experienced a lull in active publicity. Note the corresponding dip below the floor during that time. This suggests that not only is American Atheists activity responsible for upticks, but the lack of activism is responsible for downturns, advancing my hypothesis of a causal relationship of firebrand activity to nationwide interest in atheism, into the realm of dependence. That is, it seems (from these admittedly few data points) that nationwide interest goes down when we go quiet for a long period of time, which also makes sense.

Yes, I know many factors are at play here—I'm not saying this is exhaustive research. I *am* saying that there appears to be a strong correlation between searches for the word *atheist* and the activism of American Atheists since I took over in October of 2010.

Proof of causation? No. But this is definitely supportive data for the assertion that loud atheism leads to more people looking at us.

To give you a sense of scale, I also performed a comparison between the terms *atheist, Christian, Catholic, Muslim,* and *Jewish* (Fig. 7). This shows you how far we have to go compared to these other terms (note: *Christian* is also a name, so searches for people named Christian would affect this search—this is just for illustrative purposes). I will tell you how warm and fuzzy I get when I look at the steady decline for the top three lines of *Christian, Catholic,* and *Jewish. Muslim* is steady, and, almost imperceptibly due to the scale, only *atheism* is rising.

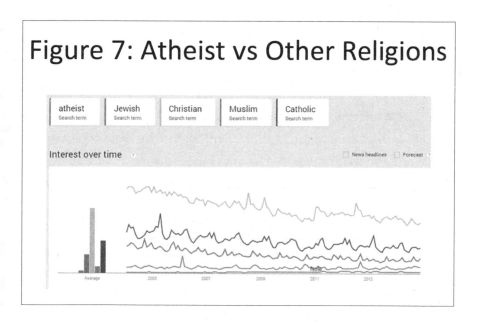

Figure 7: Atheist vs Other Religions

Some might say this increase in searches for *atheist* is just a result of the growth of atheism, and that the rise in people searching for *atheist* is just a symptom of the growth of the whole movement. I don't think so. If the whole movement was rising, and the searches were rising along with it, then we would expect to see other terms with similar curves. But that's not what we find.

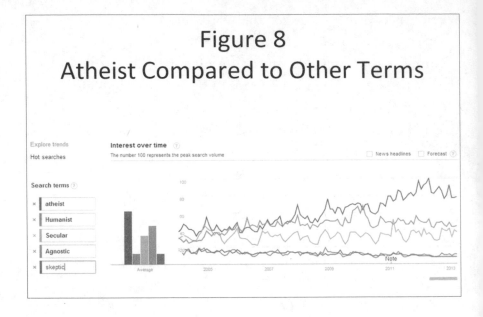

Figure 8 shows the search results for the same times for similar words. Searches for the word *humanist,* which one would expect to see increase because of all the humanist ads that went up, actually decreases over time, with its floor on a steady decline. Searches for *agnostic* and *secular* remain steady. Only *atheist* increases. Obviously the change is word-centric, not movement-centric. This shows us the growth of *atheist* is unique, not a result of a "rising tide that raises all boats," an increase in general Internet usage, or other factors that would increase the use of multiple terms.

But is it because of American Atheists? Do we have any correlation between searches for the word *atheist* and American Atheists activity?

Yep. Figure 9 shows searches for *American Atheists,* with another graph of the searches for *atheist* right above it. Every peak in searches for *American Atheists* since I took office correlates with an ad campaign, and all but one correlates with an increase in the searches for *atheist* (the exception is the "Atheism Is Patriotic" flyovers in July of 2011).

Figure 9
Atheist v American Atheist

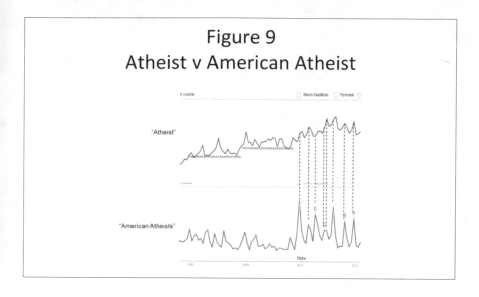

Figure 10
Atheist v American Atheist
Same Scale

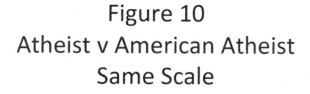

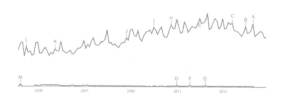

It should be noted that although the scale above seems to indicate the number of searches for *American Atheists* is about the same, this is not true. Searches for *American Atheists* are minute compared to the number of searches for *atheist,* so the number of searches for *American Atheists* is not a major component of searches for *atheist.* Figure 10 shows the same searches as above on the same scale to prove this point.

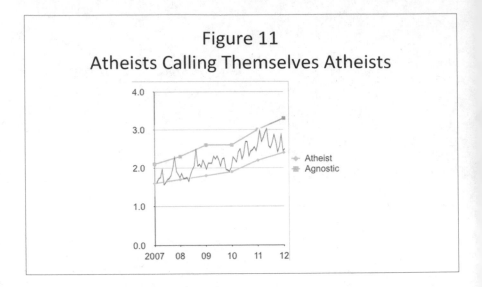

Figure 11
Atheists Calling Themselves Atheists

Here's more. Since 2010, the number of atheists identifying them-selves as such has shown a substantial increase. Note the Pew 2012 data in Figure 11:

The middle line is the same middle line from Figure 6, showing the peaks and floors of the rising use of the word *atheist* in searches, seemingly caused by American Atheists campaigns (with only the time scale retained). You can see how nicely this ties in to an in-crease in the number of people calling themselves atheists. The slope of the line representing people who self-identify as atheists (as op-posed to *nones*) increases at the same time as the searches for *atheist*.

Agnostic as an identifier follows the same pattern over the same period. This is interesting since again there is no increase in searches for the word *agnostic* in the same time frame. So, while use of the word *atheist* seems to follow searches on the word itself, use of the word *agnostic* seems to correlate with searches on the word *atheist*. This implies people are searching for *atheist* after seeing our ads, then us-ing *agnostic* as a stepping-stone term, or they are looking at the movement and deciding to take a softer label. This is more data sug-gesting hard-line atheism is helping the movement's softer side.

I'm not suggesting that searches for *atheist* will always rise in line with people identifying as atheists. Rather, I'm showing the same activism that apparently increased the searches in this case seems to have also resulted in an increase in the number of people identifying as atheists (which makes sense). This growth is important because it creates a snowball effect—the rise in conversation with and about atheists will lead to a greater awareness of atheism among the general population, which will lead to the de-demonization of atheism in general. In turn, this will relieve some of the societal pressure others feel to stay in the closet, yielding still more out-and-proud atheists.

So let's bring it home. If American Atheists activity is directly influencing the rise of people calling themselves atheists, then Figure 12 actually represents the quantitative impact American Atheists' firebrand atheism is having on the country. For those using *atheist* as an identifier, the difference between where the line was trending before our activity and the uptick apparently caused by our activity leads to an increase from 2.1 to 2.4 percent, which yields about 1 million Americans who call themselves atheists because of American Atheists. Additionally, if you look at the data point for *agnostic* in 2009 to be an outlier (a reasonable but impossible to prove assumption for this exercise), the number of people who call themselves agnostic as a result of

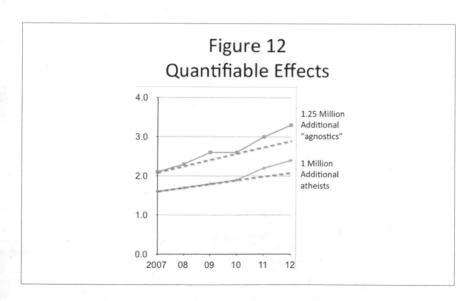

American Atheists' activities goes up from 2.9 to 3.3 percent, or an increase of 1.25 million more people as shown in Figure 12.

Here's a little more support for my argument. A *USA Today* article is one of many places you can go to find positive news about how atheists are gaining acceptance—in the same time frame as our activities:

- "For the second time in less than a year, the Gallup poll reports that a majority of Americans would vote for an atheist for president."
- "We have seen an enormous change over time in the willingness to vote for an atheist."—Karlyn Bowman, American Enterprise Institute for Public Policy Research[9]

Additionally, a 2015 Gallup Poll shows 58 percent of Americans would vote for an atheist (an all-time high), up from 54 percent in 2011 and 45 percent in 2007.[10] So not only does the data support my assertion that loud atheism attracts more attention, it also correlates with an increase in acceptance, which supports my position that we are successfully de-demonizing the word, leading to less of a stigma toward, and greater acceptance of, atheism (changing religion from *without*). The rise in assertive advertising positively correlates to a rise in searches, which positively correlates to an improved reputation.

Therefore, charges that I may be turning people off from atheism, thus worsening the reputation of atheists, appear to be totally unsupported. What *is* supported, and strongly, are the following:

- American Atheists' firebrand activism has a distinct, unique, and measurable effect on searches of the word *atheist*.
- Searches for *atheist* correlate to growth in self-identification of both atheists and agnostics.
- Growth in searches for *atheist,* but not for other like terms, implies the growth is word-centric.

- Word-centric growth of searches for *atheist,* and not *humanist,* in the face of ample billboard and TV advertising for humanist groups, implies a much higher level of efficacy for atheist billboards than for humanist efforts, the latter of which seem to have no effect on the searches for the word *humanist.* This makes sense—humanist billboards don't make news, probably because nearly 90 percent of the population doesn't understand the word.

- As our activity seems to be affecting the growth of *agnostic* as an identifier, it makes sense to argue that atheists are finding the movement because of us, and then finding their place within it, benefiting the whole movement; again, *the diplomats are beneficiaries of firebrands.*

- Claims that we sometimes hurt the movement are seemingly unfounded, and in fact as atheism grows, respect for atheism grows, and willingness to vote for atheists (as opposed to *nones*) grows. Again, this just makes sense.

Thus American Atheists' "firebrand atheism" appears to be directly improving the country for atheists. This is exactly as I predicted, exactly what I've been saying, and all according to plan.

I asked Dr. Ryan Cragun, associate professor of sociology at the University of Tampa and author of *What You Don't Know About Religion (but Should),* to comment specifically on my data for this book, and his reply confirms what I've asserted:

It is clear that there has been a very strong and consistent correlation between interest in atheism, generally, and interest in American Atheists, specifically, over the last three years. Causality can be more clearly determined when it comes to interest in the organization itself; the activities and events of American Atheists regularly result in heightened interest in the organization.

Serious social progress is not achieved without the help of those who raise their voices *and* their (metaphorical) fists. Malcolm X let the country hear Black America's righteous anger in plain words and sometimes brutal honesty, all the while knowing (by moving the Overton window) he was making Martin Luther King Jr. look moderate. Act Up raised awareness of the fundamental immorality of those who were both antigay and gay by exposing and outing people. Its activism brought the need to come out of the closet into the forefront of discussion, and, yes, (by shifting the Overton window) it made those "less fanatical gays" look closer to the mainstream. New York Radical Women, the "bra burners,"[11] similarly delivered their extreme message of equality to America while making those "less radical feminists" seem much less threatening.[12] These activists weren't considered the "nice guys" of their respective movements, but their impacts were unquestionable.

This is why I believe it's our duty as atheists to our country, our movement, and the theists themselves to shout the truth from the rooftops and wear it on our sleeves. Everyone needs truth exposed—except the liars.

On the WTF Face

I certainly can't write a book without discussing the "What the Fuck?" meme.

One of the perks of the job is being the face of American Atheists—both literally and figuratively, but this meme face concept took the expression to a whole new level.

I'd been on *The O'Reilly Factor* once before, as a spokesperson for the now-defunct Godless Americans Political Action Committee. A clip from this visit was used by Senator Elizabeth "Liddy" Dole in her 2008 campaign to make her opponent Kay Hagan look like an atheist supporter—a strategy that backfired miserably because the good people of North Carolina are not all raging atheophobic bigots as Mrs. Dole apparently is. Hagan was flooded with over thirty-six hundred donations in the forty-eight hours following Dole's ad, from atheists and theists alike.[13]

In that first episode some ten years ago, my off-camera contact with Bill was brief and insubstantial. However, this time, before a 2011 appearance about the "Scams" billboard, I had a few minutes to talk with him before the show. The surprise was that he was knowledgeable. He knew about Madalyn, past-president Ellen Johnson, and others from the movement. He was calm and rational. I went on the show admittedly disarmed, expecting a civil, intelligent conversation.

Silly me.

During the show, I tried to corner him into admitting he was not being skeptical about his own religion. I was about to succeed when he went into defense mode and exclaimed, "I'll tell you why [religion's] not a scam, in my opinion: tide goes in, tide goes out. Never a miscommunication. You can't explain that."

Okay. Here was this intelligent man giving the stupidest argument for the existence of God: I don't know, therefore God did it, which is the Neanderthal-era mentality (that ignorance is equal to evidence), to which I earlier referred. This total non sequitur to our off-camera discussion caught me by surprise.

So I made the Face.

He was playing me. He was feeding me a line to divert me from the subject. I responded with the analogy of Thor, explaining O'Reilly's argument could be used for any god. At any rate, the WTF face[14] quickly went viral, thanks to the people at reddit (r/atheism). At first it was just the standard face, but then it evolved into multiple races, gender expressions, and all sorts of designs. They had fun with it!

Yes, it stokes my ego, but it's far more important than that. The meme helps to normalize atheism, at least to some degree. It reaches

Figure 13
Two Faces

a whole new audience of Internet users who are not involved with, or even aware of, the atheist movement, and should they find out about its origin, it informs/reminds them that we are here working for their rights. It also reminds atheists of our penetration into the mainstream when they see my face being used outside the movement. I like it and promote it, because it is guerrilla-esque in its penetration. Masked by a funny face is a serious statement about religion, and the lies/deceptions/diversions that some will use to protect religious (in this case Christian) privilege.

Chapter 6

BE EVERYWHERE

There is nothing more difficult to take in hand, more perilous to conduct, or more uncertain in its success, than to take the lead in the introduction of a new order of things.　　　　　　　—Niccolò Machiavelli

One change always leaves the way open for the establishment of others.
　　　　　　　—Niccolò Machiavelli

Everyone in this country knows more atheists than they think they know, but between those still in their proverbial closets and others using theist-approved substitute terms, atheists are viewed as a much smaller minority than we really are. This has to stop if we are to succeed in taking our rightful place in this country.

If we intend to show America and the rest of the world that atheists are *here,* we must go beyond that with another truth—atheists are *everywhere*. In nearly every neighborhood, every town in every state, there are atheists. We are not a small minority who can be overlooked. We make up a major portion of this country, though we are only now making ourselves known.

This ubiquity must be demonstrated.

Since religion thrives where it can remain unquestioned, where it can demonize an out-group to divert attention from its many weaknesses, we must, as a movement, penetrate the places where religion seems to have the tightest hold. Religion will try to stake out "atheist-free zones" to protect itself, but such zones don't exist. We are already everywhere.

I'll set out examples of this mentality below, but ask you, the reader, to understand this list is far from exhaustive. Everywhere religion has a stronghold, there are atheists who must proudly add their voices to the chorus.

The Conservatives—CPAC

The extreme right wing gathers every year at CPAC—the Conservative Political Action Conference, led by Christians who today run Conservatism. Sarah Palin and Newt Gingrich are among the mainstays—the heroes—and Conservatives come from all over to hear about how gay marriage is attacking 'Murica, and, yes, how Jesus wrote the Constitution. It is a hotbed of "real" Christianity.

At least that's what Christianity would like you to think. Christianity wants to own Conservatism, as it has for a few decades now, and it loves to give the impression that the two are inextricably linked. This linkage tells us that all Conservatives are Christians, and most important, that Conservatives need to court Christians, nearly to the exclusion of everyone else, thereby promoting Christianity's legitimacy via government endorsement. In effect, the religion of Christianity has successfully and permanently taken over half the political system, or so they want us to think.

It's the perfect place for atheists to infiltrate; a closed, large group of people with the impression, but not the definition, that it is all religious. However, we all know that link isn't real. We all remember that Conservatism used to be separate from Christianity. We all know that libertarians and fiscal conservatives exist, and they are often atheists, and most important, we can see these people are completely ignored by the larger Conservative movement—ripe for rallying.

Our first attempt at infiltration (note: not disruption) was to simply buy a table at the 2014 event in Washington, DC, to make the statement that atheists exist in Conservatism. We paid our fee (the check was cashed) and had special marketing materials made up just for the event. Targeting our efforts, we were not there to spread atheism or to jar closeted atheists to come out to their friends or family, but rather to spread awareness of atheists already within the ranks of Conservatism with the following points:

1. There are Conservative atheists, and in fact nearly half of atheists think a small government is important, but only 20 percent of atheists call themselves Conservative, meaning about 30 percent of atheists nationwide are good candidates for the Conservative movement, but do not identify as such.
2. Those numbers can reasonably be extrapolated to say tens of millions of registered atheist voters are not voting Conservative but otherwise might, if not for non-fiscal-policy-related reasons (enough to swing an election).
3. To be "socially conservative" is not Conservative at all. It's really a euphemism for theocracy, which runs directly counter to what Conservatism stands for. How is marriage regulation, prayer in schools, and laws against stem-cell research "small government"? How are laws restricting death with dignity or abortion consistent with the platform of keeping government out of the lives of Americans? They're not—they are the antithesis of true Conservatism and go against atheist ideals as well.
4. The social (i.e., theocratic) side of today's Republican Party is pushing away the atheist votes needed for real (fiscal) Conservatives to win elections.

That's it. Nothing offensive by any means—only good, old-fashioned, awareness-raising facts we hoped would spur discussion among the rank and file of American Conservatism.

But our facts, as facts do, scared the hell out of the Christian Right, and when they heard of our intentions, they made up a reason to refund our money and refuse our table.

The reason they gave? We are too aggressive. Why? Because I said in an interview that the Religious Right should fear atheist infiltration into CPAC because we threaten their stranglehold on Conservatism, so some CPAC organizers asserted, "People of any faith tradition should not be attacked for their beliefs,"[1] as if we'd attacked people.

Anyway, having lost our table, I decided a little hard-line activism was in order, so I bought a ticket, donned a FIREBRAND ATHEIST T-shirt, adorned myself with atheist buttons, and went to the conference. I did not go to listen to any speeches, but rather to give out flyers to anyone who would take them. I wanted to show attendees that at least one atheist was at CPAC.

I would soon find out there were *hundreds.*

At one point early on I stood outside the main ballroom, where Sarah Palin was speaking, and waited for the capacity crowd of ten thousand Conservatives to pile out. This was intimidating and scary—watching thousands of motivated Conservatives piling out of an auditorium and down a hall, with me standing in the middle of the hall waiting to hand out atheist flyers (see Fig. 14). My heart was pumping and my adrenaline flowed.

"Why are the atheists at CPAC?"

"What are atheists doing here?"

"Conservative atheists—find out more."

Those were the phrases I proclaimed (not too loudly) as the crowd began to envelope me.

And then something amazing happened.

They turned around, came back, and took flyers. More and more people came and took my literature and thanked me for being there.

Figure 14
Atheist Flyer Photo

My view of the oncoming deluge of ten thousand Conservatives.

(Photo: David Silverman)

Yes, I had a few stereotypical conversations about hell and the like, but surprisingly, I found a lot of supporters—and even more surprisingly, a lot of atheists. Libertarians, Ayn Randians, and many others came over to tell me how wonderful it was that I was there just to push atheism awareness. Atheists came out of the woodwork to take my buttons and *wear* them. Several atheists came out to me, and to the friends they were with (and guess what—their friends did not freak out in the least), and even the Christians I met supported the idea that atheists ought to be able to buy a table.

The press was all over me. In interview after interview, I talked about Conservative atheists. Discussion ensued. People called in to comment—usually positively!

Here's the most interesting part—most of the people I met strongly disagreed with the management of CPAC on so many issues that it had become a joke among the participants! It appears that the decision makers do not *remotely* speak for the attendees, many of whom were *not* religious nuts. They are openly just waiting for the old guard to die out so new, more reasonable people can reclaim the Grand Old Party.

Think about that.

Now, it seems quite reasonable the Christian Right should fear atheist infiltration into Conservative ranks because their hold on said ranks seems to be tenuously based on the authority of old people with younger, more secular members ready to take over. If we keep up this pressure, which was in this case instituted primarily by one small team, we could potentially undermine and outlast Christian domination of the Conservative wing of American politics. Big words, big goal—but one that I believe is achievable.

Because we went where we weren't expecting to find support, we learned this goal is plausible, that we already have a support base, and our message has resonance. Furthermore, if we are successful in separating Christianity from Conservatism, we, the good guys, will win in a big-picture way—Conservatism will no longer represent a threat to the separation of religion and government.

See why fundamentalist Christianity's fear is warranted?

If Conservatism reverts back to the pre–Moral Majority era when it lived just fine without Christian dogma in its platform, most of our problems will wither away. We wouldn't know this was possible if we'd listened to what religion wants us to hear—that Conservatism is Christian—and stayed out of CPAC. Atheists are everywhere, including within the Conservative ranks, and by going where we weren't wanted, we proved it's even more prevalent than we (any of us) thought.

That proof, as we had hoped, led to progress. In 2015, organized atheism was granted its first presence at CPAC, booth and all, and we even had an atheist activist (American Atheists board member Jamila Bey) *onstage, speaking as an atheist!* Overton window: shifted. Again. The strategy worked perfectly, and atheists are out, loud, and proud inside Conservatism.

See you next year, CPAC!

Side note to Conservative atheists: I hope this section spurs you to shout your atheism loud and proud at Conservative events. It's scary, I know (as you can see, I've been there), but it's so important that we penetrate Conservatism with awareness that atheists are already in its ranks, and it's as easy as wearing an atheist T-shirt and smiling a lot when people talk to you about it. I found it a positive experience, and an opportunity for much-needed atheist activism.

The Progressives

Being everywhere also includes being where we are wanted or expected, but not prominent. For example, under my leadership American Atheists has begun attending and speaking at liberal events where one would expect to find atheists, but where oddly there was (before us) no organized atheist presence at all.

For instance, we were the first atheists to have an official presence at Creating Change, in 2014, one of the nation's largest LGBTQ events, which was so popular, multiple organizations followed in our footsteps and purchased tables at subsequent events. We are loud and proud supporters of the LGBTQ movement because LGBTQ equality is mainly an issue of the separation of religion and government. I'm happy to say our allegiance was welcomed with open arms, so much so that we are arranging for atheist panels at the next event.

Another good example of where an atheist presence was missing is Netroots Nation, the large progressive/technology event, where once again we were the first atheist organization to have a table specifically as atheists promoting atheism. To say we were welcomed and well received is an understatement. The majority opinion was that it was about time the atheists showed up—people were *relieved* we were finally there! Many attendees came to our booth to sign up and to get my autograph (I am still not used to that).

The National Organization for Women (NOW) conference also welcomed us, first inviting us to set up a table and then asking us onstage. I was able to send loud and proud women atheists (including

Amanda Knief, who was instrumental in the development of this effort) to NOW to underscore our combined fight against the religiously backed patriarchy that advocates second-class citizenship for half of our population based on their misogynistic mythology. Although some of the more religious attendees did not like our message, that was to be expected, we can justify our positions (you can do that when you're completely right), and the majority of NOW attendees clearly agreed with our assertion: religion is one of the main barriers to women's equality in the United States and elsewhere.

These are examples of where atheism is and should be, but was not obviously present before the firebrands went there. While the conservatives and the progressives differed in their reactions to us, I'd like to point out some similarities. In all cases:

1. We met many atheists; indeed, many more than we expected.
2. We found many theistic people who supported our presence.
3. We encountered no violence or outright hostility. Even at CPAC, the most virulent opposition never raised a hand, and only moderately raised a voice.
4. We added substantially to the conversation, bringing the atheist argument where it had not been. Nobody who goes to any of those events thinks there are no atheists there anymore, and indeed, many now understand we are plentiful.
5. The atheist argument was positioned to further the plans of the listener/organization. Even at CPAC, atheism was positioned (honestly) to show that by embracing atheists Conservatives would benefit.
6. Other organizations from the secular movement are following suit.
7. We made members and friends.
8. The experience was generally positive.

Religion craves dominance and despises anything that remotely resembles competition or criticism. As in war, religion finds strongholds in society from which to gain support and prepare to launch attacks on other targets. As in war, strongholds are a major part of eventual domination and conquest. As in war, such strongholds must be conquered or destroyed.

The Conservative movement is an excellent example of such a stronghold, and attending CPAC and making our presence known *and* garnering support because a lot of quiet atheists are within the Conservative ranks is a major blow to the perceived ubiquity and dominance religion has on the right-wing side of politics. What will happen if those quiet atheists are roused by our presence? What if we can motivate them to be more vocal about the theocratic side of their movement? That would be a major blow on behalf of the good guys, as it would eliminate one of religion's most prominent strongholds.

Being everywhere also includes defensive moves. The theocrats have successfully begun to infiltrate the left (as they did the right), and it is up to us to put up a fight, beat them back, and shore up the left as a stronghold for atheism. This is doable, since behind all the politics and political correctness, many progressives have moved beyond religion (mainly because they are used to fighting religion from the political right). So where we already exist as a force, or in the cases of NOW, Creating Change, and Netroots Nation, where we were absent but acceptance was expected, it behooves us to expect religion to attempt to infiltrate our perceived strongholds even as we build our presence.

Again, these are just examples—this has to happen *everywhere*. Attacking religious ubiquity is attacking privilege. This is why I wholeheartedly endorse atheists participating in as many interfaith events as possible. Excluding ourselves from these events separates us from society, creates and preserves atheist-free zones and in turn preserves inequality. This is also why I support atheist chaplains in the military—if religion is there providing religious guidance to theists, atheists should have chaplains to provide godless guidance. Because equality.

You could consider any place you don't see atheists as one of those religious strongholds and infiltrate. Where there are no atheists, atheists should go, loudly and proudly, for the good of the country and its citizenry. If no atheists are in your local government or on your school board or even in your circle of friends, assume it's a stronghold for religion and treat it as such. This goes for almost any situation because religion wants to be exclusive everywhere.

Chapter 7

ON DEFINING MORALITY WITHOUT GOD(S)

The Good Life is one inspired by love and guided by knowledge.
—BERTRAND RUSSELL

There is a huge difference between being tolerant and tolerating intolerance.
—AYAAN HIRSI ALI

As you can expect, I get asked where atheists get their morality from, absent religion, ad nauseam. This is mainly because religion claims it is needed for morality (a lie). When I give my answer, I preface it by stating I am about to ask a trick question, then continue as follows:

"Let's say your pastor said something from the pulpit you found morally offensive. What would you do?"

The answers range from "I would ignore it" to "I would object to the pastor" to "I would leave the church and find another, more moral church." But again, this is a trick question. Nobody has *ever* offered me the one right answer: "That can never happen because morality comes from my religion/church/pastor."

This highlights my point—morality comes from within. Religion simply takes the credit, convincing believers their morality came from the god as taught by the church, not their own minds.

People have their own morality, and they go to a church that shares (which itself is probably a product of religious indoctrination) their positions. This then reinforces their belief that their god thinks they are right, and the church, in turn, claims credit for this morality, which was theirs in the first place. "You're welcome, and here is the collection plate so you can properly thank us."

It's all part of the scam.

All humans have their own morality, which is fluid between people, and, on a societal level, across space and time. That's why Muhammad had sex with Aisha when she was nine years old—it was moral *at the time.* That's why some Christians owned slaves with the blessings of their church—it was moral *at the time.* That's why anyone claiming morality is fixed is simply ignorant of world history, or even American history, not to mention the state of the world today. Sam Harris, in *The Moral Landscape,* posits a big-picture objective good, said good being the benefit of human well-being.[1] I'm not arguing this macro-level point. Rather, I'm saying that which is considered "moral behavior" changes on a societal level over time, and therefore no morality that is espoused by any culture can be viewed as objectively good or bad.

Many people categorize certain issues as "moral" concerns when it's really about religion inserting itself into non-adherents' lives. These issues give us plenty of fronts on which to fight, particularly relating to sexual reproduction and women's rights.

For example, abstinence-only education is one of many ways religion tries to insert itself into other people's lives, in this case by dumbing down the way kids are taught about sex. Its advocates say, in the true religious tradition, that ignorance yields abstinence—if we don't teach kids about sex, they won't do it—which for some reason is good. But abstinence-only education doesn't work. A report in the *Journal of Adolescent Health* (2006) states:

> *A recent emphasis on abstinence-only programs and policies appears to be undermining more comprehensive sexuality education and other*

government-sponsored programs. We believe that abstinence-only edu-
cation programs, as defined by federal funding requirements, are mor-
ally problematic, by withholding information and promoting questionable
and inaccurate opinions. Abstinence-only programs threaten fundamen-
tal human rights to health, information, and life.[2]

A later article from the same journal on the same subject in 2008
quotes a study:

Adolescents who received comprehensive sex education were significantly
less likely to report teen pregnancy . . . than those who received no for-
mal sex education, whereas there was no significant effect of abstinence-
only education. . . . Abstinence-only education did not reduce the
likelihood of engaging in vaginal intercourse . . . but comprehensive
sex education was marginally associated with a lower likelihood of
reporting having engaged in vaginal intercourse.[3]

The data goes on and on that sexual ignorance is not effective
against STDs, pregnancy, or even teen sex itself, yet certain government officials try to push it any way they can, ignoring the data that
shows they are hurting kids. The only reason: their preachers say God
doesn't want your kids to have sex. Once again, religion proves
Hitchens right and poisons society—in this case, keeping teens ignorant in the name of God.

As a result, these teens are equally likely to have premarital sex,
but much less likely to use a condom because they don't know how and
have been told condoms are not that effective anyway. Abortions are
bad too, according to religion, so in some states, religion-inspired
abortion restrictions force teens to keep their unwanted fetuses to
term. But that's okay, because that makes baby Christians—religion
grows through breeding and indoctrination. See the machine?

Tell me again how religion hurts nobody.

Now look at contraceptive regulation (same machine, different part). Here we are in 2015, and this is still a subject of debate because a religious institution, the Catholic Church, wants your boss to use his or her discretion as to what kind of birth control, if any, you can access on the company insurance plan. They pretend it's about the company owners, but those that oppose your using contraception just happen to be echoing their church. So once again, their religion gets into your life, and you lose personal freedom in the name of religious freedom.

The same goes for the morning-after pill. All of a sudden, some pharmacists get to stop their customers from obtaining a medicine because its against the pharmacists' religious views. They call it a "conscience clause," but no conscience is involved here—just religion asserting control. These pharmacists' customers are victims of religion calling the shots (which in this case means women lose body autonomy), while politicians parade these "moral objections" around as if they were ethical. They're not.

Morality is individual, and I am in no position to push morality on anyone, but often issues of the separation of religion and government are marketed as "morality" issues, and American Atheists gladly steps in there when needed.

Gay marriage and adoption equality. Abortion. Sex education. Contraception. The morning-after pill. These are *all* mainly issues about the separation of religion and government that get wrongly categorized as "morality" issues, and they affect each citizen of this country. In these areas and more, religion has infiltrated politics and attempted (usually successfully) to make non-adherents obey religious dogma under rule of law—just as many Islamists want to do via political correctness and, in some cases, sharia. It's about *them* controlling *us*.

Many of these issues are a part of a larger machine to make baby Christians because their argument is so damned weak, they can't depend on converting people to sustain themselves. The Religious Right uses its size and money to wield power in politics to create as many situations as possible that make Christian babies (poor sex education + contraception regulation + abortion restrictions, etc.).

This is a numbers game. I can think of no position that any Christian church has ever taken that would result in fewer babies being born, because that's the antithesis of their objective: Christian babies become Christian adults who tithe and obey. Christian leaders don't care if these policies also affect non-Christians (except that making non-adherents obey religious dogma legitimizes the church), but creating an environment that produces more Christian babies is one of Christianity's highest objectives, and many of its positions combine to support this effort.

> *Not to have children is a selfish choice.*
> —Pope Francis, February 11, 2015

This is why we are the good guys and they are the bad guys. There is no bill in any state trying to force atheism on anyone. *All of our moves are defensive or equality-based,* all the time. Take the religion out of science class and keep science neutral. Give women their full rights over their own bodies, including the right to birth control and abortion as they, not you, see fit. Get that religious icon off public property, or give us our own; it's our public property too. Take the religion off the money, and out of the Pledge of Allegiance, so neither religion nor atheism is preferred. Everything, every lawsuit, every complaint, every fight we fight as a movement, is all defensive, all pro-equality. We demand religion stay out of our lives, and we are hated for it by those who know we are right, but are unwilling or unable to admit it.

I said earlier that all theists are victims of religion. Make no mistake, to a significant degree we are *all* victims of religion because we *all* have fewer rights because of it.

It's time we shut that shit down.

Chapter 8

ON FIGHTING UNPOPULAR BATTLES (BUT BEING RIGHT)

We have fought long and hard to escape medieval superstition and I, for one, do not want to go back. —JAMES RANDI

The secret of happiness: find something more important than you are and dedicate your life to it. —DANIEL DENNETT

American Atheists began with a mother, a child, and a court case.

After Madalyn won her epic court battle (in conjunction with other plaintiffs) banning mandatory Bible readings in public schools, she started American Atheists for the sole purpose of continuing the fight for atheist equality, freedom of conscience, and the separation of religion from government. Since then, American Atheists has fought legal battles that may be politically incorrect or unpopular, but are nonetheless vital to the continued evolution of this country.

Today, American Atheists has a specific legal philosophy to which we adhere. Simply stated, we fight battles to win. While that may seem obvious, this means we don't file cases for show or for publicity alone. We design and take cases with the intent of triumph.

We choose battles to maximize the win potential while minimizing the potential for loss. Many don't understand that when the good guys lose a lawsuit, the bad guys win a lawsuit (!), and this may set a precedent in the wrong direction, creating new, bad law with long-term and wide-ranging ramifications. Well-intentioned people have contributed to the creation of bad laws with lawsuits that should not have been filed, and I don't want to be one of them. So while we only pick cases we intend to win, we might turn down a case if what we could win doesn't outweigh the risk of losing.

We look for cases where our equality is infringed, even if they are small infringements, because each unchallenged infringement is the next case's precedent. Never should we stand by and say, "It's okay, that infringement doesn't mean much to me," because these small-looking cases are never the endgame, but are merely stepping-stones to the next assault (analogous to drawing Muhammad). This is an important point worth repeating—our opponents assail our rights using baby steps, not huge leaps, and we must make sure those "small assaults" to our liberty don't go unchallenged.

Having explained the philosophy, let's look at some legal issues of particular concern.

Government-Imposed Religious Privilege

Churches and other religious institutions have special rights above and beyond those of other nonprofits because of laws that elevate religion. Such laws are fundamentally contrary to the separation of religion and government. Religious organizations are given more perks, more breaks, and more money because they promote religion; secular clubs get less, simply because they don't (unless they call themselves religious). It's a clear, deliberate, legalized advantage for religion, and it's rampant.

For example, thanks to the Faith-Based Initiative, churches provide many services using our tax dollars that should be provided by secular charities, yet the churches do so without the same oversight or employment rules. If there is any glaring example of unfair policy that favors religion that President Obama could easily have fixed, it is this one. (Obama promised to do just that during his run for office, but he must have forgotten.) This policy allows churches to say they will be performing a community service, get federal funds, and spend it without the accountability to which secular charities would be subjected. Sure, they are supposed to perform the services, and some do (and if they do it without preaching or discriminating in hiring, like other nonprofits, that's legal), but we taxpayers don't know how well or how efficiently because of inadequate oversight. Everything we hear on the subject is hype—no numbers, no reports.

The churches could be keeping the money and not providing the services. They could be providing the services poorly. They could be preaching their mythology as they provide the service (illegal, as they are using public funds to lure in potential converts). We don't know because *the public doesn't get to know.*

Moreover, when this money goes to religious organizations whose personnel are trained to preach religion as a primary goal, and not to trained professionals whose primary goal is to provide social services, the government ends up paying underqualified people to perform social services *because* they are religious, or members of a particular religion.[1] Churches get federal tax money to provide services in which they are not experts, while secular experts go unemployed, and the government thinks this is a good idea.

Then these organizations use their status as social service organizations to—guess what—try to influence public policy on religious-freedom issues. In 2011, the Chicago-based Catholic Charities were supposedly on the side of children as they took federal funds to run an adoption agency. But apparently their religion-based hatred for gay people was far more important as they shut down rather than place kids in gay homes when marriage equality came to Illinois.

They claimed—get this—that the government was forcing them to break their religious rules by making them obey the same rules as other organizations (and not discriminate).[2] And this is happening all over the country, including in Colorado[3] and Washington, DC (where they also threatened to shut down their help for the homeless if marriage equality passed),[4] in an attempt to sway public policy by holding their social services hostage to promote and preserve bigotry in the name of God. So now those kids will suffer, the community loses a supposedly secular asset, and according to them *it's the government's fault!*

Are you angry yet? These organizations are supposedly set up as charities and social services, get government money to do so, but when they have to be fair and nondiscriminatory, their compassion goes in the Dumpster, and children get screwed. And when they shut down, they cry discrimination because they can't make society obey their silly religious rules. And they claim to be ethical.

It gets worse, because the Faith-Based Initiative is not even the best (worst) example of unfair government treatment of religion. That award goes to the IRS tax code.

Nonprofits serve as pseudo-extensions of the government that provide a broad range of services. In general, they are supposed to help their community in some way. The idea is that corporations without stock ownership (the government owns all the stock of nonprofit corporations) are formed by experts to provide services not adequately addressed by the government, and as such they are exempt from some taxes and receive other benefits. Contrary to what one might think, nonprofits can and do earn profits, but they are restricted on how they spend their profits, they cannot sell shares, and donations are tax deductible.

All nonprofits have a degree of oversight and are regulated at the state and federal level, as one might expect of an extension of the government. We must declare our income and expenses, and how much we pay for salaries and spend on our social work. All this information is public, as we (this includes American Atheists) serve the general population.

Did I write *all nonprofits have oversight*? That's wrong. What I should have written is *all nonprofits that are not religious* have oversight, because religious institutions are not subject to such rules. In fact, churches and religious institutions have a completely different set of rules to which they must adhere. Because God.[5]

The IRS tax code lists "advancement of religion" as an official charitable activity, right between "relief of the poor, the distressed, or the underprivileged" and "advancement of education or science."[6] Additionally, it adds an "if religious/then benefits" statement that provides religious institutions benefits that other nonprofits aren't granted.

These benefits include:

- A substantially streamlined application process. Religious institutions get nonprofit status by default, avoiding bylaw reviews, wait times, and (of course) fees. The Reason Rally Coalition, the 501(c)(3) (educational) organization set up to run the rally, took months to become official, but if we'd declared ourselves a religious organization, it would have been cheaper and nearly instantaneous.

- Donor privacy. Donate $5,000 or more to American Atheists and the government hears about it, as does the general public, because we have to declare you on our yearly tax forms. Donate *$5 million* to the Church of Scientology and your privacy is assured because they don't have to declare anything. Think about how that works to prevent major donations to causes such as American Atheists, which might be considered controversial, while contributions to religions are completely confidential.

- Lack of oversight. Religious institutions are *assumed* to be ethical and efficient, so they are not required by the government to report income or expenses in any way, to anyone. According to the IRS, "Generally, tax-exempt organizations must file an annual information return (Form 990 or Form 990-EZ). Tax-exempt organizations that have annual gross receipts not normally in excess of $25,000 ($50,000 for tax years ending on or after December 31, 2010) are not required to file the annual information return; they may be required to file an annual electronic notice, however. In addition, *churches and certain church-affiliated organizations are excepted from filing*"[7] (emphasis mine).

- Churches are only audited by the IRS in extreme circumstances (in fact, the IRS has special rules limiting its power to conduct such an audit, so it rarely ever happens),[8] but secular organizations are subject to strict rules and regular oversight. In 2009, for example, an IRS agent investigated the Living Word Christian Center in Brooklyn Park, Minnesota, and found inappropriate politicking and possible financial improprieties, but the judge in the case ruled the church didn't have to comply with the IRS audit because—get this—the auditor was of *insufficient rank*; only high-ranking IRS officials may audit churches.[9] Try that one the next time you get audited!

- According to Professor Ryan Cragun, churches cost America about $71 billion per year in nonprofit property-tax exemptions alone. That's enough for twenty-eight missions to Mars per year,[10] or *1.5 million* teachers[11] or *1.4 million* police officers[12] per year. This does not include sales-tax breaks, parsonage-tax exemptions, or side businesses such as child care or coffee shops in churches that should be taxable, but thanks to the absence of oversight (churches are assumed to never lie) are sometimes folded into the church books and hidden. How much is all that? We don't know because the government says we don't *need* to know. Cragun states these subsidies (that's what they are) need to go: "As the perceived 'benefit' to society of religions becomes increasingly irrelevant as more and more Americans cease to utilize their 'services' by disaffiliating, it will also be increasingly unfair for a large percentage of nonreligious Americans (almost 40 percent in some states) to subsidize the recreational activities of others. These subsidies should be phased out."[13]

Again, the only reason churches and other religious organizations get this perk is because they are religious. This is entrenched religious favoritism by our government.

What if the government treated every nonprofit organization equally, regardless of whether it preached about a god? What if the Mormon and Catholic Churches were actually required to declare their income and expenses just like every other 501(c)(3)? What if the government provided oversight of religious nonprofits (arguably one of the most corrupt industries on the planet) to the same degree it oversees nonreligious nonprofits? What if religious nonprofits had to disclose to their parishioners and the country at large just how much they are spending on helping people, *just like everyone else*?

We'd have a very different country. Churches that wanted to do good things would do them, file their forms, help people, and reap the tax benefits, just like all the other nonprofits. Churches that didn't want to obey the equally applied nonprofit rules would become for-profit churches, with full ability to pay stockholders, hide money, and, yes, preach politics from the pulpit (I don't like that last part, but it would be fair). Just like everyone else.

This is how it should be, and this is why American Atheists is suing the IRS. That "if religious/then benefits" statement *is religious discrimination incarnate*. It has no basis in secular law and promotes religion in America. We demand its removal, and if that means churches have to make a choice whether to be nonprofit or for profit (like every other company in America), then so be it. It's not our problem and it's not our government's problem that churches will have to adapt to equality.

The churches will complain. They will call it an "attack" because every attempt to equalize is seen as an attack by those losing special rights. They are blinded by their own privilege. But once everyone sees the inherent inequality of assuming all religious activity is by default a "social service," while nonreligious organizations enjoy no such assumption, they will be forced to admit taxing churches equally and with the same oversight as other nonprofits is fair (and compliant with the "do unto others as you would have done unto you" mantra).

We have to realize those who complain the most probably have the most to lose *because* they are benefiting from a flawed system. I am reminded of a 2012 radio debate I had on the subject with a pastor of a Nashville megachurch, which had both a coffee shop and a gymnasium inside its building. The IRS had told the church they had to file tax returns on the side businesses, but the church replied that the side businesses were "integral" to church business and contested the ruling.[14] During the dispute, the side businesses remained closed, indicating (1) they were *not* in fact "integral" to the church and (2) the church was concerned about disclosing any earnings to the US government, so much so that it would rather close the "integral" businesses than disclose the numbers. Smells like someone hiding something, doesn't it?

By far the most telling moment of that interview occurred when I spoke about oversight, and the pastor, who had apparently lied to the IRS about the importance of his coffee shop and gym to the functioning of his church, actually proposed that churches should self-police!

Interestingly, Conservatives are prone to respond to demands for fair taxation with an odd and counterintuitive "But without the church tax exemptions, churches would go out of business! Taxing churches is therefore an assault on religion!" This counterintuitive response makes more sense when you think about how the politicians are in the pockets of the preachers. This is akin to saying the government is in the business of supporting religion via a recurring bailout, as it's taking extra taxes from the citizenry to indirectly fund the churches through tax exemptions they do not otherwise deserve.

The government has bailed out scores of corporations. ProPublica has a "Bailout Tracker" because it and many other people (mostly Conservatives) oppose bailouts from the government. They believe in the free-market system—capitalism—and therefore businesses that fail should be *allowed* to fail.

Yet when it comes to the continuing bailout of the religious system, we as a nation turn a blind eye. We somehow feel it's a bad thing to let sick churches fail, and that it's the government's job to keep them in business. Even those who oppose the most defensible corporate bailouts support the government's funding of religion in this manner and accuse us of attacking churches when all we seek is fair taxation. They are wrong.

Churches that cannot support themselves should fail, and it's not our problem. It's certainly not the government's job to keep churches open and pastors paid. The government's current system is clearly illegal and un-American, and we, as taxpayers, deserve the right not to support the dying religion industry by force of taxation. In this very real way, the government has been keeping religion alive long after it should have withered and died.

According to ProPublica, the US government bailout for Morgan Stanley was $10 billion. Again, according to Ryan Cragun, religion gets bailed out (via tax exemptions) to the tune of $71 billion per year on property taxes alone. So we, the people of America, bail out the religion industry to the tune of *seven times the US government bailout of Morgan Stanley, every year,* on property taxes alone. Yet nobody (except us) complains, and the politicians do nothing.

The counterintuitive Conservatives are only partially right—taxing the churches fairly will result in the closure of some churches—but *only* the ones that refuse to actually perform nonprofit services will be affected. Any church, even the poorest of the poor churches, could perform a community service, declare its income, and stay open as a nonprofit, if it wanted to. The only churches that would close as a result of fair taxation are the ones that refuse to provide *real* community service ("outreach," which many churches call "community service," is not real community service, but rather marketing) and to disclose their funds like everyone else, yet cannot support itself with non-tax-deductible donations. I have no problem with that.

We must admit that religion is a corrupt, or *at least* corruption-friendly, industry that requires at *minimum* the same basic oversight as everyone else, and we must be willing to say it loudly. That religion is given such a widespread bye on laws, oversight, and accountability damages every citizen in tangible ways, and it's the biggest problem we face in our fight for equality, as well as the most cherished possession of the corrupt preacher.

We as taxpayers have been making the choice to sit silent while our government and our wallets have been bled dry by religion, with some pastors flying in private jets and some priests living in stately tax-free mansions.[15] According to *Business Insider,* the Vatican is the third-largest landowner in the world,[16] and all the Catholic churches, schools, and most of its other holdings pay no property taxes at all. Again, because God.

And what does that even mean, really? Since all religion is individual, and the gods to which people pray are actually invented by the individual believers themselves, "God wants" actually just means "I want" and "God believes" just means "I believe." It's a great Nuremberg-style of defense ("I don't want to break the law, but my god wants me to." "I'm not a bigot, my god is.") that allows religious people to separate self-interest from their demands/opinions, riding religious privilege to benefit their personal goals.

Remember: "God wants this" = "I want this." So when we are talking about religious exemptions, we are talking about exemptions from laws *only* because some people *want* to be exempted, and are using their god to legitimize and elevate their wants and desires above civil law. This is why the RFRA and laws like it are so dangerous—they allow people to break laws if they say they *think* their god (which *always agrees with them*) wants them to.

I say we've had enough, and we need to make a change.

There is no reason for religion to appear anywhere in the legal code, except to protect free exercise (which does *not* mean freedom to break the law or to gain special privileges from the government or to infringe on other people's free exercise). To include any exception or special right for religion elevates it without need or warrant. To say religion gets special treatment of any kind promotes religion, usually at the expense of other religions or the atheists, and that's not what government is all about (indeed, it is the exact *opposite* of what our government is all about). Any place the law provides an exception for a religion is illegal, prejudicial, and un-American and harms the population by creating huge opportunities for rampant corruption, and it must be recognized as such.

While I'm talking about privilege, I need to mention the confidentiality of confessionals, aka priest-penitent privilege.

An *accessory* to a crime is defined as "one who, without being present at the commission of an offense, becomes guilty of such offense, not as a chief actor, but as a participant, as by command, advice, instigation, *or concealment; either before or after the fact* or commission"[17] (emphasis mine).

Concealment after the fact. If I know you committed a crime and I stay silent, I'm an accessory to that crime, which makes me guilty of a punishable offense, and the accessory is generally punished with the same severity as the person who committed the crime.[18]

This is a good law. After all, if I know you molested a child and I stay silent, I leave you on the street to molest more children.

The bad part of this law is that, once again, the law is not handled evenly, as every priest in the country who hears confession is protected from this crime. All across the country, crimes are being reported to priests, who are bound by canon law not to reveal the secrets heard during confession. But Vatican canon law is not American civil law. You'd think the civil law would be paramount, but, no, we in America have religious exemptions from our accessory law. According to Andrew Chow at FindLaw.com, "Statements made to a minister, priest, rabbi, or other religious leader are generally considered privileged or confidential communications. State laws generally exempt a pastor from having to testify in court, or to law-enforcement, about what was discussed in a church confession."[19]

Priest-penitent privilege, as it is called even though it refers to any confessions made in confidence to any clergy, began in 1813 with a case called *People v. Phillips*. The court stated in its opinion, "It is essential to the free exercise of a religion, that its ordinances should be administered. . . . The sinner will not confess, nor will the priest receive his confession, if the veil of secrecy is removed."[20] Essentially, the court found that the free exercise of religion outweighed the secular need to require preachers to testify. We've been building on this flawed concept for over two hundred years.

Today, priest-penitent privilege is regulated on a state and federal level. While most states laws have exceptions that mandate preachers report child abuse learned in confession,[21] our legal research has not yielded a *single case* where any preacher has revealed the contents of a confession, even to save the life of a child,[22] and we've found no exemptions in any state for murder, rape, or terrorism. In addition, the federal Rule of Evidence 501 recognizes "Communications to a Clergyman" as a privilege in federal cases.[23]

There is no way to tell how many criminals are walking the streets today because priests stay silent, and there is no way for us to know how many more crimes have been committed because these known (to priests) repeat criminals are protected by exemptions that shouldn't exist. There is no way to know how many of our nation's children have been hurt because of this truly asinine legal policy.

The accessory law has some secular exemptions, the most obvious of which is for psychotherapists. In many cases, they are exempt from accessory laws for reasonable, secular reasons, but these exemptions end where someone else's life is in danger. As described by Nolo.com:

> *Most states have an exception to the psychotherapist-patient privilege for dangerous patients, often referred to as the* Tarasoff *duty.* (Tarasoff v. Regents of Univ. of Cal., *17 Cal.3d 425 [1976].*) *Depending on the jurisdiction, the exception either allows or requires therapists to report statements by patients that indicate dangerousness. In California, for example, therapists must disclose statements when:*
> - *the patient presents a risk of serious harm to others, and*
> - *disclosure is necessary to prevent that harm.*
>
> *The therapist's required course of action depends on the circumstances, and can involve notifying the potential victim, the police, or both.* (United States v. Chase, *340 F.3d 978 [9th Cir. 2003].*) *For instance, if a patient tells her psychiatrist that she plans on shooting her ex-boyfriend, the psychiatrist may have to notify the police and warn the former beau.*[24]

Psychotherapists are required by law to put their confidentiality with their patients aside in the case of imminent danger to someone else. That's good and reasonable because it places the needs of the many innocent people over the need of the one (patient/criminal).

Another well-known confidentiality privilege is that of attorneys and their clients. One might think that anything one says to a lawyer is confidential, but again, this is not true according to Nolo.com:

The confidentiality of attorney-client communications usually does not extend to statements pertaining to future frauds or crimes. The government can compel a defense lawyer to testify to a client's statement about a future crime. In emergency or life-threatening situations, a lawyer might have to reveal such a statement to the police even before a crime is committed.[25]

So we have a law that protects confidentiality, with some reasonable exceptions to that law so as *not* to place anyone in imminent danger. All exemptions from accessory laws end when a person seems about to commit a crime against someone, in which case people are expected to do the right thing and turn in the person.

Unless we're talking about religion. If the accessory is a priest, there are *virtually no limits to the exemptions*. Priests can choose not to turn in any criminal and get away with it, even when the criminal commits crime after heinous crime, over and over. The reason? Canon law prohibits disclosure. That's all. Whatever you did, your secret is safe with the Catholic Church, and you are absolved of your sin. You're going to heaven. You're welcome—here's the collection plate.

Wait. Did I just imply the Catholic Church is resisting turning in criminals because criminals have money and they make huge donations to the Church in exchange for absolution? Yup, and we let it happen, to our own detriment.

Cathy Caridi, JCL (licentiate in canon law and founder of Canon-LawMadeEasy.com), writes about this on Catholic Exchange and explains how a priest turning in even the worst of the criminals would be "impossible":

Canon 983.1 tells us right up front that the sacramental seal is inviolable, and thus it is absolutely wrong for a confessor in any way to betray the penitent, for any reason whatsoever, whether by word or in any other fashion.

If, for example, a person confesses that he is the serial killer who is being sought by the authorities, and the priest recognizes his identity, he cannot contact the police and reveal it. This is true even if the person indicates that he intends to commit another crime.[26] *[emphasis mine].*

We are not talking about psychotherapists or lawyers, where confidentiality might have a secular purpose. We are talking about churches saying nothing about dangerous criminals as a matter of *tradition*, affecting the safety of every person in the country.

That's US law subverted by religious law to the direct and dangerous detriment of every citizen in the country. We the citizens put up with it because of tradition, and if we challenge it, we're being "hostile" to the Catholic Church. They do wrong, and if we complain, we're the bad guys.

I hope you can see the parallel between this law and the IRS law I mentioned earlier:

- They both provide extra perks to religion and only religion.
- They both harm the citizens at large, either financially via higher taxes or by increasing the likelihood of violent crime.
- They both put religion on a pedestal over secular law.
- Most people think tax *exemption* laws are the same for secular and religious 501(c)(3) organizations, but they are not the same, and religious organizations get substantial advantages over their secular counterparts, to the financial detriment of the citizenry, for no reason other than tradition. Similarly, most people think *confidentiality* laws are the same for secular and religious institutions, but they are not the same, and religion gets substantial privilege, even to the detriment of the citizenry, for no reason other than tradition.

Every priest who hears confession is, by definition, an accessory to every crime he hears about and does not report to the authorities.

If canon law requires a priest to remain silent about what he hears in confession, canon law is immoral—"My god wants me to break the law" is not a legal defense, or at least it shouldn't be.

Here's an example. A new case making major news is that of a priest in Baton Rouge who would rather go to jail than testify about child abuse, *even though the penitent waives confidentiality.* This case involves "a girl who was 14 in 2008, who said she told her parish priest—Father Bayhi, pastor of St. John the Baptist Parish in Zachary—in the confessional that she was abused by a now-dead lay member of the parish."[27] But even though the penitent wants what she said to be revealed, the Catholic Church is calling it an attack on their freedom—*their freedom*—to have to obey the same laws as everyone else!

This is an important example because the state supreme court has determined "that the privilege of confidentiality can only be claimed 'on behalf of the person' (penitent). Since the female minor had waived her privilege, Fr. Bayhi could not claim confidentiality to protect himself from testifying."[28] The court's statement, while heading in the right (ethical) direction, underscores that if the penitent does *not* waive confidentiality, the priest is within his rights to keep silent.

The Baton Rouge Diocese complains in its response: "A foundational doctrine of the Roman Catholic Church for thousands of years mandates that the seal of confession is absolute and inviolable. Pursuant to his oath to the church, a priest is compelled never to break that seal. If necessary, the priest would have to suffer a finding of contempt in a civil court and suffer imprisonment rather than violate his sacred duty and violate the seal of confession and his duty to the penitent." The statement notes, "For a civil court to inquire as to whether or not a factual situation establishes the sacrament of confession is a clear and unfettered violation of the Establishment Clause of the Constitution of the United States."[29]

So their defense is "we've done it this way for a long time," followed by an obviously disingenuous "even inquiring about whether this is valid is against the law." No, it does not break the law for us to consider legislation that usurps religious tradition in favor of the safety of children, and of course they know that. Unfortunately, even after all the pedophilia scandals in the Church, they still have not learned to put people first—they still seek to hide criminals. If a civil law has a purpose, that purpose is not negated because of Vatican tradition and thousand-year-old oaths.

Caridi opines:

If, however, our laws were to change dramatically and our priests were legally obliged to report the confessions of penitents who had admitted committing certain crimes, it is impossible to imagine that the Vatican would permit them to do this. The principle of the sacramental seal is . . . so strong and so absolute that it is, unfortunately, easy to imagine a priest being obliged to violate the laws of his local jurisdiction rather than betray the trust of someone who had confessed his sins to him.[30]

How this change would affect the Vatican should not be anyone's concern, especially when the safety of our citizenry is involved, but I speculate that the Vatican would respond the same way it has always responded when justice is forced on it—it would evolve to meet the situation. The Vatican would find a way to justify a change (either by revelation or reinterpretation), and—*poof*—they can change their practices and stop helping criminals. The Church becomes more moral and helps put bad people in jail instead of telling them God forgives them and setting them free on the population to do it again. Of course, we can't look at the Vatican's past performance with regard to the safety of the population and expect them to just do the right thing (writing that gave me a chuckle), so we need to change the laws to make it happen.

Current federal law (the previously mentioned RFRA) requires the government to show "compelling interest" before restricting free exercise of religion. *People v. Phillips* asserted that the free exercise of religion outweighed America's need for preachers to divulge what they hear in the confessional. But, especially when we are talking about penitents who repeatedly engage in murder, rape, terrorism, pedophilia, or other heinous crimes, I assert that we as American citizens have a compelling interest in mandating reporting (with actual penalties for noncompliance) for these crimes that supersedes preachers' freedom to exercise confidentiality. Indeed, if the immediate safety of others, including children, doesn't constitute a compelling interest on behalf of the state, it's hard to imagine what would.

Removing religious exemptions to accessory laws, *at least* to the same degree as lawyers and psychotherapists, is good for everyone except the criminals, and that it is against religious tradition or canon law does not negate this truth—or this need. The safety of the many, the few, or the one outweighs all the combined ego and tradition of the Vatican.

While American Atheists works the issue, we as a movement need to let our politicians know that this real problem affects all of us and benefits the very, very few. We need to make this an issue, for our own sake.

In summary, it's time to treat religions fairly. It's time we tax them fairly, treat their employees fairly, and hold them fairly accountable for all their actions. It's time we hold politicians responsible for defending religious discrimination in our nation's laws. It's time we demand extreme religious equality.

Obey the law, even if you think your god says you don't have to.

Simple stuff.

The 9/11 "Miracle Cross" Case

On September 11, 2001, religious terrorists murdered almost three thousand Americans in the name of their god. They were not selective in their murders—they killed everyone equally, regardless of religion or lack thereof.

The Twin Towers were made of crossbeams, and thousands of those beams survived the carnage. One Christian worker selected one of these crossbeams and attached religious symbolism to it, imbuing holiness to the wreckage. He supposed this specific crossbeam was not scrap metal like all the others, but was rather a sign from heaven that "God had not abandoned us."[31]

My original thoughts on this still stand: "The World Trade Center Cross has become a Christian icon. It has been blessed by so-called holy men and presented as a reminder that God, who couldn't be bothered to stop the terrorists or prevent three thousand people from being killed in his name, cared only enough to bestow upon us some rubble that resembles a cross."

My quote for our press release angered Sarah Palin, who quoted me in her vacuous book *Good Tidings and Great Joy* and responded with a stereotypical deflecting comment, "So much for not wanting anyone to be offended," before she tried to make it about atheists persecuting Christians by demanding equality.[32] Yes, that was her response to my assertion that God, who knew 9/11 was going to happen and did nothing to stop it, told us he hadn't abandoned us (after he abandoned us) by giving us a piece of metal that looks like a cross. The statement is true if God is real, but her only response was to say it was offensive and evade my point. This evasiveness only hints at how far the religious will go to defend their god's uselessness.

Anyway, NYC priest Father Brian Jordan seized the opportunity, and a "holy relic" was invented. According to reporter Becky Garrison, "hardly any" first responders and a "few other" volunteers and workers began holding weekly services with Father Jordan at the cross, but the money and publicity machine around the cross had begun. The cross was moved, repaired, mounted, and exploited.

Lies about the Miracle Cross began to surface. Suddenly, the services at the cross supposedly drew hundreds of people, not just a few. Suddenly, the cross was unique, not one of thousands. Suddenly, the cross was formed miraculously by God, not a human in the Towers' construction crew. And suddenly the Miracle Cross was for sale— in the form of trinkets purchasable through church gift shops and Web sites.

Hallelujah!

For years, the cross sat in front of St. Peter's Church, earning money through both purchases and donations. There the worshippers further modified it, carving JESUS on the top, etching prayers on the side, and removing, adapting, and replacing the "shroud" (the metal that covers a piece of the cross) to make it look even more overtly Christian.

Then, with little notice, the cross was installed in the World Trade Center (WTC) museum in a religious ceremony led by (who else) Father Jordan, who pronounced the cross representative of *all people of faith*. He then *consecrated the public land* on which the museum is built and the cross was lowered in.[33,34]

Then, to justify the inclusion, the WTC Memorial Foundation Board declared the cross "secular."

The museum holds artifacts and photos from before, during, and after 9/11, including a fire truck that was damaged in the rescue effort. Was the fire truck installed by a priest in a religious ceremony? On consecrated land? No. Why? Because *this* is a secular item. Only religious items would be installed in religious ceremonies.

The Miracle Cross is Christian and Christian only. It does not represent all faiths, but rather one specific faith, and we all know it. Subtract the Christianity from the cross, and you've got scrap metal, like all the other crossbeams that survived the event.

Furthermore, it must be made clear that the cross is not neutral to non-Christians—it's a symbol of oppression and intolerance to adherents of many other religions and atheists, and this is a good example of why. To place the seventeen-foot-tall cross in the WTC museum is simply using the fact the towers were made out of crossbeams to justify installing a huge and unambiguously Christian salute to greet all visitors. The cross's inclusion is an attempt to Christianize 9/11, implying Christians were the main victims and pushing the rest of us off to the side.

The WTC board contends this cross is a "secular artifact," but its actions concede the point that it is not. In July of 2011, the 9/11 Memorial Foundation confirmed that a small Star of David and a Jewish prayer shawl had also been included.[35] These are not artifacts by any definition but were added for inclusiveness—Jews apparently didn't like being represented by a Christian symbol.[36] Hindu holy water was also included—a comparatively tiny religious icon—to represent the Hindu people who were also, apparently, not happy being represented by the Miracle Cross.[37] Even when combined, these religious symbols are dwarfed by the seventeen-foot-tall cross.

If the WTC board is going to install a Christian memorial, they should not lie and say it's not Christian. Rather, they should admit it is religious, just as the Star of David and the Hindu holy water are, and in compliance with federal law they should include equal representation for the estimated five hundred atheists (far more than the number of Jews and Hindus lost) who died in these religiously motivated attacks.

We demanded from the board what we could legally demand—equality. The way it was accomplished (by removing the cross or acknowledging the atheists) would be up to them. American Atheists even offered to pay for an atheist memorial at the site and to allow the WTC board to approve a design, or even to dedicate an existing exhibit to the nonreligious victims. This would have meant nothing more than putting a sign next to an existing exhibit—an easy enough solution. But they turned us down, and we were called un-American, unpatriotic, and insensitive for making the request. They were not serious about seeking inclusion and diversity. Once again, we were bad for demanding equal treatment.

Why won't they honor our just and legal request? Because it would further dilute the Christian monopoly to have other religious demographics represented. Fairness would equalize what they most obviously want to be unequal.

Equality is an all-or-nothing concept. Public officials (or those who manage public property or use public funds) do not get to say some religious positions are okay and others are not. We *all* have equal rights, and America's atheists are not being treated equally at the WTC. If the WTC board insists on bringing in religious symbols, it needs to include everyone who wishes to be included. It can keep the Miracle Cross, the Star of David, and the Hindu holy water, but then we must *all* be represented. Equality from the government is fair, legal, and the American Way.

It is not important that people on the WTC board don't like atheists, we are equal anyway. It doesn't matter that the cross is one of thousands of wrecked crossbeams—it's still unmistakably Christian. It doesn't matter if it is inconvenient for the WTC board to include multiple religious icons—if they include one, they have to include everyone. That's the law they've broken in an attempt to Christianize the events of September 11, and that's why American Atheists filed this case.

An Unfortunate Addendum

The Second Circuit Court upheld the dismissal of our case by the lower court, and this, unfortunately, is going to kill the case for now.

In effect, the higher court, while affirming our standing, stated this is not a First Amendment issue because museums can have religious art, so this museum can have the cross. It doesn't matter that *this is not art*—it's rubbish that looks like a cross because it was built that way—but the court seems to think that it's better for the WTC to include a religious icon by pretending it's "art" rather than account for everyone equally in a place that only exists because of religious intolerance. It also came out in statements before the court that the other religious icons had not been installed after all (at least not yet).[38] In accordance with our legal philosophy, I've observed that the current makeup of the Supreme Court is simply not conducive to reversing cases like ours, and I do not want secular "art" crosses to be the law of the land, so the case will die here, unless something happens to improve our chances of winning.

Of course, the issue is not dead. We will see this issue again. I predict the next step will be replicas of the 9/11 cross, or paintings of it, or carvings, on public land and other future memorials. These in turn will be used as a justification for more "secular" crosses, including inside courtrooms. Baby steps.

And we will be there.

Benches and Other Atheist Monuments

Another place we see this intrusion of religion into the public sphere is in the blatantly unconstitutional act of placing the Decalogue (aka the Ten Commandments) on public land, alone, regardless that most of these commandments are contradictory to American civil law. Indeed, seven of the Ten Commandments (eight if you're Catholic) are not laws, and some directly contradict the American Way.

Read and consider them for yourself:

1. Thou shalt have no other gods before me (exact opposite of freedom of religion).
2. No graven images (unless you're Catholic, and also exact opposite of freedom of religion).
3. Remember the Sabbath and keep it holy (exact opposite of freedom of religion).
4. Don't take God's name in vain (exact opposite of freedom of religion and speech).
5. Honor thy mother and father (not law).
6. Don't kill (hey, this one doesn't contradict American law! It's a shame it predates the Old Testament by hundreds of years).[39]
7. Don't steal (that's two! But also not original to the Old Testament).[40]
8. Don't lie (not a law).
9. Don't covet thy neighbor's stuff (coveting is the fuel of capitalism. Of course you covet your neighbor's Mercedes, otherwise there is no incentive to work hard and buy your own).
10. Don't covet thy neighbor's wife (not law).

My point is to show you how far apart biblical laws are from American law, and how we must all be cognizant of the implications of religious declarations of stronger linkage.

In 2013, American Atheists negotiated with Starke, Florida, to allow us to achieve yet another first for atheists—a permanent monument representing the atheist perspective on public land. Once again, this was a defensive move, as a huge Ten Commandments display had been placed on public land in the center quad of the town's municipal building. This was clearly illegal, despite what certain Christian apologists would have you believe, and the city had no choice but to allow us equal time and equal prominence if it wanted to keep the Decalogue.

To be clear, this is *not* what we wanted. We wanted the Ten Commandments removed and the town square clean and green, but we don't get to make that decision. As in the World Trade Center memorial case, we have the right to demand equality, not the right to choose the method by which that equality is granted. There was inequality in that the one monument clearly endorsed one religion, and the city had to fix it. However, the option of giving us the monument versus taking down the Ten Commandments was up to them. The city chose the former, and had we decided not to take them up on the offer, the Ten Commandments could have stayed there permanently and without opposition.

We designed the bench (see Fig. 15) as a team, led mainly by Ken Loukinen (American Atheists director of regional operations). It includes quotes from America's founding fathers, Madalyn Murray O'Hair, and the Treaty of Tripoli. We further included the punishments in the Bible for breaking the Ten Commandments (most of which are death).

Figure 15
Atheist Bench

We included the punishments to drive home an important point— the Ten Commandments are not some benign laws on which all good people can agree. It's not enough to combat the lie (previously addressed) that they are the basis of law in this country. We must take the next step, read the commandments in context, and see them for what they are—hate speech. And, no, I'm not being hyperbolic.

According to USLegal.com, hate speech is "the expression of hatred for some group, especially in circumstances in which the communication is likely to provoke violence. It is an incitement to hatred primarily against a group of persons defined in terms of race, ethnicity, national origin, gender, religion, sexual orientation, and the like."[41]

The First Commandment reads, "I am the Lord thy God, thou shalt have no other gods before me," which, according to TheologyNetwork.org, Martin Luther interpreted as "Thou shalt have [and worship] Me alone as thy God." Luther went on to say, "Therefore it is the intent of this commandment to *require* true faith and trust of the heart which settles upon the only true God and clings to Him alone."[42]

The parody (but delightfully accurate) site LandoverBaptist.org describes the penalties for breaking this commandment: "Genocide. Entire cities with men, women, children and animals must be killed. (Deuteronomy 2:33–34, Numbers 21:34–35, 1 Samuel 15:2–3, Joshua 6:21. Joshua 10:40). In some cases you can keep the girls alive for raping. (Numbers 31:15–18)."[43] This surely qualifies as inciting violence, yet it sits on our government property.

So what is placed on the public lawn is a statement that, read in context, requires atheists, polytheists, and believers in gods other than the one cited in the Ten Commandments to be killed by order of God solely for their religious beliefs (or absence thereof). Yes, the other commandments have different punishments, including the one Catholics decided to omit (Catholics skip over the "No graven images of anything that is in Heaven" commandment because it was apparently inconvenient to obey it).[44] But my point here is that the posting of the Ten Commandments on public property is not something atheists should ignore—it's hateful, it has inspired and still recommends *murder of us and a whole lot of other people,* and it should not be tolerated as something that should ever be promoted by the government.

We placed those punishments on the monument to highlight the barbarism of the Old Testament, and the rules contained therein. I've said it before and will continue to repeat, *in America, atheism's greatest problem is that Christians don't read their Bibles.* We hope that by placing the punishments on the monument, people will see just a small piece of the Bible for the horrid immorality it represents and will be motivated to read the rest.

This is not new information. The Christians who run the organizations trying to place the Decalogue on public land know it's horrible in statement and implication and defend it with statements like "Well, in the New Testament Jesus changes things." Why then are they not placing the words of Jesus on public grounds? Why are we talking about commandments that promote intolerance, and not a plaque of the Sermon on the Mount, for instance, which is much nicer and more representative of what many of today's Christians represent? Why aren't Christian organizations championing the placement of the Golden Rule?

Simple—the Christian organizations want and need to include the Jews. They don't want to fight the Jewish organizations, who would probably, *selfishly,* want to put up their own monument if the Christian monument didn't include them (like when they demand a menorah be placed next to a manger scene). They want the Jewish people on their side, not on ours, so they place something that, at least on the surface, includes them, even if the message is antiquated even by "modern" Christian standards, because they know that when most people see the Ten Commandments, they think about Christianity, not Judaism.

This issue is about perceived endorsement. Once again, religion is weak and cannot thrive without the government pushing it. Christian organizations place these monuments not so anyone will read or think about them—indeed, they are counting on the opposite. They want people to walk by, see the Ten Commandments, associate that with Christianity (sorry, Jews, but this isn't about you after all), and walk away with a clear perception that the government is endorsing the Christian religion. Once again, this is all about Christian privilege.

Before the atheist monument went up in Starke, the Men's Christian Fellowship (the group that originally sponsored the Ten Commandments monument), had exactly what it wanted. In no way could someone walk into the main courtyard, see the huge Decalogue, and not perceive it as an endorsement of Christianity. Then, with one monument, we changed that around completely. Now, with both monuments in view, the unmistakable perception is that the city of Starke does *not* endorse any one religion. With the bench, the statement went from *definitely endorses Christianity only* to *definitely does not endorse Christianity only, and by the way, atheists are equal,* thereby completely negating the unstated intent of the Decalogue's sponsors while normalizing atheism.

The good news is that the law is on our side. *McCreary County v. ACLU, Van Orden v. Perry,* and the Supreme Court made clear distinctions as to when religious displays are allowed on public land. Simply put, if they are a part of a larger display, it's okay to include a Decalogue as a part of a free speech zone. If, however, a Decalogue sits alone, it's illegal.[45,46] These cases gave us clear guidance on where we as atheists are entitled to equal representation in the public square.

This is why there will be more monuments—because to the Christians pushing these monuments it's not about speech or expression, but rather favoritism and legitimization. We can and will use the same strategy—using "free speech zones" according to *Mc-Creary* to promote an atheistic perspective wherever Christians try to use them to gain preferential treatment. In doing so, we will use the law to negate and indeed deter further placements. When a Christian group wants to stick a monument on public land, they need to know we are waiting to do the same. When a municipality considers free speech zones, they will remember we have free speech too, and placing a Christian monument means they'll soon be placing an atheist monument. We hope they will choose to keep their quads green, instead.

One final note: When I say I want a green quad. I mean it. We don't want *any* monuments up at all, including ours. We only put up ours as a defensive move when a religious display is already installed (or planned). Therefore, when the city of Starke (or any future municipality) decides that it wants all monuments removed, American Atheists will gladly pick up the tab to remove our monument *after* the Ten Commandments are removed. Starke's quad can be monument-free again, anytime the city wishes.

In the meantime, please visit Starke, Florida, where Roadside-America.com now lists our monument as a "tourist attraction."

Utah Highway Patrol Association Cross Case

I often say we are the good guys who get treated like we are the bad guys. Nowhere is this better illustrated than in Utah, where American Atheists (before the WTC memorial case) fought successfully to have roadside crosses removed.

Utah had a law that disallowed roadside memorials, which was later modified to allow memorials for fallen state troopers. However, the only monument *design* allowed for a trooper was a twelve-foot-tall cross. The Utah Highway Patrol Association (UHPA) would not allow a deviation from that design even if the dead trooper had not been Christian.

But that's *not* what they said, and that's *not* how they argued. In an August 19, 2010, debate against me on *Fox News Live,* the Utah attorney general, Mark Shurtleff, asserted, "We've offered. . . . If a Jew dies and they want to put up a Star of David, that's fine."[47] However, in the Tenth Circuit Court of Appeals decision on December 20 of that year, the judges noted, "Notwithstanding the UHPA's position, the State Defendants, in oral argument before the district court and in their briefs and argument before us, asserted that they would not allow any change in the memorial, whether to accommodate other faiths or otherwise."[48]

Did the attorney general go on TV and get the main point of our contention wrong, or did he attempt to cover up the truth? If he got it wrong, he was incompetent, which is difficult to accept from a person in that position. If he was covering, why?

Perhaps he was hiding the true intent of the monuments in the first place. They could have memorialized the troopers with obelisks like the Washington Monument (Shurtleff asserted, "Nobody would know what that means"), flags, or statues. Instead they chose the cross and *disallowed* other monuments. Had they chosen the cross and *allowed* other monuments, there would have been much less room for a legal challenge (but that would be an admission the cross is Christian). If they had used a nonreligious symbol, there would have been no challenge at all. If the crosses were on private land, there would have been no challenge at all.

Why then would they choose to place religious symbols on public land to memorialize the troopers *and* not allow for deviation in the case of religious difference *and* claim on TV they would allow for such deviation, which stifled opposing arguments? All questions lead to one answer—they wanted to set a precedent that crosses are secular. The Utah Highway Patrol Association asserted that the *cross is a secular representation and not religious,*[49] and therefore mounting giant crosses up and down the highways of Utah was not a violation of the separation of religion and government.

Much like the argument in the World Trade Center cross case, Christians used dead people to shield their attempt to *cloak* the cross in false secularism. If the cross is declared a secular object, then anyone can place "secular crosses" in any public school, courtroom, or anywhere, without worrying about equal representation. You can imagine a school shooting, followed by grieving parents being manipulated by the local church to place a "secular cross" on school property, using the UHPA crosses as a valid precedent (remember: baby steps). Besides, who would fight against the bereaved parents of a dead child who want to put a cross on public grounds?

We would.

When we fought against the lie in Utah that the cross is not Christian, we were accused of "fighting against the grieving families of dead troopers"! How *horrible* we atheists must be! In reality we were fighting against people apparently *using dead troopers to push a dishonest agenda* of creating precedent for the "secularizing" of the cross, for the sole purpose of getting it on public land, once again for the actual purpose of securing Christian privilege.

Now that's a horrible thought, but if you were really trying to memorialize the troopers, and all you had to do was have a secular symbol *or* allow multiple religious symbols *or* place them on private land, why would you choose to break the law and incite a lawsuit instead? Why would you fight it all the way to the Supreme Court? Why would you (apparently) misrepresent this policy on television (remember—what is represented on TV may sway public opinion, but it is not legally binding)?

The troopers died in service to a Constitution that Shurtleff and the UHPA were apparently trying to circumvent, using the troopers as a shield. Yet American Atheists and I were accused of being the bad guys for trying to stop people from using dead heroes to break the law.

This is what we do, and this is why we do it—popular opinion be damned. In a Rasmussen Reports poll, 72 percent of Americans disagreed with our case,[50] but they were wrong, so we swam upstream *and we won.* Meanwhile, this case cost Utah residents nearly $400,000 in legal bills.[51]

(Credit: Artist J. Andrew World, Right-About-Now.com)

We are going to see this kind of encroachment again, and we will fight it again. The nationwide attempt to create legal precedent for a secular cross is pervasive and wholly dishonest.

Secular crosses are impossible in today's society. It doesn't matter that the symbol itself predates Christianity, any more than the swastika used to be a sign of peace and predates Hitler. Today, the cross is Christian, undeniably so, just as the swastika is unavoidably a Nazi symbol. To say otherwise is pure sophistry.

The argument for "secular" religious symbols is certainly one we expect to see more of, and it isn't unique to the cross.

In July of 2013, headlines were made over objections by the Freedom From Religion Foundation to a proposed Holocaust memorial for the Ohio statehouse lawn funded with public money. The problem? It was adorned with a Jewish star, and *only* a Jewish star, ignoring the 40 percent of the victims of Nazi atrocities who were not Jewish. I opposed this structure because it followed the same logic as the Utah and WTC crosses. Yet again, proponents said the religious symbol (the star) was secular—that it represented the Jewish "people" or Israel, or wasn't solely Jewish.

That's all crap. Just as anyone who drove by a huge steel cross would clearly think *Christian* or drove by a swastika and think *Nazi,* so too would any reasonable person who drove by a Jewish star think *Judaism*—and only Judaism. Predictably, I was called a dick (and worse) by religionists and tabloid atheists as well, but I remain unapologetic. If the star is ultimately allowed to stand, it will surely be used as a precedent for crosses in the near future, with Christian cries of "You let the Jews do it, so if you don't let us do it, you're discriminating." Wait and see.

Assaults on the separation of religion and government will remain a fixture of the American political and cultural landscape for the foreseeable future. American Atheists will continue to follow its legal philosophy in picking its battles.

Just as Bill O'Reilly attempted to reclassify Christianity as a "philosophy" in order to justify government endorsement of religion, so too are other religionists willing to lie about the religious nature of their symbols to get them on public land and preserve the legitimacy and privilege religion desires so badly. It's understandable given the nearly inevitable demise of religious power in America, but it's also dishonest and illegal, and American Atheists will continue to call it out and fight it because in the service of good we're not afraid to risk being called bad guys.

Chapter 9

ON THE REASON RALLY

I distrust those people who know so well what God wants them to do because I notice it always coincides with their own desires.

—SUSAN B. ANTHONY

Power is not only what you have but what the enemy thinks you have.

—SAUL ALINSKY

The first atheist rally on the Mall in Washington was the Godless Americans March on Washington (GAMOW) in 2002, sponsored mainly by American Atheists but also involving the Council for Secular Humanism and a few other organizations. This event boasted twenty-five hundred attendees, which we considered a huge success. A subsequent Atheists in Foxholes March was much less successful (it was held during the week, so few people came and it looked bad following GAMOW).

In 2010, Margaret Downey, my friend and president of the Freethought Society, was pushing the concept of a movement-wide convention. It didn't have much support, but she was absolutely correct on the need for unity to achieve the common goal of advancing secularism and reason in America.

Rather than a convention, I felt we needed a movement-wide *rally* that promoted unity within the movement while also raising public awareness. We needed another GAMOW, only this time with the whole movement involved. At the 2010 HEADS meeting (HEADS was an annual meeting of the leaders of the secular movement) I floated the idea of a movement rally. I was not officially suggesting we create the rally or that I run it. I was just throwing the concept out there, but the idea was immediately supported by movement leaders Roy Speckhardt, Fred Edwords, Bobbie Kirkhart, and soon Richard Dawkins. With that much oomph behind me, I prepared to propose the rally formally at a future meeting.

At a long table in the hotel restaurant where the subsequent HEADS meeting was held, I outlined my idea to the twenty-five to thirty leaders attending from all across the movement. The idea, which I called the 40 Million Reason Rally, garnered more support than I had anticipated. The movement was ready for this, and more important, it seemed ready for me to run it, which I had not expected.

Details began coming together and more organizations came on board—the Brights, the Society for Humanistic Judaism, the Secular Coalition for America, Atheist Alliance. We formed a board and invited the entire HEADS group as a default list for sponsorship. We offered two sponsorship levels: one for the larger groups that could afford to pay more, and one for the smaller groups to ensure they would not be excluded. With six major sponsors, we focused on a single-location, ten-thousand-person event with a budget of $150,000. A shoestring budget for sure, but enough to make something happen.

And then in walked Todd Stiefel.

Todd is a philanthropist with a keen business sense and a clear view of the big picture. He knew the rally was going to be important, and he knew it was going to *need* to be successful. If the rally was a failure, it would not be forgotten like the Atheists in Foxholes event—Fox News would see to that. He knew, as did we all, this needed to succeed for many reasons and on many levels. We needed a band. We also needed a producer (I was insistent on this, as I didn't have any experience and this was no place for beginners). So, Todd called me one day and pledged six figures to the event.

I think it's important to underscore how much this changed things. It not only kept me away from the blatant conflict of interest of raising funds for the multi-organizational event while also being president of American Atheists, but it also highlighted to other donors just how much they could impact the movement. Todd's donation changed everything. All would-be philanthropists need to understand the huge marginal impact their donations can have on this movement versus those movements with far larger budgets.

So the rally began to take on a life of its own. In these early days, the event's personality was in flux. What *kind* of event was it going to be? I remember one evening I told two of my closest friends about this upcoming protest/rally that might happen. They wished me the best of luck, but indicated tactfully that rallies and protests weren't their thing, and they probably wouldn't make it to DC. So I asked, "What if it was a party or a celebration? The largest atheist party ever?" One quickly replied, "Oh, I'd definitely be into that!"

I flashed back to the parties and the pub crawls at conventions I'd attended and realized/remembered that *fun* was the draw, more so than speakers. This was not to be a protest—this was to be a happy event. The *celebration* in the event tagline, "A Celebration of Secular Values," came from this discussion and impacted my attitude throughout the life of the event.

The sponsors were lined up. The band Bad Religion signed. The Reason Rally was on budget. The movement was behind us.

Things were getting busy.

As an aside, I had the pleasure of having dinner in 2011 with Christopher Hitchens at his last public appearance. I'd exchanged e-mails with him several times, but during this convention we had our one and only one-on-one conversation. He knew about the upcoming rally by then, and I invited him to speak. He looked at me with expressive eyes and said, "I'll not likely make it." I told him that I would save a place for him, and that if the day came and he woke up able to come to the rally, he could come down and I would put him onstage, without his even calling first. He smiled, thanked me, and our conversation diverged. He died before the rally, and Seth Andrews put together a great video in tribute.

But how many people would come? Well, we needed famous people, perhaps from outside the movement—and fortunately we were able to get Paul Provenza (a fantastic emcee!), Tim Minchin, Adam Savage, and Eddie Izzard. We had our draw.

But how many people would come?

This question came up more and more frequently, and we still had no idea. We were saying ten thousand, and that seemed right. After all, ten thousand is a *lot* of people, it's what we originally proposed, and still far more than attended GAMOW, so ten thousand is what we started telling everyone was our goal. The truth was we had no idea.

I knew if we were going to get even that many we needed more buzz, and that meant we needed news. The problem was the Reason Rally Coalition (even though I was president) was not going to place billboards that would get any real press because so many of the participants were not firebrand organizations and would oppose ads with edge. This is when I pulled out an idea I'd had a while back— billboards targeting Islam and Judaism.

The concept was simple. We needed to challenge Islam on its own turf and dispel any idea that it had some kind of post-9/11 protection from all criticism.

I realized that if we posted the same message to Muslims and Jews at the same time, we would get each community watching the other. I figured the Islamists wouldn't freak out if we were saying the exact same thing to the Jews and the Jews weren't freaking out. I felt quite strongly that if we didn't do something to confront the veils against criticism for both these religions, they would just get more difficult to pierce.

It worked. We put up two billboards (see Fig. 17) and issued a statement that read, "The purpose of these boards is to raise the awareness of the Reason Rally to the atheists in those communities." The press went crazy, as we knew it would. It was a great story with a great message, and every report carried a mention of the Reason Rally.

Figure 17
Arabic and Hebrew Billboards

And nobody rioted or even protested, except the Jewish landowner who refused to allow our billboard on his property and made us move down the street. The rally was advertised over the national news networks, the buzz around the rally became a roar, and the veil against criticizing Islam and Judaism was pierced.

Time grew short. With two weeks to go, the long-range weather forecast was for a bright, sunny day (curse you, long-range weather people!).

Day by day the forecast got worse. Occasional showers became occasional thunderstorms. Then just thunderstorms. So going into the event, it was going to be expensive, sparsely attended, and fucking rainy.

Will there be a rain date? people posted on our Facebook page, asking about alternate venues and dates. *Nope—rain or shine. Bring ponchos. It rained on Woodstock too.* I knew it was a lame response, but that's where we were. A rally in the rain. Hopefully, some people would still come.

The Wednesday before, all was well and set at American Atheists HQ. The skeletal staff of two had shipped everything, both for the Reason Rally and the American Atheists National Convention, which would follow on its heels. My car was packed, and I left for DC. Clouds were on the horizon, the forecast sucked, and all I was hoping for was that the few people who would show would actually have fun. After all, the lineup was great, so how bad could it be?

I walked into the hotel where the convention was being held and immediately spotted some familiar faces. It was nice to see smiles. Oh, and they showed me their umbrellas to underscore their dedication to coming and staying, no matter what the weather. That was great the first time.

And the second.

And then the third.

From there it grew. Strangers and members showed up wearing ponchos. Posts on the Facebook wall and my Twitter: *Buy lots of ponchos and give them away!* These became a badge of honor demonstrating defiance against the weather. These activists—*my* activists—were coming!

But how many? We knew we could use the weather as an excuse if the crowd didn't show.

The rest of Thursday and Friday were a blur, almost as if they didn't happen. The next thing I knew, it was Saturday.

It was time.

We arrived at 8:30 a.m. for a 10:00 a.m. start. The crowd was already assembling. I looked out and saw a few familiar faces in the VIP area, took a few pictures from the stage, and ran out into the VIP area to shake some of the early birds' hands. I saw my buddies who'd come all the way from New Jersey set up on the lawn—they'd come for the *celebration,* and I intended to deliver. But I had no time to exchange anything but nods with them.

The videos started playing. People started cheering. I had to run back to prepare to start the show. The rain came—I *hated* that rain. That rain was going to screw with my rally. I remember it got progressively worse over a short period, deluging the early birds and just pissing me off even more. But while I wasn't looking, the crowds came too. With umbrellas and ponchos in hand, they filled the place up and overflowed onto the sidewalks. And the next park section.

So what was the final tally? In the end, we estimated thirty thousand in that rain. That's more than for the Glenn Beck rally (although our friends at Fox News called ours a "little rally about nothing")— more than we'd hoped given the weather. Thirty thousand smiles on the faces of cold, wet, wonderful activists, making a statement to the country en masse, in the rain:

We are here.

At one point early on, a staffer came backstage and caught my eye. I thought she had a new problem for me to fix, and I was ready to handle whatever it was—*the donation tent wasn't up. The American Atheists booth is not functional. The other sponsors are angry.* I was ready for anything, except what I got:

"It's all good."

"Really?"

"Yes, everything is . . . fine, Dave." She shrugged—she had obviously expected the same problems I had and was seemingly just as amazed to say there weren't any as I was to hear it. That's when I looked out on the crowd, now all the way back to the tents and beyond. In the rain. Smiling and cheering. The weight lifted and all was well. The rally would be better than expected. I began to have fun. Lots of it.

Indeed, words cannot convey how much of a good time I had

that day. It was all of us atheists, making the loudest and boldest state-ment on atheism in American history. It was everything we'd dreamed of. The plan had come together.

After dancing with my wife to Bad Religion behind the band, it was over, and I gave the good-bye speech, for which I had not planned, so it came straight from the heart.

Then it was done. Then it was history.

But that was far from the end. Since the rally I have been getting tweets and wall posts about people I've never met coming out, at-tending their first meetup or joining the movement. A snowball ef-fect is still happening.

One of the most important accomplishments of the rally was the cooperation among organizations. In the past, we had worked against each other, and the result was stagnation. The rally was the first time in our movement's history that all the major organizations worked *together* toward a common goal, and the result was a huge success and our supporters showed their emphatic approval. If the organizations want the continued support of their members, we'd better be ready and willing to do it again, and again.

But why is the Reason Rally an example of firebrand atheism?

- It went where we were not—Washington, DC.
- It used the press for publicity, especially with the Arabic/He-brew billboards.
- It spurred cooperation between groups, making us stronger as a movement, making us appear larger as a movement, and fos-tering future events.
- It told the truth and did not apologize for being atheistic. The pride in our atheism was very apparent.
- It showed our breadth and the big picture to all the attendees—every side of atheism was represented. It provided a platform

Figure 18
Picture from the Reason Rally Stage

This picture includes Richard Dawkins, my mom (just a few months before she died), wife, daughter, sister, and brother-in-law, and my face on a banner. It's a good picture. (Photo credit: Dave Silverman)

for firebrand and diplomat alike, and we mutually delighted in our diversity of approach.

- It showed and motivated activism, spurring people to join the movement on an unprecedented level.
- It allowed us to shout.
- It allowed us to be heard.
- It's happening again! Stay tuned for Reason Rally II in June 2016! (reasonrally.org)

Chapter 10

RELISH THE FUTURE

Extraordinary claims require extraordinary evidence.

—Carl Sagan

We are all connected; To each other, biologically. To the earth, chemically. To the rest of the universe, atomically. —Neil deGrasse Tyson

I've spent the majority of this book ranting about how religion deserves to die because it harms people, believer and nonbeliever alike. But one question remains: *Can* we win this? Can we actually defeat the Goliath that is religion, fighting against money and power with will and truth alone?

Yup. Here's why.

As I've mentioned before, atheism is the fastest-growing religious segment in all fifty states,[1] and I want to take a few moments to crunch some numbers with you to illustrate the point that this growth, if managed and maintained, is the key to humanity's victory once and for all over mythology.

Before I begin, let me make a blanket statement for the purposes of this analysis only: people who declare their religion as "none" are atheists.

Okay, that isn't a perfectly true statement because 24 percent[2] of people defining themselves as such are believers,[3] but this assumption yields much more data and, for the most part, these folks have freed themselves from the shackles of organized religion as a stepping-stone to dropping all of it. Once you realize organized religion is all wrong, it's only a small step to admit religion is all individual and relative, which is a baby step from saying it's all made up.

Furthermore, any people who declare their religious belief as "none" but are truly religious are far outweighed by the atheists who call themselves Jews or Christians. Assuming such closeted atheists *only cancel out* those 24 percent who declare no religious affiliation but are truly religious is extremely conservative. I'll support this statement, and back out the theistic nones, later in this chapter, but for now, let's look at some data.

Figure 19 shows a 2013 Gallup poll estimating a 17.8 percent population for atheists (*nones*).[3] When this poll came out, the news was consistent and obviously slanted—the growth of atheism (they also conflate the terms for nonbelievers without the explanation I provided above) had slowed, if not stopped, and so the growth trend seemed to be ending.

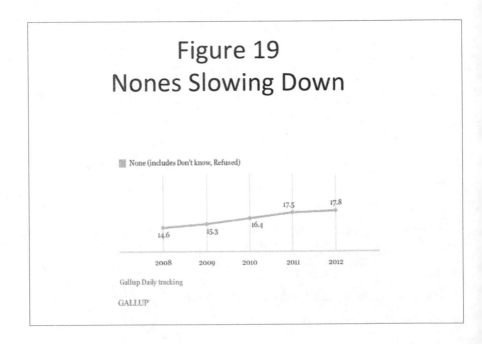

Figure 19
Nones Slowing Down

■ None (includes Don't know, Refused)

17.5   17.8

14.6   15.3   16.4

2008   2009   2010   2011   2012

Gallup Daily tracking

GALLUP

Looking at the chart, you can see how at first glance their asser-tion seems correct. This plays well with the narrative pushed by those who want to see us fail. But take a second look, one level down (see Fig. 20),[4] and you'll see something very different.

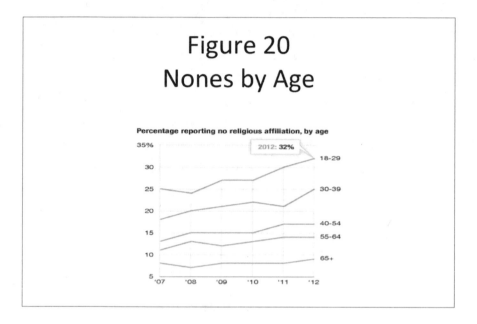

Figure 20
Nones by Age

Percentage reporting no religious affiliation, by age

2012: **32%**

18-29

30-39

40-54

55-64

65+

This changes perspective a bit. As you can see, the older you are, the more religious you are likely to be (statistically speaking). The older generation is far more religious than the younger, and this is consistent across all age groups, with the youngest age group reaching 32 percent *none*.

But old people die, and the trend for the younger generations is obvious growth at a rate much higher than for the older ones (due, I strongly suspect, to the regular use of the Internet, and therefore a constant exposure to alternative viewpoints, critiques, and data that support atheism).

Back to the data. We can see the overall data being "held down" by the older folks, but nobody has taken the time to extrapolate the trends and make decent predictions about growth in the future. In-stead, the pundits at Fox News and those who echo them have looked at Figure 19 and decided we are done. It's time for the Religious Right to celebrate.

Wrong.

For this analysis I've looked at a few different sources and completed the extrapolation and predictions myself. Please note these are not scientific predictions, which would entail using the same sources to ensure consistency. As a result, my numbers don't match up precisely, but I think this effectively illustrates my point.

First, I took the Gallup data above and applied it to the actuarial tables and population data supplied by the US government. This gives me the likelihood of people dying over a given ten-year period. Then, I extrapolated the five-year trend in each age group toward nonreligion and multiplied the expected growth to the expected population in the same time frame.

Here's what I got (see Fig. 21):

Figure 21
Trends Chart

			Growth of Atheists / Nones to 2025				
	Percent Atheist / None in Year						
Age Range	2007	2012	US Population (000)*	US Population in 2025**	# Atheists today	# Atheists in 2025	% Atheists in 2025
18 to 29	25	32	42,000	30,180	13,440	15,150	50.2
30 to 40	18	25	39,000	91,833	9,750	39,672	43.2
40 to 55	14	17	63,000	65,052	10,710	16,133	24.8
55 to 65	11	14	37,000	-	5,180	-	21.8
65 and up	8	9	41,506	65,052	3,736	7,546	11.6
Total			222,506	252,117	42,816	78,501	
Current total percentage of atheists/nones in US			19.24%				
Projected % of atheists / nones in 10 years:			31.14%				

* Source: US Census Bureau, Current Population Survey, Annual Social and economic Supplement, 2012
** Source US Census Bureau, National Population Projections 2012 - Age sections differ from Pew research, leading to omissions in 55-65 age group

Today, according to my numbers, atheists are about 19.24 percent of the (18+) population. This does not match the 17.8 percent in the chart above, due to the different sources and the growth from 2012 to 2014 (the year in which I am writing this).

Note that the new numbers for the youngest age group are larger mainly because I have not moved people down the age groups as they get older, because this is irrelevant. What I am looking for is overall population, so the age distribution in the final analysis is not relevant. The trends of growth are for the people in the age groups and are not directly related to the ages themselves. One does not get less likely to be atheistic as you age, but older Americans *today* are less likely than their younger counterparts to be atheists. It *does* matter that I remove those sixty-five-and-over people when they die, and add the ten- to eighteen-year-olds when they age (and I assume they are equally as religious as the eighteen-year-olds today, when the trend would clearly support the assumption they are even less religious). Today's young people will continue to use the Internet and be exposed to alternative ideas as they age.

Enough disclaimers—let's look at the data. If all current trends continue, we will hit 31 percent *none* in ten years based on numbers alone. This does not take into account the important fact that younger people are becoming less religious at an increasing rate—I took a five-year average to be conservative. If I took a one-year average, the rate would be much higher than 31 percent, but I did not think that would illustrate a truly defensible point. This point is defensible: given current numbers and five-year trends, the number of religiously unaffiliated people will rise by a fat 63 percent in ten years.

In 2025, the US will be nearly one-third openly unaffiliated, and that's without pushing, advertising, or the escalation of the religious wars that are so effective at turning people away from religion. That does not take into account the snowball effect of the increase in visibility leading to a decrease in bigotry and in turn a faster increase. This does not take into account the rest of the closeted atheists who call themselves Christians and Jews. This is just straight line.

That's a massive voting bloc. More than the Catholics, Jews, Muslims, Buddhists, and Hindus combined.[5]

Here's a sanity check: The five-year average for growth in atheism for the two youngest age groups is 7 percent. That is, the 18–39 age group is growing more atheistic over time, to the tune of 7 percent in five years. At this rate, in twenty years the group that is currently the 18–29 group will be 38–49, and they will be 60 percent atheist, and the current 30–39 group will be 50–59 and be 53 percent atheist. Assuming the younger folks are at least as atheistic as their older counterparts, in twenty years more than half of the people under sixty will be atheists.

For a second sanity check, I looked to *Psychology Today*. There, Dr. Nigel Barber took a still different approach, the Existential Security Hypothesis, which posits a link between religion and the need for basic necessities, concluding that "the entire world population would cross the atheist threshold by about 2038."[6]

Now let's go back to that statement I made earlier about atheists who call themselves Christians or Jews far outweighing those who define their religion as *none* but are in fact theistic. We have some data to support this claim. Barna Research, after conducting a 2009 survey of Christians nationwide, published a study entitled "Most American Christians Do Not Believe That Satan or the Holy Spirit Exists"[7] stating, "All 1,871 self-described Christians were asked about their perception of God. In total, three-quarters (78%) said he is the 'all-powerful, all-knowing Creator of the universe who rules the world today.' The remaining one-quarter chose other descriptions of God—depictions that are not consistent with biblical teaching (e.g., everyone is god, god refers to the realization of human potential, etc.)." So according to Barna, 22 percent of self-proclaimed American Christians see God as a metaphor for something real, but not as a literal living supernatural entity, aka, atheists calling themselves Christians (when God becomes a metaphor, you become an atheist).

Moreover, according to Pew (2015), 70 percent of the population describes themselves as Christian.[8] This brings us to an easy calculation of 316 million (total population[9]) x 0.7 x 0.22 = 48 million atheists who call themselves Christian, *more than the total of those who call themselves atheists/none today!* These are the church-pew atheists.

According to Harris Interactive, a whopping 52 percent of people who call themselves Jews are actually atheists.[10] Therefore, 2.2 million atheists call themselves Jews.[11]

This tells you that about 50 million atheists are sitting in pews or otherwise representing a lie.

Taking an aggressive-but-reasonable approach, if outed atheists number 32 million (42 million *nones* less the 24 percent who are still believers), that means we as a country are already at 82 million—26 percent atheist *today*—almost half the size of all believing Christians, and nearly twenty times those identifying as Jews!

Think for a moment about our growth. Why should we worry about converting believers if all we have to do is convert closeted atheists like these folk into outed atheists? How many of those closeted atheists will come out over the next ten years, once the bigotry against us is minimized by our activism?

None of the polling data reflects the trends among the closeted wing of atheism, so we can't track or predict it. I can't tell you (with support) if the growth of atheism is coming from closeted atheists coming out, or religious people converting, because they both look the same in the polls. Therefore, for the sake of the analysis earlier in the chapter, and to make the point that religion is losing, I equated people who declare themselves as none with atheists, and pretended that closeted atheists *only evenly* compensate for the 24 percent theistic *nones*. The truth is the numbers are actually far greater, and my numbers should therefore be considered conservative.

But wait, there's more. In May of 2015, just before this book went to press, Religion News Service announced, in an article entitled "Christians Lose Ground, 'Nones' Soar,"[12] that Pew came out with new data confirming the continuing trend of the growth of

atheism. Specifically, the percentage of Americans who call themselves *atheists* has increased to 3.1 percent, up from 2.4 percent—about
a 30 percent growth—and the percentage who call themselves *agnostics* rose from 3.3 percent to 4 percent—a 21 percent growth—since
I began to write this book two years ago (see Fig. 11, page 142). Both
statistics show not only an increase, but yet another *increase in the rate
of increase*. Other notable findings include:

- The Percentage of Americans who now count themselves as
  Christian dropped 8 points (to 70 percent)—more than 10
  percent—since 2007
- There are more than four former Christians for every convert
  to Christianity
- Generational change, as I spoke about earlier, is the driving
  factor
- Nones now make up 22.8 percent of the population, a 42
  percent increase over 8 years.
- Former Christians represent 19.2 percent of the population[12]
- More than 1 in 4 American men are religiously unaffiliated
  today—that's more than Catholics.
- Among nones, the share of people identifying as atheists and
  agnostics has increased from 25 percent to 31 percent since 2007,
  suggesting a decrease in apathy.

So, yeah, we can win. In fact, we are already winning. The snowball effect is happening as predicted, and it's showing no signs of
slowing down. America's atheists are taking their rightful place in
society, outside of the closets religion made for us.

How will America look when the atheists are free to live as atheists
without bigotry? How will we be organized? How will we wield
the power that our numbers will give us? How will we shape politics

and be represented in the press? How will we penetrate the schools to champion tolerance for atheists, and what will that mean for the following years? What will happen to the stigma attached to atheism when we are everywhere *and* out? How will our kids feel when their atheism is no big deal in school? All those hopes and goals are within our reach, and will be attained within our lifetimes.

So we will continue to focus on those 50 million closeted atheists sitting in the pews, urging them to come out in any and every way possible. If the trends are not straight lines, and our methods and activism continue to work as they have been, we will seriously do damage to religion by simply convincing the closeted atheists to come out sooner, resulting in an increase in the rate at which people do so, while believers convert as a result of the increased penetration of atheism into America's conversation, as a part of the snowball effect. Then our numbers go wild.

And so does our influence.

That's the plan.

It's up to us. This generation faces the responsibility of preparing for our next. We have the opportunity to create the country we want, and indeed, in the long term, the world we want. All of it can happen in our lifetimes, and the power is in our hands. All we have to do is focus on our goals, challenge apathy with vigor, and ignore those who naysay us for money and power. The numbers are on our side. The naysayers can choke on them.

Chapter 11

MOVING FORWARD

To live for a principle, for the triumph of some reform by which all mankind are to be lifted up, to be wedded to an idea, may be, after all, the holiest and happiest of marriages. —Elizabeth Cady Stanton

I'm a Pakistani journalist living in Karachi and born into a Muslim family. I just wanted to let you know that your TV interviews posted on You-Tube contributed significantly to helping me admit to myself that religions are a scam. I haven't come out publicly about my atheism because of very real security concerns here, but it is important that I have come to terms with it myself, and my friends. Just thought you might like to know that your work is having an effect half way around the world, so thanks! —Anonymous e-mail to American Atheists

As I just mentioned, the number of atheists in America today approaches 82 million. If we add up all the members of all the atheist organizations in the country and assume all of them are unique to the organizations (no crossovers, no double memberships), the combined number might be seventy-five thousand today.

That's 0.09 percent (nine-hundredths of 1 percent) of the atheists in this country who belong to the movement designed to protect and preserve the rights of atheists and all Americans.

We are nonprofits, and that means we have a purpose beyond

making money and adding members. We are here to serve our country. Indeed, the purpose of any nonprofit is to go out of business (or transition to a new business, as did the March of Dimes)[1] in the long term, because that would mean the need for which the nonprofit was formed had been addressed and no longer existed. Our combined long-term goal is a lack of need for an atheist movement.

However, at present the need for an atheist movement is very real, and fortunately, ours is great, diverse, and growing. We are succeeding, and I hope this book has moved you to consider joining this—*your*—movement.

Your money is not just a donation—it's a purchase. You are buying activism for this country, and, yes, the more the better. You can see how much we do with 0.09 percent. Just think of what we could do as a movement with 0.5 percent of America's atheists backing us!

I wish I were wrong. The bad news is I'm not.

There is no god to help or reward us, and unfortunately, everybody dies. This is the truth. It sucks, but it's the truth, and we can say it with all the certainty we have when we talk about other fantasies and myths.

And I'm not being rude, obnoxious, or dickish when I say that because it's important information people need and deserve to hear, so that some who agree may know they are not alone, and those who disagree may reconsider. Telling the truth in the face of a horrible lie is a good deed.

We, the firebrands, are having a measurable effect on this country, and the society in which our children will live. I leave you with the following summary thoughts:

1. If you don't have a belief in any gods, whatever the reason and whatever your philosophy, you're an atheist. You can be an atheist and a humanist, an atheist and an agnostic, or

anything else (except theist), but you *are* an atheist if you have no belief in a literal, extant god. Hiding behind theist-approved euphemisms and using other labels is dishonest and counterproductive. Using the A-word is honest, humanistic, and supports the cause—calling yourself an atheist, if you can, is activism in and of itself.

2. Beyond the rhetoric, everything I do, and everything we should do, revolves around equality and acceptance. We fight for equality against a foe that says we already have it or don't deserve it, neither of which is true. We strive to level a playing field, which means the elimination of special privileges and advantages for theists. Some theists take this as an "attack," but it is no more than the assertion of our equality—whatever they can do, we can do—and the elimination of bigotry against us. That we seek equality and acceptance, and *only* equality and acceptance, makes us the Good Guys.

3. *Religions preach both immoral and moral things.* Everything from "love thy neighbor as yourself" to "kill your neighbor if he thinks the wrong way" is in there. This is why *all religion is cafeteria religion.* Whatever the religion and whoever the theist, people make their own moral judgments, dismissing the immorality in their holy books out of habit, and sticking to the stuff they like as if it were divine, objective, and/or perfect.

4. Since religion's claimed objectivity creates an ever-present lag in its prescribed morality relative to the rest of society, religion must inherently be referred to as a bad source of moral teaching, or rather, a *good source of old morals.* Religious morality is forever behind the times, and therefore immoral by definition when it comes to today's morality. As such, it would be ridiculous to seek current moral advice from a holy book.

6. *In the history of the world, the number of times a supernatural anything has been proven true is zero.* Every god, ghost, spirit,

devil, possession, and miracle ever claimed true is a lie. No exceptions. The number of times an atheistic (godless) argument has been proven wrong by a theistic argument is zero. *In contrast, every time a theist-versus-atheist argument has been settled, an atheistic argument has won* (the "shrinking God of the Gaps" argument). This does not mean science is antireligion; it just means (or rather, strongly implies) religion is wrong. The "God of the Gaps" argument has a 0 percent success rate, but it is often repackaged to look deceptively fresh. I challenge anyone to find any scientifically valid testable proof of *anything supernatural, ever.* If you can prove it, even once, I'll quit my job. I'm not nervous, as it has never been done in history, because it's *all* a lie.

7. Many so-called believers are people who do not really believe—they just *choose to pretend* to do so because of societal pressure, thereby doing the wrong thing by supporting immoral institutions for personal interests. These people hurt themselves and others by living a lie, and it is their responsibility to come out, or at least seriously contemplate why they feel the need to hide.

8. If theism is harmful because it takes credit for good people's morality while promoting, protecting, or supporting immoral behavior, if this harm permeates society, inserting itself into other people's lives in a clear attempt to control non-adherents, and if theism facilitates hate, terrorism, and reinforces bad behavior with a false morality, *then how can a moral person be apathetic toward religion?* How can one not care that we, as a society and as a species, are being endangered in real ways because people are too reverent to the liars and victims who run religion out of nothing more than tradition and political correctness?

9. *Since religion is inherently and demonstrably harmful to society and moral progress, atheism holds the moral high ground.* Therefore,

the most moral choice of behavior as an atheist would be the behavior that has the most positive impact for society and against religion.

10. The numbers in this book show a positive correlation between firebrand atheism and the exact desired results—more people talking about atheism, more people calling themselves atheists, and more theists liking atheists and willing to vote for atheists. Firebrand atheism, while unpopular and politically incorrect, *benefits society and the believers far more than the diplomatic approach,* which just reinforces the legitimacy of religion. Say it aloud: "I respect you, but not your religious beliefs."

11. *We see little progress on a societal level from the nice-guy approach, which is exactly what we'd expect, as our place at society's table is not governed by the flock.* Rather, it is pastors and the politicians in their pockets who have serious skin invested in our inequality who stymie our progress toward acceptance. That's why we need to shatter their unearned respect, dispel their lies, and challenge their immorality in public on a grand scale. We are not trying to be liked by theists—we are taking our equality from those who use lies, greed, and ignorance to keep it from us.

12. *We must consider our moral responsibility to help cure theists of their affliction.* It does not matter that this looks like religious proselytizing; we still are morally obligated to help them. While I am not advocating door-to-door proselytizing, I do think we should reconsider any knee-jerk negative "that looks like religion" reaction to an activity that clearly facilitates a positive outcome.

13. *"I respect your beliefs" is a lie told by atheists for their own benefit (it's easy and pleasant), to the detriment of the theist (and to the atheist).* We walk away with a warm, fuzzy feeling, but we

have reinforced the poison in the mind of the theists ("Even the atheists respect my beliefs"). It is harder for us, and better for them, if we tell the truth—that we *don't* respect their religion, and that it's silly to believe in a god in this day and age—and that makes firebrand atheism humanistic. We may upset them, and we may create hard feelings, but it's undeniably the right thing to do, for them and us, to help theists accept that their religion is a lie, unworthy of the respect it so fervently demands. We all prefer to be nice—it's more important to be effective in doing good.

14. Don't be confused by the polling numbers that suggest we are small. These numbers reflect that atheists are hiding behind other terms for whatever reason. Reasonable calculations suggest the number of atheists is already huge and will continue to grow. Truth is winning, and that has religion scared. I love that, but it doesn't mean our victory is assured. Our apathy can stop us.

We are going to win this fight *if we keep pushing,* this I can promise. The opponents of religious equality may have money, power, and numbers, but *we* are going to win because their gods don't exist, their preachers tell lies, their claims about morality are false—and slowly but surely, everyone is figuring it all out. The Lie of God, which apparently started with the Neanderthals, is nearing its end, and good riddance.

The death throes of religion will not be calm; the greatest lie ever told will not walk silently into the night. Even now, religion is encroaching on secular parts of the world and continues to threaten the foundational principles of our country.

The next several years will see many demands from those who insist on being revered for no other reason than tradition. They will tell us we must believe or at least follow along silently in respect.

They will tell us we must tithe via higher taxes so religious institutions can pay none while they preach hate against us. They will tell us they deserve respect, because they say so. They will demand we never question or criticize, saying their way is flawless and perfect, and that when we find them wrong and say so, we are being disrespectful to that which must be considered valid and important by default. They will claim discrimination is their religious right, that hate has merit, and that believing—or pretending to believe despite ample evidence to the contrary, which of course is lying—is a virtue.

Meanwhile they will continue to line their pockets and control the deluded.

To hasten religion's demise, we, the firebrands of the atheist movement, must remove its societal protections against criticism and its government assistance. This means we must attack religious privilege and the hold that religion has on society and all of the individuals therein.

The firebrand atheist will hasten the end of religion's influence on society and ensure our children will enjoy true freedom of thought in America. The firebrand will fight not with arms, but with truth and honesty. The firebrand will truly preserve and protect the American Way, which requires equality for everyone, no matter what they think about gods.

While we fight for good, we will be called evil and yet fight on anyway, even for the benefit of religion's victims, against whom we are pitted.

That's what makes us the good guys. That's what makes it important that we win not only the small battles, but the war itself. This is why I believe it is the ethical duty of every atheist to help this movement succeed.

Fighting God is fighting a war for freedom of thought, which is the most important freedom we have. If we win, *everyone wins*. With the rise of atheism, the availability of information, and proven tactics by a well-organized movement, we can win—if we work together, and tell the truth.

Thank you for your attention.

My name is David Silverman, and I am an American atheist.

Appendix 1

FREE WILL

On Free Will and the Sonic Screwdriver

Note: This is fun. It was originally printed in the American Atheist *magazine, Web edition, in 1998. Back then,* Doctor Who *was far from mainstream. It was only on TV at odd times on PBS stations, and viewership was relegated to hard-core geekdom. I've edited this little, so please remember it was written for an audience that had never heard of the now-very-popular-and-it's-about-time show.*

Doctor Who is a campy sci-fi TV show produced in England about an extraterrestrial good guy (the Doctor) who flies around in time and space going on adventures. The original series to which I'm referring here ran from 1963 to 1989, with multiple actors having starred in the lead role.

As an extraterrestrial, the Doctor has knowledge and tools far beyond current Earth technology; his most famous (next to his spaceship) was his sonic screwdriver. This useful tool is great for opening prison cells, locked boxes, and virtually anything else, as long as the plot allows. However, when it is inconvenient for the plot to allow the sonic screwdriver to work, there is always a lame technobabble reason it doesn't ("ionization in the atmosphere," etc.).

Now, let's talk about "free will."

The God of the Old and New Testaments is supposed to be omniscient, seeing the past and the future with equal clarity. Omniscience is a necessary part of omnipotence, because one cannot be all-powerful if one can be surprised. Therefore, we have a Garden of Eden, with Adam and Eve, a talking snake, and an all-powerful, omnipotent deity. Since this deity is omniscient, this god knew, way back then, that I would be writing this article and that you would be reading it. He knew everything, so the story goes.

And this deity made a decision—he wants to plant a Tree of Knowledge of Good and Evil in the garden. He knew, since he is omniscient, that if he put it there, Adam would eat from it, causing the fall of man, and billions of souls would go to hell. Yet he put it there anyway. He didn't put it where he knew Adam *wouldn't* eat from it. He put it where, with 100 percent certainty, he *knew* Adam would eat the fruit.

Adam had no choice at all—God's foreknowledge took away his free will, because God knew with zero room for error that Adam would eat it. And he did, as God knew he would, and so God punished him, and us, by sending souls to hell, causing women to suffer pain during childbirth, and enacting other penalties. God supposedly gave Adam and Eve free will, but God's foreknowledge trumps and negates that, because neither Adam nor Eve, nor the talking snake for that matter, had the ability to do anything that God did not already know they were going to do. From God's perspective, everything we do is preordained, with no freedom to deviate whatsoever.

I love the free will argument because it's an imperfect tool to use against the perfect question: "Why doesn't he just show himself and fix our problems?"

"You see, God gave us free will," say the theists, "and by showing himself or solving a problem for us—like disease, hunger, etc.—God would take away our ability to disbelieve in him, robbing us of free will. We would no longer have a choice but to believe."[1]

Okay. So now we have a tool, the free will argument, which works great when asked some questions. Note that I said *some* questions, because this sonic screwdriver of an argument only works when the plot allows.

For instance, let's take the story of Jesus (you may have heard of this). This man walks on water, cures illness, and changes water into wine in front of people. Surely these miracles, which according to the text were witnessed and believed by many, would take away the free will to not believe in him of all those who saw them, right? Therefore, it is logical to assume that all the apostles, who knew and believed Jesus was the son of God, had no free will.

Moreover, we must assume from this argument that all other people who saw these miracles would also lose their free will.

Hmmm . . .

Now let's do the Old Testament. This guy, Moses, leads his people into the sea, and God parts the sea for them to run through and thereby escape their pursuers. So all these people lost their free will to disbelieve, right? God must have chosen to let them live without free will rather than see them subjected to slavery. They were, after all, God's Chosen People. Of course, those who pursued the Jews witnessed the event and survived, yet somehow did not immediately convert to Judaism, thereby keeping their free will. Similarly, the Jews themselves, who had to have lost their free will to disbelieve in God because they saw a miracle, decided to pray to an idol.

Hmmmm.

Now, time warp to the 1940s, during which 6 million of these same people are being tortured and murdered. God must somehow have thought that the fate of the Jews in a concentration camp was far better than doing something—anything—to save them. I'm sure those people were happy they died slow, painful deaths the likes of which you and I could not imagine, but at least they had free will because their deity didn't show up to save them.

Doesn't make all that much sense, does it? Free will is apparently more important now than anything else on the planet, or else God would do something divine such as ending disease, hunger, or natural disasters. However, in the Bible, miracles were commonplace, so I guess few people had free will back then. Perhaps humans lost the ability over time to view a miracle and retain free will. Perhaps God took this ability away from us so he wouldn't have to perform any more miracles.

Or maybe, just maybe, the Bible is a work of fiction like *Doctor Who,* and the free will argument only works like a sonic screwdriver, when the plot of the Bible needs it to work. When it doesn't work, well, there must be some ionization in the atmosphere.

Free Will Addendum (2014)

In a recent debate, my opponent asked me if I DVR'd a football game and accidentally learned the final score of the game before I watched, would the players still have free will? I responded "no" because the recorded images of the players on my DVR would have no choice but to end the game the way it ended. They throw, tackle, and try to outsmart the other players, all without having any chance of doing something different—every decision having already been made. The players on the DVR are robots—tools unable to change the score in any way whatsoever, yet completely unaware of their inability to change their minds.

This is what God's omniscience does for humanity. God's foreknowledge usurps free will by definition. You and I, and everyone on the planet, are physically incapable of surprising him. He knows what we are doing, what we have done, and, with absolute perfection, what we will do. Do we then really have a choice? God has the DVR remote and has already watched every detail of our football game of life. Do we have the ability to make a different play or change the game in any way, even slightly?

From our perspective, it certainly seems as if we have free will—that God's foreknowledge would not stop us from making choices—but if God exists, we have no choice to do anything except that which he expects. From God's perspective, we have no free will at all, because he knows our "choices" in advance. There can be no free will in any religion where the deity knows everything; we are free-will-free pawns dancing a useless dance before our creator deity.

This brings us back to the Garden of Eden. If Adam had no free will, then he did not make a choice. God, due to his perfect foreknowledge, put the tree where he *knew* Adam would eat from it. I could hold out a rock and drop it and have less certainty that it will fall to the ground than God had about the Fall of Man as an inevitable result of his placement of the tree in Eden. So God, quite deliberately and directly, *made* Adam eat that fruit, then punished the pawn and all his descendants for falling uncontrollably into his glorious trap (hallelujah).

Adam and Eve didn't fall from grace—they were pushed and then told it was their own fault. This deity, this Yahweh, then sent billions of souls to hell (however they are defining it) and blamed it on his children, when it was all predesigned and predetermined from the start.

This is why the god of the Bible is not only unworthy of praise, he is worthy of scorn and hate. He knows our actions completely in advance, knows who will be saved and who will not until the "end times," and yet he grants us no free will, merely the illusion of (and wish for) such. He demands we praise him, yet he knows who will or won't. He demands we convert, but he already knows who will be saved, when, why, or why not. He demands everything when he needs nothing. It makes no sense at all—mainly, of course, because it's all fiction.

Appendix 2

MY REASON RALLY SPEECHES

Opening Reason Rally Speech

Ladies and gentlemen, *good morning!* I am David Silverman, president of American Atheists and chair of the Reason Rally Coalition, and I would like to welcome you all to this, the largest atheist and secularist gathering in world history!

This event was conceived to raise the awareness of the secular movement, but what we have planned for you goes far beyond lectures and speeches.

We are here to celebrate secular values, those values which we accept as Americans but have no religious basis—diversity, equality, charity, compassion, and reason, just to name a few.

Nationwide, the nonreligious population is both the fastest growing and the most despised. I ask you all, why is that? Why are we hated when we endorse no violence, incite no racism or hatred, and demand nothing more than equal treatment? I'll tell you why: it's easy to hate what you don't know, and the theists don't know us. Actually, they do know us; they just don't know they know us, because most of the atheists in this country are closeted. Bigotry is born of ignorance, but ignorance can be cured. If the atheists weren't closeted, it would be harder to hate us, because in the end, you can't hate what you already love.

But it's about more than just equality of atheists. So many of our major battles being fought today only exist because of our silence, including marriage equality, stem-cell research, death with dignity, school prayer, and intelligent design. These issues only exist because the atheists in this country are quiet. We could make a thunderous noise, yet we are defeated by our own silence. We are the fastest growing in all fifty states, and we think we are alone. We are weak only because we think we are weak. The bad news is, it's our fault. The good news is, it's under our control. We can choose to be loud. We can choose to be proud, and we can choose to be a part of the organized movement designed to take this broad country into a future of true equality, respect, and even love from our community.

That is the purpose of the Reason Rally. The sponsors of this event are as diverse as you are. Whether you're a hard-liner or "accommodationist," if you prefer to support politics or charity, students, military, or even little kids, and no matter how you define yourself, you will be able to find a sponsor that suits you. Join them! Lend your voice to this movement and be heard! Because when you have a support mechanism, it's easier to come out as nonreligious to your friends, family, and neighbors. Make sure nobody you know thinks they don't know any atheists. The road may be bumpy, but it is absolutely necessary if we are going to fix this country.

This is our movement's biggest and greatest event ever and we are here to deliver a message to America. We are everywhere, you already know us, and you already love us. And, oh yeah, we will never be closeted again. If we can deliver this message to America, it will evolve into a fairer, more modern country, right before our eyes. In years to come, the Reason Rally will be seen as the beginning of the end of the Religious Right's grip on America, and on behalf of America's sane and reasonable future, thank you for making the Reason Rally a success.

Second Reason Rally Speech

Ladies and gentlemen, good morning once again! As I mentioned before, I am David Silverman, and I am privileged and honored to be the chair of the Reason Rally, but I am also the president of American Atheists.

American Atheists was founded in 1963 by Madalyn Murray O'Hair, who led the fight to remove forced prayer from the public schools. Since then, American Atheists has been known as the Marines of the free-thought movement. You see, sometimes things need to be said and fights need to be fought, even if they are unpopular. Minority points of view are often overlooked unless they are shouted. Rights are trampled unless they are protected. Equality is never granted if not demanded. That's our job.

We are the atheists with the picket signs and the megaphone. We are the radicals. The hard-liners. Some call us extremists, but that's just because we are extremely right. We file the lawsuits to keep religion and government separate, like our current lawsuit against the World Trade Center memorial. Yes, we are the crazy ones who say that a big giant cross with JESUS inscribed on it is a Christian symbol, and we will not allow the five hundred atheists who died on 9/11 to be ignored. We demand equal treatment by our own government, even if the Christians don't like it.

The message we deliver is undeniably true, even if it may be politically incorrect. *God is a myth and reason is inherently atheistic.* Our methods deliver our message to the unaffiliated and closeted atheists: you are not alone and you deserve equality. We also deliver a message to the theists: we are here and we will never be silent again.

And now, I have a message for you. I am here today to propose our first-ever nationwide, movementwide policy. A zero-tolerance policy towards bigotry and hate. I am asking every atheist everywhere to call out people when they deride us, every time they deride us. When charities turn away our donations, they should be shamed—got that, American Cancer Society? When politicians insult us en masse, the press should hear from us, en masse. Got that, Newt? And when the press lies about us, we need to call them liars, loudly, *Bill.* Bigoted teachers need to be fired, bigoted athletes should be traded, and bigoted politicians need to be called out in front of cameras and voted out on Election Day. Zero tolerance. Bigotry is stupid, and it's not okay no matter where it's directed. I am therefore calling on all of you, and all the organizations sponsoring this event, to adopt this simple proposal, of not taking any more crap, from anyone, ever.

My friends, this country experienced a lot of progress in the last hundred years. Women, African-Americans, and the LGBTQ Community have made monumental strides in their respective quests to achieve full equality in society. For each cause, there is a beginning, and a time when the task seems monumental. But then there is a precipice, which, once passed, allows the struggling movement to flourish, and grow, and succeed. Ladies and gentlemen, we are at that precipice right now. We have the numbers, we have the momentum, and we have every right, and indeed the responsibility, to demand an end to bigotry and hate. I want to personally invite all of you to join American Atheists and come to tomorrow's convention and take part in the righteous fight for our reasonable future. *Thank you!*

Appendix 3

ON OPENING THE ATHEIST "CLOSET"

First published as "Atheism: The Other Closet," American Atheist magazine, Web edition, Read Me column, October 1998. Adapted for this book.

Coming out of the closet is a phrase most associated with people announcing to the world that they are gay, bisexual, or transgender. Most are better off having done so, having found their way to a more open and satisfying life. But there is another closet hiding a different minority: atheists. Many of us hide in the shadows due to fear of hostility and aversion to confrontations.

But we can't stay in the closet any longer. Since the 1980s, the Christian Right, in its never-ending quest to make everyone Christian, has unleashed an unparalleled slew of efforts aimed at Christianizing the country. On top of legislation, constitutional amendments, and publicity, the Religious Right has engaged in a war of words and slander against its greatest enemy: the logic and common sense of atheism. The Bible goes so far as to forbid contact with atheists (2 Corinthians 6:14), thereby stifling debate and preventing logical, nonreligious ideas from entering the flock. Similar behavior is seen in religious cults, where new members are not even allowed to contact noncult family members.

Because of this policy, atheists are vilified as anarchistic and evil antireligionists, who want nothing more than to rob other people of their right to practice their beliefs. Only a small portion of atheists are open (out of the closet) about their atheism, and as a result we are viewed as a much smaller percentage of the population than we really are. In turn, the legislators pay far less attention to us than they should. In many cases, they pay no attention to us at all.

We need to help reverse the progress made by those who oppose free thought by assisting nonbelievers in being more open about their atheism. For some people, coming out as an atheist can be as difficult as anything else they've ever done, but this is not always necessarily the case.

Why Come Out?

While the reasons for staying in the closet seem valid, the reasons for coming out may far outweigh those for hiding.

If you are closeted, you are hiding a big piece of yourself that you're not allowing other people to know. As a result, those who love you are ignorant of a side of your personality. Would it change their minds about you should they find out? Possibly, but wouldn't you rather know for sure? Do you really think they'd reject you completely if they knew? In most cases, this is not so. In fact, a huge percentage of atheists I know—most of them, in fact—have at least cordial relationships with those family members who are religious. In all reality, religion is rarely as important as the love of a family member, even to the most pious.

There is also a good possibility for pleasant surprise. Many times I've heard from people who have come out that things weren't nearly as bad as expected. Many times we remember our parents, friends, and family members as they once were, without considering that they may have changed in the many years that have passed since then. Take a step back and look at them as they are today. Do your parents have any atheist friends? Have other family members come out yet? How bad is this *really* going to be?

How do you feel about hiding? Don't you feel that you're being oppressed for no reason? Do you feel like a second-class citizen, or that your acquaintances think atheism is something of which to be ashamed?

The fact is that there is nothing shameful about atheism. Rather, it should be viewed as a major accomplishment. Most people stick with the religion in which they were raised, never thinking or examining the reasons why. Those that switch religions (or sects of a particular religion) often never truly question the belief in a god. Those that do should be proud that they have searched and reached an educated conclusion, and so should you.

As an atheist, you have broken out of the cycle of doing what you're told because someone says god says so. You think for yourself, you are self-reliant, and you are responsible for your actions and decisions. Showing yourself is your next great decision.

Degrees of Outness

There are degrees to which one is open about his or her atheism. While there is often overlap, these are the degrees as I see them:

Degree 1: Completely closeted. Not even your spouse knows. You tell everyone you're a believer, and you may even attend church services to convince those around you. You're living a lie, terrified that someone may learn the truth.

If you fit into this category, something should change in the near term, if at all possible. Your spouse, who loves and trusts you for who you are, needs and has the right to know.

Some people feel they cannot escape this space, that the ramifications of coming out as an atheist would be too devastating to their lives if they did. It is for them (and others) that we fight. The more, and the louder, we come out today, the easier it will be for those who can't do so until tomorrow.

Degree 2: Mostly secret. Your spouse knows, but most of your family and friends don't. You avoid the subject at all costs at work, and if it does come up, you will hide your atheism.

Degree 3: Somewhat open. Some family members and most friends know, but you are hesitant to bring it up in conversation. It's still a secret at work, unless you are close friends with a coworker or two, who know. You have friends who are atheists and may belong to an organization such as American Atheists for moral support and connectivity. You may write a letter to a congressperson, but not to the local paper, because you don't want your atheism published. You may avoid the subject when it comes up, but if pressed, you will not call yourself a believer (though you may soften the blow by using the term *agnostic* or *freethinker,* even if you're an atheist by definition).

Degree 4: Mostly open. Almost anyone who knows you knows you don't practice religion. Coworkers, perhaps including your boss, all your friends, and your entire family are aware. You don't shout it from rooftops, but you make no effort to hide your atheism when it comes up in conversation, and you may occasionally raise the topic yourself.

Degree 5: Completely open. Every time the subject comes up, you state your disbelief with pride and frankness. Anyone who doesn't like you because of your atheism is a bigot and is not your concern. You've written letters to the editors of newspapers on the topic, and you may have an atheist bumper sticker on your car (or a license plate that reads ATHEIST).

Coming Out: How, and How Soon

If you find yourself in the first two degrees, then you have work to do. Your self-isolation is unhealthy, both mentally and physically (IMO), and you need to rectify it. Your goal is degree 3 (ultimately 5, but 3 is the short-term minimum), and it's actually quite easy to get there.

The first step, after admitting your atheism to yourself, is to be with people like you, and the easiest way to do this is to join an atheist group. No, this is not a shameless plug for you to join American Atheists, but it is a plea to join something. You have no idea how great it is to walk into a room full of people and know that they are *all* atheists and think you're right. It's the easiest way to make atheist friends and develop a power base from which to draw when confronting the other people in your life.

There are three types of people in everyone's life that have influence: friends (including spouses), family, and coworkers. My experience has been that coming out to people in this order is usually best.

Friends are easy to tell about your nonbelief. Why? Because we choose our friends. People tend to prefer to be with those like themselves, so while it may not be that your friends are atheists, it is unlikely that these people are so intolerant toward atheists that they are going to reject you for it. Chances are, since they are *your* friends, they will support you and continue to be your friend even if they don't agree with you. Advice: to pick which friends to tell first, look for any association with science or science fiction, or anyone with an advanced (nontheological) degree, as these have high likelihoods of prior exposure to, and therefore tolerance of, atheists.

Truth be told, if you are a recent convert from a hard-core religious belief or cult, your friends in that religion/cult may not be receptive. If this is the case, then you will possibly need to find new friends with like interests, as your old friends, still being pious, may reject you—at least at first. Again, the Bible actively prohibits association with atheists. You may try to point this out to your friends as the bigoted text that it is, and if your friendship is worth something to them, you may still be able to keep the friendship alive. If none of your friends look like good candidates, find and make new friends if you can or just go straight to family.

Family may be the most difficult to tell. On one hand, you feel a need for support from parents and siblings (and sometimes children) whom you love, yet on the other hand, you feel guilty for holding back such a significant secret. With family, you don't have the same advantage as you do with friends, in that people from the same family can more often have extremely different beliefs. Therefore, the possibility exists for rejection and cold-shouldering from your own flesh and blood.

Despite that family members may not like what they hear, for the most part they need to know. Religious parents are often the most dismayed, having "failed" to bring up a good religious child. In all frankness, however, deep down they would not rather you lie to them or hide such an important aspect of yourself from them.

The exception to this rule is if you are a child or are otherwise dependent on parents you are sure would expel you from home if they knew. Freedom of religion and respecting yourself are important, but not more important than having a roof over your head. In this case, you may want to wait for independence before announcing your atheism.

Coworkers are easy. They usually don't care, and it's frankly none of their business in the first place what your beliefs are. You can go all the way through degree 4 and still not tell your coworkers. As with a parent, don't come out if you think you're going to lose your job. If you are uncomfortable with the situation, postpone your announcement until the situation changes and you are more secure.

Some of your coworkers are your close friends and therefore fall into the earlier category. However, remember that those who are not close friends may spread your news faster than you can, and that people whom you'd really rather not know this information may find out. It is therefore important to remember that this decision is different from coming out to friends and family and needs to be handled independently. If you decide to come out at work, follow the same rules as for friends (find supporters at work by finding like minds, telling them in confidence, and then spreading the news as you see fit using your supporters as a base).

Coming Out—Doing It

Okay, so now you've decided/realized that you're an atheist, and you're about to tell the people you know about it. Exactly how is it done? There are some simple rules to follow when coming out as an atheist that I've found to be quite helpful.

Be confident. Don't come out by saying, "I'm thinking that I'm having some doubts about religion." This will only invite people to try to "save" you before it's "too late." When you tell people, state it in no uncertain terms, in the present tense, and make sure to convey that you've come to an educated decision. Try something like "After a lot of soul-searching and talking to a lot of people, I've decided to give up on religion" or "I've been an atheist for some time now, so I won't be going to church with you anymore."

Smile. This is an accomplishment, not something shameful. This is a good thing you want to share with loved ones. If you convey this attitude, the people you are telling may receive these signals, which may make the situation go a little easier.

Be compassionate. Yes, *you* should be compassionate to *them*. Understand that the people you tell love you and actually believe in God and their preachers' teachings. They are victims—just as you were—of the lies and falsehoods told by religious organizations, the only difference being that they may still believe those lies. They may express their emotions as anger, but a little education and steadfastness mixed with understanding might allow them to get over that hump quickly.

Make sure you tell your parents that they succeeded (instead of failed) in raising you as a person who makes one's own decisions and does not follow blindly. They did a good job. Tell them you're happy, and at the end, slip in that this is your decision and that they have no reason to be hurt or to judge you and that you're grateful for their acceptance and love.

Hope for the best, but prepare for the worst. The best is obviously "I'm an atheist too" or "So what?"—but don't count on it. As I said earlier, friends are easier than anyone else and are less likely to reject you because of your atheism. I've lost potential friendships because of it, but never an established friend (even the most pious ones). However, be prepared for all the standard responses—"You're going to hell!" "Does this mean you pray to Satan?" "How could you do this to me?"—from loved ones and family members.

The best defense for this is to have answers at the ready. You know your people better than anyone else and are best suited for guessing what those questions might be. Below are some frequently used statements and some suggested counterpoints for your reference:

Atheists have no morals since they don't believe. What a sad world it is when people can seriously say that humans need to fear eternal damnation in order to do good. Humans have the idea of right and wrong embedded in them by their own brains, as well as their upbringing and society. Atheists do good, not out of fear of reprisal, but because it's the right thing to do. We value family, society, culture, and, of course, freedom. Many of us will—and have—defended these values with our lives.

Examples:

Slavery was not only acceptable two hundred years ago, it was considered a good deed by many and defended using the Bible. The Bible was also used to justify the Holocaust, the Crusades, and the Spanish Inquisition. This shows that the Bible can be used to defend even the most immoral and unethical ideals and is therefore not an adequate yardstick to measure moral or ethical behavior.

Mention bad religious people. Remember that Hitler was a Catholic, and that Jeffrey Dahmer said grace before he ate his victims. Mention also that one need only open a newspaper to find yet another story about allegations against priests for sexual misconduct, often with children.

Along with these statements always note that while atheists make up 15–20 percent of the population at large, we only make up 0.21 percent of the population in prison (1997 Federal Bureau of Prisons statistics). I mean, think of it, what if 15–20 percent of the population (on top of all the religious criminals) decided it was okay to steal, rape, and murder? We'd have chaos! These will prove that religion and ethical behavior are not even slightly related.

Atheists believe in evolution, but that doesn't answer as many questions as creationism. Atheism is not a scientific theory; rather, it is a lack of religion. We do believe in the proven process of science, and that all questions will eventually be answered with science (or rather, that as in history, no questions will ever be answered with a deity) even if they are not answered today, but we readily admit that not all answers are known right now. That is no reason, however, for inventing a fictional god to whom to give credit, especially when all it does is create more questions. Ignorance of fact is not evidence for fiction. Science has done well so far, giving theories regarding evolution, geological movement, and the big bang, all supported by evidence, but not necessarily endorsed by all atheists.

Atheists cannot know there is no God since you cannot prove he doesn't exist. Again, this is a two-sided coin, but the theists are loath to admit the other side. Atheists don't need to prove the nonexistence of God any more than we need to prove the nonexistence of Zeus or Santa Claus. Can theists prove the existence of God over any alternatives? Of course not. Nobody can prove God exists, yet theists will stand on their heads saying they're sure. Well, if they can be sure despite evidence to the contrary, we can be sure in light of evidence in support of atheism.

Atheists seek to remove religion from society, and to force all people to be atheists. Absolutely wrong. We seek only the freedom for people to make their choice on their own, free of intervention from the government or public school system. We seek the freedom not to support religion through taxes, forced participation, or special privileges of any kind. That being said, your thoughts are your rights, and none of our business. Wear your jewelry, celebrate your holidays, and pray in your house, church, or in public if you like. Just don't force your religion on other people. That's what we're all about.

Atheists are so closed-minded they can't see that miracles happen every day! Some people look for miracles where none exist. Allow me to put things in perspective: someone's cancer going into remission is no miracle (nor is the cancer's existence in the first place), but we can talk when disease suddenly disappears from the face of the earth overnight without help from medical science. Food getting through to a hungry village—human perseverance. Starvation vanishing overnight from the earth without a reason? Miracle. One more time: a premature child survives—science. The spontaneous end of birth defects—miracle. Got it?

Just for good measure, I also wanted to list some good questions to have as support for your reasoning to be an atheist, particularly when speaking with Christians. These may start or worsen a fight and are to be used sparingly. They are dangerous questions that can only be answered with "The Lord works in mysterious ways" or the like. You might also get the old "You're asking questions about God, so you must believe in him" speech.

This is easily countered by saying that it's easier to prove the Bible wrong using the Bible itself, and that your arguments do not constitute an acknowledgment of God's existence any more than a discussion about Greek mythology would prove a belief in Zeus.

Use these only when you are sure of a congenial discussion, and be prepared to agree to disagree.

- If God is all-powerful, why did he take six days to create the universe, resting on the seventh? Why didn't he just snap his proverbial fingers and create everything all at once and not need rest afterward? Doesn't sound so all-powerful to me.
- If God knows the future, why does he make mistakes? He should have known he would regret the flood, and that Sodom and Gomorrah would be full of sinners, etc.
- Why does God need to be "served," and why can't we do it from heaven?
- God already knows who will sin, who will accept him, etc., for all eternity (since he has perfect knowledge of the future). Why then, are we here? Why not just send our souls to heaven or hell, depending on what he knows we'll do?
- Why does God care if he is praised? If he is this all-knowing superbeing, why does he care whether we mere humans give him credit for creating the universe?
- How can you justify that this merciful, loving god sends all non-Christians to hell, no matter how good they are? Even those from before Christ was born went to hell. However, terrible people, including Hitler and Jeffrey Dahmer, can go to heaven if they accept God before death.
- Why does this wonderful, forgiving God hold Adam's sin over all our heads? Why did God put the Tree of Knowledge of Good and Evil in the Garden of Eden in the first place if he knew with 100 percent certainty that it would cause Adam to eat it and trigger the Fall of Man? Why must we all pay for this by being permanent sinners? If God was so pissed, why didn't he just kill Adam and Eve and start over? Again, this is God's choice, so they're going to have to explain why God *chooses* to hold this incredible grudge.

- Where did God come from? How was he created? Why is it a valid argument to say that he "always existed," but an invalid argument to say the same thing about matter and energy?

Once you've both agreed to disagree, you've successfully outed your-self to that person. Avoid that awkward postdiscussion silence, making sure the discussion is complete, and not that the other person is searching for words to continue. The best thing to do is change the subject to something positive, smile, and get on with your relationship with this person. The person may need some time to adapt, but it will be made easier if you are yourself and show your happiness at being free of the closet.

Be a proud, open, honest atheist, not another closeted victim of the Christian Right. I ask all who can without serious consequences to take a deep breath, shout your atheism from the rooftops, and listen for echoes of approval and appreciation. If you hear nothing, shout louder.

Appendix 4

MY SPEECH AT STARKE, FLORIDA

Ladies and gentlemen, I am thrilled to be here with you today on this warm summer day for this historic event. Today, America's atheists take another step forward in our struggle for equality, and we as a nation take a step forward toward the American ideal of a pluralistic, melting-pot society. Across our country, public lands are littered with religious monuments, most notably those depicting the Ten Commandments, like the one I stand beside. Out of ignorance, most people believe the Ten Commandments to be some bland, benevolent set of ethics on which all nice people can agree; these are the people who have never read the Bible, or the context in which the commandments are given. As our bench reminds people, the Ten Commandments are not benevolent but barbaric; most of the commandments are regularly ignored because they are irrelevant to modern society, and only three of the ten have any similarity to US law. But one thing almost all the commandments have in common is the God-prescribed death penalty for things many of us do every day. The second commandment prohibits graven images of anything that is in heaven, so I guess that's pretty bad for Catholics who wear or display crucifixes carrying graven images of Jesus.

The fact that the Catholic Church actually removed this commandment proves that Church officials agree that this version of the Ten Commandments contradicts the Catholic dogma, and the penalty is death. Commandment five, work on Sunday? The Old Testament says you deserve to die for your labor. And then there's commandment four, taking God's name in vain. Goddamnit, that carries the death penalty too! Imagine—the death penalty for a disrespectful child or a cheating spouse! Indeed, coveting is the very basis for capitalism, so America itself would cease to exist if this commandment were obeyed. Nearly every Christian in America ignores most of the commandments because the commandments deserve to be ignored. They are ignored because they are mostly irrelevant, and it's a bad thing when the government allows groups to preserve their relevance out of a misguided allegiance to primitive, pre-American morality. But then there's the first commandment: "I am the lord and your God, thou shalt have no other gods before me." Martin Luther paraphrased this commandment, I think correctly, as "Thou shalt have and worship Me alone as thy God." Once again, the penalty for not observing this commandment is death by stoning. That's where we come in, and this is obviously our strongest objection. The demand to worship one god of one religion under penalty of death is the very essence of theocracy. Taken in context, it's the exact opposite of religious freedom and fits the definition of "hate speech" as it incites prejudicial action and violence against nonadherents—and it's sitting on the front lawn of the courthouse—the seat of justice for the county!

The good news is the Constitution requires all branches of the government to be fair and neutral when it comes to religious viewpoints, so atheists nationwide are able to counter religion's morality of yesteryear with one of honesty, compassion, and equality. In that vein, American Atheists offers an alternative monument which tells the verifiable truth, with no underlying threats at all.

The first thing you will notice about our monument is that it has function—atheists are about the real and the physical, so we selected to place this monument in the form of a bench, so Starke's residents can gain something they once did not have—another place to rest for a bit on a sunny Florida day.

The inscriptions on the bench include one from my predecessor, the founder of American Atheists, Madalyn Murray O'Hair. Often called the most hated woman in America by those who wished her silent, Madalyn demonstrates one very important thing missing from the Ten Commandments—compassion. Madalyn states, in her brief to the Supreme Court: "An Atheist knows that a hospital should be built instead of a church. An Atheist knows that a deed must be done instead of a prayer said. An Atheist strives for involvement in life and not escape into death. He wants disease conquered, poverty vanished, war eliminated."

Some people lie about religion's importance in the founding of this country, so we also included inscriptions of verifiable quotes to set the record straight; even though some of our founding fathers were religious, they all agreed, and indeed went out of their way, to create a secular Constitution, with a wall of separation between religion and government. Furthermore, few people know about the Treaty of Tripoli, the country's first treaty, which was written under order of George Washington, ratified unanimously by the founding Senate, and signed into law by John Adams, which states specifically that "the Government of the United States is in no way founded in the Christian Religion."

This treaty and these quotes aren't what religious historical revisionists would like you to believe—these are not indicative of people who founded a Christian theocracy, they are the actions of religious and nonreligious people who understood that government and religion must be kept apart and who designed a free and diverse nation. Our message to America is clear—atheists are everywhere, and we demand equality from our government. Of course, equality is an all-or-nothing prospect, so in "free speech zones" like this one, where one religion is promoted, all other religious and nonreligious positions, including atheists, satanists, and Muslims, are allowed. Our message to believers is also important: read your Bibles and holy books. One of atheism's biggest problems is that not enough Christians read their Bibles. This allows preachers to interpret the Bible's contents as they see fit because nobody who owns what they claim to think is the "perfect word of God" can actually bring themselves to read it.

It's no mystery why so few believers actually read their Bibles—they are afraid that if they did, they would understand how flawed it really is. In short, ignorance of their own Bibles keeps Christians Christian and empowers crooked preachers and politicians to do as they see fit in the name of God with parishioners' money, without challenge. Indeed, Christians who don't read their Bibles are allowing religious freedom to be endangered, hurting themselves and their country on the whole. I will give this Bible to any Christian who promises to read it cover to cover!

Ladies and gentlemen, we are here today not only to unveil a new monument, but a new ongoing project for American Atheists. This is not only the first permanent atheist-sponsored monument on public land—it's the first of many. I'm pleased to announce that thanks in part to a generous and anonymous donor, we are embarking on a mission to place fifty monuments on fifty public lawns and walls where religious monuments currently stand. Local atheist organizations are encouraged to seek out places where the Ten Commandments or other religious propaganda are placed on public land, and American Atheists will work with those local groups to ensure that the truth is placed next to the lie, and that civility is placed next to barbarism. In most cases we expect to accomplish this goal without substantial legal costs, as we have the right to place our monuments anywhere they place theirs, and this has been confirmed by the Supreme Court. However, we are prepared to fight any legal battles that emerge in this effort, so in the cases where the local politicians are so entrenched in the bigotry business of religion that they insist on spending taxpayer dollars to preserve inequality by refusing to allow our monument next to where a religious monument stands, we will be ready to take legal action, win, recover court costs from the municipalities, and place our monument there anyway. We will expose the Ten Commandments for the religious intolerance they represent, and the violence and hate they endorse and command. We will educate people about the true and provable secular nature of our country and highlight the lies religious leaders tell their flocks. And we will do it nationwide.

Diversity. Equality. Democracy. True American values never mentioned in the Bible but elemental to our great nation and required for any ethical society. Religious intolerance had a lot to do with the founding of the colonies. Religious intolerance is the reason we have a secular Constitution. It's time to reexamine Christianity, to expose its nearly insignificant role in the founding of America and the framing of our Constitution, and its lack of value in today's society. Today we begin to spread the truth and raise awareness of American Atheists in a new way—expanding on the methods of those who wish to hide or distort the truth—by using the Constitution in the way it was designed by the religious and nonreligious founders—to have our say as equals in the melting pot that is America.

United we stand.

Appendix 5

RELIGIOUS DOGMA IN SCHOOLS (UNPUBLISHED)

Posting the 10 Commandments or other religious declarations like "God Bless America" in public forums is un-American, unconstitutional, and unpatriotic. Many people believe that prohibitions against such displays are attacks against religion, when in fact they are necessary when Freedom of Religion is of paramount importance.

First, it must be noted that there is a significant difference between pro-atheism and neutral. A lone display on public land reading "There are no gods" is pro-atheist and just as un-American as pro-religion displays. On the other hand, an absence of religious opinion is neutral, as it makes no mention of the issue. In a neutral environment, everyone is treated equally, which is what we Americans call "freedom."

Our founding fathers did some things very wisely. Many, like Patrick Henry, were very religious, and others, like Thomas Jefferson, leaned toward atheism. There is no doubt that they discussed this issue and concluded that religion and government needed to be separate. To that end, they intentionally left God out of the Constitution, protected all religious theologies in the First Amendment, wrote about the "wall of separation between church and state" in postconstitutional writings, and unanimously signed the Treaty of Tripoli, which specified that the government be not in any way founded in Christianity.

In other words, the founders (religious and not) remembered what today's Christians have forgotten: that true religious freedom only comes when the separation of religion and government is absolute.

But we would be wrong to say that just because the founding fathers specified it, it must be right. We should not look at eighteenth-century writings as gospel (pun intended) for today's society. After all, the founders owned slaves and forbade women from voting, so to take their words without question would be unwise. We must *begin* with them, but then we must evaluate whether their writings are still appropriate for 2005.

We need to determine where we want our own country to go. Do we want a country that prefers one religion (or a few) to the others, or do we want one that treats all theologies equally? Do we want government spending time and money promoting one particular theology, or even theology in general? Do we want a majority religion to have control over a minority, or do we prefer to give the minorities the same freedoms enjoyed by everyone else? In short, do we want the Christian church to merge, even partially, with the government?

We say no. American Atheists asserts that in this case, the founding fathers were exactly right, and the government does not need to be in the business of promoting something which, by its very nature, is both exclusionary and divisive.

The government should be neutral, just, and fair. The separation of religion and government is already blurred (religion is exempt from taxes, zoning laws, etc.), and to worsen the problem by having the government promote one theology over others would harm America on the whole, while serve no positive purpose whatsoever.

We are not talking about removing religion—we're talking about protecting religious freedom. Freedom comes from equality, and equality comes from government neutrality. Neutrality should therefore be the ultimate goal of American government.

However, some religionists prefer the display of religious doctrines, even when they admit that there are many whose religious nature is contrary to such practice. Why? The motivation is simple and logical. The only purpose of posting a religious message is to pressure those who don't observe a religion to do so.

The same can be said of school prayer. Nationwide, any child can pray to any god they wish at any time, so why do we need organized prayers in schools? To pressure those who don't want to pray into doing so, and for *no other reason.*

Advocates insist that this is not really a factor, but simple logic dictates to the contrary. Peer pressure has been noted as the primary cause for drug use, and religious leaders know it cannot easily be ignored. Despite the fact that peer cliques have been blamed as a central cause for violence, they suggest we inject another divisive factor (let's single out the different ones!) into an already troubled system.

Would the posting of the 10 Commandments solve our violence problems? Hardly. Even the hard-hitting right-wingers will admit that most if not all of the major violence in schools is committed by children who have had religious instruction. There is no reason, then, to support the assertion that posting this religious doctrine would have had any effect, or that it would in the future.

By posting the doctrine in an official manner, the school will legitimize one religion, as opposed to another or none at all. One suggestion has been to post the doctrines of several religions in the classrooms, so as not to single out one religion or sect as preferred. Even if one of those plaques included atheism (which the right-wing religionists would never permit), this idea is implausible. While again solving no problems, we would soon be flooded by lawsuits to require the doctrines of all religions and any cults that define themselves as religions. This would ironically place Christian and Jewish parents in the same place as atheists, as their children would be exposed to theologies contrary to their own, behind the parents' backs. The choice of doctrine would be "all or nothing," because anything in between would be the government preferring one religion over another, and in that case we might as well live in Iraq.

Again, neutrality (not pro-atheism) is the easiest and fairest alternative.

Instead of trying to change the nature of our country, imposing new and divisive pressures into our schools, or employing useless posturing, we should be joining forces to remove divisiveness and increase the awareness of the benefits of diversity. The government is there for everyone, not just the majority.

Appendix 6

MARRIAGE EQUALITY IS A SEPARATION-OF-CHURCH-AND-STATE ISSUE

Excerpt from my marriage equality speech in Trenton at the Garden State Equality Rally, December 5, 2009.

Has anyone here ever heard a logical and rational reason why we shouldn't have marriage equality? I haven't. I've heard catchphrases and euphemisms: "Gay marriage hurts the sanctity of marriage." What does that even *mean*? I've heard a lot about Adam and Eve and Adam and Steve, but no statistics to support the assertion that gay marriage harms anyone or anything. And where I haven't heard any sound logic, there is one thing I've heard in abundance—religious dogma.

This is why, if you come to an atheist convention, you'll meet people from both sides of many issues, but not on this issue. While I can't speak for 100 percent of atheists everywhere, I can speak for every atheist I've ever met, and there are a lot of them. We all agree gay marriage opponents have no logical legs on which to stand.

The reason nobody is offering any logical reasons for opposing marriage equality is because there *are* no logical reasons to oppose it. The *real* reason people oppose marriage equality is religious in nature. Marriage equality is therefore not *only* a civil rights issue, but also a separation-of-church-and-state issue.

The enemy of gay marriage isn't all religions, just a small, rich, and politically savvy minority, and, boy, do they get around! The enemy of gay marriage also wants *religion taught as science* in the classroom. The enemy of gay marriage *also* boycotts companies for saying "Happy holidays" instead of "Merry Christmas." The enemy of gay marriage wants *you* to be (or at least act) like *them,* whether you want to or not. It is not enough for them to choose how *they* live; they also want to choose how *you* live. They want control for the sake of control, and power for the sake of power.

The enemy of gay marriage is *not* the Republican Party, but rather the well-funded political-corruption machine that currently controls it—the shrinking but still rich Religious Right. The Religious Right is our only real adversary, and we all know it. They think they have the monopoly on morality and will stop at nothing to get all of us to fit their mold and follow their way.

The Religious Right *knows* that gay marriages will not affect straight marriages because it hasn't affected the straight marriages where it's already legal. But they don't care about the facts. Even though they've been proven wrong, they still pressure the government to force you to behave as they see fit. Does this seem moral to you? To me it seems barbaric and primitive, and more than a little pathetic.

It's laughable and yet it's disgusting that this Bible-based bigotry is so alive and well.

Does this mean I'm hostile to religious freedom? No. Religious freedom is one of the pillars of American society. I am, however, extremely hostile to those who make this world a worse place to live by making it less hospitable to diversity and individuality, all for the sake of their own egos, and their own wallets.

The reason marriage equality is such a problem is *because* it is a church and a state issue. Marriage is both a religious observance and a civil institution, and in that way *it's the only issue of its kind.* It's a perfect example of how poorly church and state get along when merged.

While the state must not mandate a church to perform gay weddings, neither must a religious policy dictate legal decisions for the population at large. Many religions are our friends in this fight. Some religions read the same Bible as the Religious Right, but come to different conclusions. This highlights a key reason that the separation of church and state is so important for everyone, not just atheists—there are many theological beliefs, each one's thoughts different from all the others', and none can speak for all. We are a diverse state in a diverse country, and no single person or theology can possibly speak for everyone, nor should any try to do so. *This is the very essence* of the need for separation of church and state—any one church that is entrenched with the state will inherently exclude everyone else.

There is no one, anywhere, with a rational and logical reason to deny marriage equality. If you push hard, it all comes down to Bible-based bigotry and faith-based hate. This is why this is a church-and-state issue, and why I will fight for everyone's unalienable right to live and love in absolute, unapologetic equality.

Appendix 7

UNPUBLISHED LETTER TO THE EDITOR: SCHOOL PRAYER

October 17, 2005

Editor,

> *And when you pray, do not be like the hypocrites, for they love to pray standing in the synagogues and on the street corners to be seen by men. . . . But when you pray, go into your room, close the door, and pray.*
>
> —Matthew 6:5–6

The US Supreme Court is now hearing arguments regarding organized student-led prayer at school functions like sports events and graduations. According to polls, such activities are supported by the majority of the population, and most see it as a harmless act of faith, which takes little time and hurts nobody.

Indeed, that is exactly what the Religious Right is saying in defense of such prayer. According to them, organized school prayer would preserve the First Amendment rights of the religious students while saving us from all our social ills and liberal atheists bent on destroying religion.

Wouldn't it be great if life were that simple?

Unfortunately, it's not. In fact, this type of behavior can only lead to a destruction of rights and a less peaceful atmosphere.

Organized school prayer, whether led by a student or teacher, cannot and will not include everyone—it's not meant to. Indeed, organized school prayer is designed to be exclusive, to divide the members of the "recognized church" from the others (to allow believers to be seen praying), and to make nonmembers feel left out. In the case of the sports event, all people, no matter what religion they are, must stop what they are doing and be quiet while the others pray.

We all know that peer pressure is the most powerful cause of drug use among teens. How do you think nonbelievers will feel in a stadium surrounded by praying peers, with nothing to do but stand and watch? Will it make a difference whether the person leading the prayer is a teacher or student, if everyone else is doing it?

And who is a nonbeliever? Are we talking about those "liberal atheists" I mentioned before? Hardly. In the case of organized prayer, the term *nonbeliever* is used to refer to anyone who is of a belief different from the one being preached. In fact, one case considered by the Supreme Court was brought not by atheists, but by a Catholic and a Mormon who felt harassed by the Baptists in control.

Indeed, the victims of school-organized prayer will be of any religion and any sect—anywhere they are the minority.

But what of the majority? What about free expression and the believers' constitutional rights? The answer is simple: nobody is stopping anyone from praying anytime they want. Just like in class, people in school sports games can pray anytime they want, any way, and to any god—or none at all.

The line is drawn when it stops other people from doing as they see fit. One person's constitutional right to pray does not mean he can demand that other people stop what they are doing so they can watch. One does not have the constitutional right to infringe on other people's constitutional rights.

And the benefits of organized prayer? None, except that the believers can be seen praying and exercise some control over those who disagree (by making them stop and listen). The disadvantages are far more obvious and problematic: school prayer is a perfect venue for singling people out for persecution and proselytizing, while making the minority feel manipulated and undervalued. A perfect recipe for tension, hatred, and even violence.

We've all seen the effects of cliques at Paducah, Jacksonville, and Columbine. We should be working with each other to find areas common and inclusionary to all students, instead of deliberately tossing in another divisive factor—religion—into an already sensitive situation.

Let us not be manipulated by those who want to tell us how, when, and to whom to pray. The Pat Robertsons of this world can pray when they want, but they need to learn that the schools, and school functions, are there for everyone in the community and not to be viewed as fertile ground for religious recruiting.

Appendix 8

LETTER TO RANDALL TERRY (OPERATION RESCUE)

The following letter was delivered but I never received a response.

May 17, 2001

Mr. (Randall) Terry (Operation Rescue),

I bid you greetings in the spirit of cooperation.

My name is David Silverman and I am the National Youth and Family Director of American Atheists. While we may normally think of each other as adversaries, I am writing you today to ask for your help with an issue, which may be as important to you as it is to me.

You may be familiar with the CAPTA law, which makes it illegal for parents to abuse children. You may also be aware that this law contains a provision which allows exemption from this law for religious reasons.

This exemption allows members of fringe religious groups, including cults and Christian Scientists, to withhold medical treatment for their children, even unto death.

Because I value life, I am trying to have this clause removed. Like you, I believe the government needs to protect living children even to the detriment of the religious views of the parents.

This is where you come in: you and I only differ on when life begins, but we both agree that kids are alive after they are born. Therefore, I am writing to ask for your help.

I wish to join with you in a very "unlikely alliance" to protect the born children who are suffering and dying needlessly due to this clause. I propose joint press releases, meetings with Congress-people, and perhaps a news conference. The unique teaming of our groups would surely help to highlight this issue.

Mr. Terry, I know that your teaming with me in this manner would be distasteful to some of your compatriots. To a lesser extent, I would also expect similar reactions from mine. However, I truly think you and me—together—could save the lives of children, and that is far more important than ruffling feathers.

I hope you agree. Please send me an e-mail at [redacted] with your thoughts.

Sincerely,
David Silverman
National Youth and Family Director
American Atheists

Appendix 9

DIVERSITY AT WORK

In 2000, a company called Diversity at Work contacted me. They were working with Lucent to increase diversity awareness and wanted me to write an article for their publication (to be distributed to all their clients' employees) on atheism in the workplace. Someone had noticed (and complained!) that in all their literature about religious diversity, not a word had been mentioned about atheism. Atheists weren't just a minority; they were totally ignored, even in the diversity training. So this group asked me to write an atheist's view of diversity in the workplace.

Here is what I gave them, and a follow-up article I wrote for them after 9/11.

Diversity at Work Original Letter (August 14, 2000)
It's wonderful to see all the diversity efforts being implemented in the corporate world today. Over the past decade, almost every major corporation has instituted policies of tolerance and understanding towards people of different ethnic and religious backgrounds. Race, color, and religion are now forefront issues, and discrimination due to these grounds can be met with disciplinary actions.

It's almost beautiful.

Because of these actions, people who were once silent can now be free to express themselves, worship openly, and decorate their work spaces with personal items (e.g., religious icons or pictures of same-sex partners) that would have caused a stir only a few years ago.

But there is still one group of people who are in the closet, and efforts to make them more comfortable are few and far between: atheists.

Atheists are people who have no religious beliefs, other than that all religious beliefs are false. We see all gods as equally fictional and believe that our consciousness ends with our death.

Bigotry against atheists is rampant and for the most part unchecked. We are blamed for crime, violence, drug use, and the general malaise that society is suffering, despite the fact that all the evidence is to the contrary. In several states, there are still laws prohibiting atheists from serving on juries or running for public office, and a recent poll showed that 65 percent of Americans stated they would not vote for an atheist.

In the workplace, this translates into an attitude that is distinctly anti-atheist. Because atheism is not a religion (but rather a belief about religion), we are not always protected by diversity policies. The result is an environment that, while tolerant of everyone else, can actually be hostile to the nonreligious community.

Knowledge of or experience with hostility causes many atheists to hide their opinions, isolate themselves, and reinforces a "second-class citizen" mentality. In some cases, a deep resentment builds as they watch other minorities voice their opinion openly while they sit silent. Even worse, their silence reinforces the bigotry by perpetuating ignorance about atheists.

Some companies are already beginning to combat this phenomenon. Lucent has instituted a club policy, which allows people of all beliefs—including atheists—to gather in scheduled meeting rooms at no expense. As a result, a few atheist clubs are beginning to pop up, and acceptance of these groups is growing.

But Lucent and other companies need to go farther. Atheists need to be recognized as a valued part of our corporate culture and protected from bigotry like everyone else. We need to get to the point where diversity does not just include the theists. To that end, companies need to specifically mention or allow for nonbelief in their diversity statements, provide opportunities for atheist diversity speakers to address their employees, and facilitate an open dialogue about religious differences among all people—not just the believers.

Diversity has come a long, long way. The first steps have been the most important, but the process must be completed to include every group, not just the loudest few.

Prayer Vigils Exclude Atheists (September 24, 2001) (Note how they still do!)

In the wake of the September 11 attack on the World Trade Center, nearly every American went into mourning. Across the country, people filled the streets and churches with vigils and signs of patriotic unity.

Here at Lucent, and at most other large corporations, the main auditorium was filled with a massive prayer rally. Additionally, what was originally announced as a moment of prayer was observed by the entire building, where all work was to stop for two full minutes. This was noted by a global announcement over the loudspeakers.

These rallies and vigils are usually thought of as beneficial, harmless, and community building. They are created with good intentions—to galvanize the employees and facilitate a community feel. Nobody who does not wish or need to pray is ever forced to do so as a matter of policy.

The problem is that such prayer rallies, while being beneficial to the employees who pray, may have a secondary effect of dividing those who pray from those who don't. A moment of prayer was observed by the entire building, which unifies only those who take part—those who are religious—and actually alienate those of us who do not.

In my building, this is a significant part of the population. Nationally, nonreligious people, or those who are religious but who choose only to pray in private or in churches, can reach upwards of 20 percent.

The problem is that those who attend these vigils can be offended by those who don't, or those who are religious but who choose ambivalence, indifference, or worse. Indeed, a patriotic atheist can be seen as anti-American due solely to a refusal to attend a prayer vigil. The result can mean that nonprayers can be made to feel forced to pray or face division from their peers.

Any way you slice it, the prayer vigil is an activity specifically for those who pray, and not for those who don't.

Employers need to be aware of this, and work with it. Nonreligious people have also been hit hard by the WTC tragedy, and we need to be involved in the community too, without being pressured to abandon our beliefs. At Lucent, the moment of prayer was changed to a "moment of silence, prayer, and remembrance," which did well to include the entire population. Another suggestion would be to replace the rallying phrase (perhaps on posters on the walls of the building) from "God Bless America," which excludes far more than just atheists, to the all-inclusive "United We Stand."

Also, employees need to keep in mind that people mourn differently. The silence of a person who has also been hit hard by the WTC tragedy should never be interpreted as a lack of sympathy or support, and nobody should ever mistake a lack of religious observance as antipatriotism.

NOTES

Chapter 1: Atheist, Know Thyself

1. http://www.merriam-webster.com/dictionary/atheist.
2. http://www.thefreedictionary.com/Athiest.
3. http://www.oxforddictionaries.com/definition/english/atheist/.
4. http://www.defineatheism.com/.
5. http://www.merriam-webster.com/dictionary/theism.
6. http://en.wikipedia.org/wiki/Etymological_fallacy
7. Source: Quantitative Research performed by Mercury for Openly Secular Campaign, April 2014
8. http://www.merriam-webster.com/dictionary/freethinker
9. http://dictionary.reference.com/browse/know?s=t.
10. A. C. Grayling, *The God Argument* (New York: Bloomsbury USA, 2013), 62.
11. http://dictionary.reference.com/browse/secular
12. http://www.thefreedictionary.com/Secularist
13. http://www.patheos.com/blogs/wwjtd/2015/04/happy-openly-secular-day/
14. Source: Quantitative Research performed by Mercury for Openly Secular Campaign, April 2014
15. http://www.merriam-webster.com/dictionary/religion.
16. http://phys.org/news/2011-01-religiosity-gene-dominate-society.html.

Chapter 2: The War Has Already Begun, and We Are Ethically Obligated to Fight

1. http://www.theguardian.com/world/2005/oct/07/iraq.usa.
2. https://www.secular.org/content/gingrich-says-atheists-cant-be-trusted-disregards-50-million-secular-americans.
3. Edwin Kagin, *Baubles of Blasphemy* (Austin, TX: American Atheist Press, 2005).
4. http://www.patheos.com/blogs/progressivesecularhumanist/2014/11/texas-approves-textbooks-with-moses-as-founding-father/.

5. "Human Embryonic Stem Cell Policy Under Former President Bush (August 9, 2001–March 9, 2009)," National Institutes of Health, 2009, http://stemcells.nih.gov/policy/pages/2001policy.aspx.

6. "Defining terms: theocracy?" Yahoo! Answers, http://answers.yahoo.com/question/index?qid=20070226232603AAbFltr

7. http://spp.sagepub.com/content/early/2015/04/27/1948550615584200.abstract

8. http://www.huffingtonpost.com/2013/10/20/maria-belen-chapur_n_4133164.html.

9. http://www.merriam-webster.com/dictionary/lie: Lie is defined as (def. 1b) "an untrue or inaccurate statement that may or may not be believed true by the speaker."

10. http://plato.stanford.edu/entries/evil/

Chapter 3: Telling the Truth in Action: Being the Firebrand

1. http://www.logicalfallacies.info/presumption/no-true-scotsman/.

2. Eran Elhaik, "The Missing Link of Jewish European Ancestry: Contrasting the Rhineland and the Khazarian Hypotheses," *Genome Biology and Evolution* 5 (2013): 61–74, doi:10.1093/gbe/evs119.

3. http://www.simpletoremember.com/articles/a/jewsdontbelieve/.

4. For those who don't understand the "ex-parrot" reference, please do yourself a favor and search for the "Dead Parrot Sketch" from *Monty Python's Flying Circus* on YouTube.

5. Wafa Sultan, *A God Who Hates: The Courageous Woman Who Inflamed the Muslim World Speaks Out Against the Evils of Islam* (New York: St. Martin's Press, 2009), 62.

6. Ibid., 67.

7. http://www.snipview.com/q/Timeline%20of%20the%20Jyllands-Posten%20Muhammad%20cartoons%20controversy.

8. http://www.theguardian.com/world/2015/jan/07/paris-terror-attack-what-we-know-so-far.

9. http://money.cnn.com/2015/01/07/media/charlie-hebdo-terror-attack-media-mohammed-cartoons/index.html?section=money_news_international.

10. http://www.gq.com/news-politics/newsmakers/201208/anders-behring-breivik-norway-massacre-story.

11. http://www.huffingtonpost.com/2011/07/26/bill-oreilly-media-breivik-christian_n_909498.html.

12. http://www.christianitytoday.com/ct/2003/juneweb-only/6-2-22.0.html.

13. http://flaglerlive.com/25667/pt-mcveigh-breivik/.

14. http://www.bbc.com/news/world-africa-29994678.

15. http://churchandstate.org.uk/2012/12/the-catholic-church-condoms-and
    -hiv-aids-in-africa/.
16. http://abcnews.go.com/Health/herpes-strikes-nyc-babies-ritual
    -circumcisions/story?id=18890284.
17. *Daily Mail,* April 6, 2013.
18. http://www.voicesofny.org/2012/08/ultra-orthodox-defend-oral-suction
    -circumcision/.
19. *Jewish Daily Forward,* August 5, 2011.
20. http://atheism.about.com/library/FAQs/rr/blrr_rob_taylor.htm.
21. http://www.biography.com/people/mobutu-s%C3%A9s%C3%A9-seko
    -9410874.
22. http://www.hinduwebsite.com/hinduintrod1.asp.
23. http://zeenews.india.com/news/world/hinduism-third-largest-religion-of
    -world_817591.html
24. http://www.allaboutreligion.org/hinduism-gods-faq.htm.
25. http://www.hinduwebsite.com/hinduism/h_women.asp.
26. http://www.oxfordbibliographies.com/view/document/obo
    -9780195399318/obo-9780195399318-0038.xml.
27. http://www.hinduwebsite.com/hinduism/h_caste.asp.
28. http://zeenews.india.com/news/delhi/girl-killed-allegedly-by-parents-for
    -inter-caste-marriage_1501775.html.
29. Subodh Shah, *Culture Can Kill* (Mumbai: Lok Vangmaya Griha, 2007), 90.
30. Ibid., 123.
31. http://www.oneindia.com/2011/01/10/hinduguru-swami-nithyananda
    -admits-sleeping-with-morethan.htm.
32. http://www.wonderslist.com/10-curious-scandals-of-indian-swamis/.
33. http://www.huffingtonpost.com/2010/05/05/george-rekers-anti-gay-ac_n
    _565142.html.
34. http://www.cnn.com/2006/US/11/03/haggard.allegations/index.html.
35. http://www.biography.com/people/tammy-faye-messner-9542346#televi
    sion-ministry.
36. http://www.getnetworth.com/tag/harold-camping-income/.
37. Just my opinion.
38. http://archive.randi.org/site/index.php/swift-blog/1660-popoffs-still-at-it
    .html.
39. http://peterpopoff.org/.
40. http://www.patheos.com/blogs/friendlyatheist/2012/07/05/s-e-cupp-calls
    -out-a-group-of-crazy-militant-atheists-for-wait-what/.
41. http://www.patheos.com/blogs/friendlyatheist/2012/07/09/atheist-s-e
    -cupp-i-would-never-vote-for-an-atheist-president/.

Chapter 4: Fighting the Good Fight

1. http://www.ummah.com/forum/showthread.php?226952-Did-prophet-Muhammad-marry-a-6-year-old.

2. From the hadith of Sahih Muslim, vol. 2, no. 3309, http://www.muhammadanism.com/Hadith/Topics/Marriage.htm.

3. From the hadith of Sahih Bukhari, vol. 7, bk. 62, no. 88.

4. http://www.themuslimtimes.org/2012/04/religion/islam/age-of-consent-for-marriage-of-saudi-girls-soon.

5. http://www.vice.com/read/why-sex-offenders-are-getting-slaughtered-in-california-prisons-218

6. http://www.bestplaces.net/religion/city/massachusetts/boston.

7. http://beautifultrouble.org/principle/use-your-radical-fringe-to-shift-the-overton-window/.

8. http://www.truthorfiction.com/rumors/m/madelynmurrayohair-touched.htm#.VG4TMvnF9AM.

9. http://www.truthorfiction.com/rumors/m/madelynmurrayohair-touched.htm#.VJjNCF4AU.

10. http://www.truthorfiction.com/rumors/m/madelynmurrayohair.htm#.VJjNyF4AU.

11. http://forums.spacebattles.com/threads/one-nation-indivisible-sign-defaced.169339/.

12. Leviticus 24:16 (KJV): "And he that blasphemeth the name of the Lord, he shall surely be put to death, and all the congregation shall certainly stone him: as well the stranger, as he that is born in the land, when he blasphemeth the name of the Lord, shall be put to death."

13. 1 Timothy 2:12: "I do not permit a woman to teach or to assume authority over a man; she must be quiet."

14. Leviticus 11:7–8: "And the pig, though it has a divided hoof, does not chew the cud; it is unclean for you. You must not eat their meat or touch their carcasses; they are unclean for you."

15. Deuteronomy 22:11: "You shall not wear cloth of wool and linen mixed together."

16. Leviticus 19:28: "Do not cut your bodies for the dead or put tattoo marks on yourselves."

17. http://abcnews.go.com/images/pdf/935a2Pope.pdf.

18. http://www.evilbible.com/Rape.htm.

19. http://www.evilbible.com/Slavery.htm.

20. Psalm 137:9.

21. http://www.biography.com/people/anders-behring-breivik-20617893#attack-on-oslo.

22. http://www.teabreakfast.com/kareem-adbul-jabbar-anti-islami-muslim/.

23. http://wadiyan.com/2013/04/25/boston-bombers-are-not-true-muslims -taliban/.

24. http://www.garvandwane.com/religion/early_religion.html.

25. http://www.philosophyofreligion.info/theistic-proofs/the-teleological -argument/.

26. http://www.philosophyofreligion.info/theistic-proofs/the-cosmological -argument/.

27. http://www.philosophyofreligion.info/theistic-proofs/the-moral -argument/.

28. http://www.existence-of-god.com/ontological-argument.html.

29. https://explorable.com/history-of-the-scientific-method.

30. With thanks.

31. https://answersingenesis.org/creationism/old-earth/.

32. http://www.brooklyn.cuny.edu/bc/ahp/LAD/C4c/C4c_carbon_creation .html.

33. http://onenewsnow.com/church/2014/11/03/pope-backs-evolution-vatican -calls-creation-'blasphemous'.

34. http://www.csmonitor.com/USA/Society/2014/0206/Pat-Robertson -rejects-young-earth-creationism.-Nonsense-he-says.-video.

Chapter 5: Use, or at Least Understand, Firebrand Tactics

1. Sahil Kapur, TPM, March 25, 2014, http://talkingpointsmemo.com/dc/elena -kagan-antonin-scalia-birth-control-mandate.

2. http://lgbtweekly.com/2015/04/02/indiana-rfra-and-discrimination/

3. http://www.huffingtonpost.com/2015/04/02/indiana-lgbt-protections_n _6992184.html

4. https://www.youtube.com/watch?v=CULGslK2vrw.

5. http://www.patheos.com/blogs/friendlyatheist/2013/12/31/after-making -offensive-statements-about-atheists-new-york-state-senator-issues-the -worst-apology-youll-ever-see/.

6. http://en.wikiquote.org/wiki/Sun_Tzu.

7. https://www.youtube.com/watch?v=T8yyHzA1swA.

8. http://religion.blogs.cnn.com/2012/12/20/christmas-exposes-atheist-divide -on-dealing-with-religion/.

9. http://usatoday30.usatoday.com/news/religion/story/2012-07-26/athiest -poll-president/56516466/1.

10. http://www.gallup.com/poll/183713/socialist-presidential-candidates-least -appealing.aspx

11. That's actually a myth. They just threw their bras in the trash.

12. http://womenshistory.about.com/od/feminism/a/new_york_radical _women.htm.

13. http://www.mcclatchydc.com/2008/11/11/55722/doles-mistake-godless -ad-drove.html.

14. As illustrated principally by Aris Nikolaidis.

Chapter 6: Be Everywhere

1. http://religion.blogs.cnn.com/2014/02/25/cpac-reverses-decision-will-not -allow-atheists-at-conservative-conference/.

Chapter 7: On Defining Morality Without God(s)

1. Sam Harris, *The Moral Landscape* (New York: Free Press, 2010), 11.

2. http://www.ncbi.nlm.nih.gov/pubmed/16387256.

3. http://www.jahonline.org/article/S1054-139X(07)00426-0/abstract?cc=y.

Chapter 8: On Fighting Unpopular Battles (but Being Right)

1. http://seattletimes.com/html/localnews/2011301098_worldrelief10m .html.

2. http://www.patheos.com/blogs/friendlyatheist/2011/05/29/catholic -adoption-agency-will-shut-down-instead-of-letting-gay-couples-adopt/.

3. http://www.ontopmag.com/article.aspx?id=14156&MediaType=1&Category =26.

4. http://www.washingtonpost.com/wp-dyn/content/article/2009/11/11 /AR2009111116943.html.

5. http://www.irs.gov/Charities-&-Non-Profits/Churches-&-Religious -Organizations.

6. http://www.irs.gov/Charities-&-Non-Profits/Charitable-Organizations /Exempt-Purposes-Internal-Revenue-Code-Section-501(c)(3).

7. http://www.irs.gov/Charities-&-Non-Profits/Churches-&-Religious -Organizations/Filing-Requirements.

8. http://www.irs.gov/Charities-%26-Non-Profits/Churches-%26-Religious -Organizations/Special-Rules-Limiting-IRS-Authority-to-Audit-a -Church.

9. https://blog.au.org/church-state/march-2009-church-state/people-events /court-rules-against-irs-in-minnesota-case-over.

10. http://www.businessinsider.com/mars-rover-curiosity-cost-each-american -8-2012-9.

11. http://www.motherjones.com/politics/2012/09/map-teachers-salaries-by -city.

12. http://www1.salary.com/Police-Officer-salary.html.

13. Cragun, Ryan T., Stephanie Yeager and Desmond Vega. "How Secular Humanists (and Everyone Else) Subsidize Religion in the United States." *Free Inquiry*, Vol. 32 (June/July 2012), 39–46.

14. http://www.christianitytoday.com/gleanings/2012/november/should -megachurchs-cafe-and-gym-be-taxed-as-businesses.html?paging=off.

15. http://www.cnn.com/interactive/2014/08/us/american-archbishops-lavish -homes/index.html.

16. http://www.irs.gov/Charities-%26-Non-Profits/Churches-%26-Religious -Organizations/Special-Rules-Limiting-IRS-Authority-to-Audit-a -Church.

17. http://definitions.uslegal.com/a/accomplice/.

18. http://criminal.laws.com/accessory#sthash.V3ZR9hAp.dpuf.

19. http://blogs.findlaw.com/blotter/2012/02/church-confessions-admissible -in-court.html.

20. http://www.churchstatelaw.com/cases/peoplevphillips.asp.

21. https://www.childwelfare.gov/pubPDFs/clergymandated.pdf.

22. Legal research performed by American Atheists legal director Eric Husby.

23. http://www.law.cornell.edu/rules/fre/rule_501.

24. http://www.nolo.com/legal-encyclopedia/if-i-tell-psychologist-crime-i -committed-can-i-trouble.html.

25. http://www.nolo.com/legal-encyclopedia/i-told-lawyer-i-plan-commit -crime-the-future-is-confidential-information.html.

26. http://catholicexchange.com/can-priests-ever-reveal-what-is-said-in -confession.

27. http://www.catholicnews.com/data/stories/cns/1402869.htm.

28. http://cnsnews.com/news/article/paul-lagarde/baton-rouge-priest-wont -break-seal-confession-testify-abuse-claim.

29. Ibid.

30. Ibid.

31. http://www.washingtonpost.com/politics/911-memorials-the-story-of-the -cross-at-ground-zero/2011/09/07/gIQA2mMXDK_story.html.

32. Sarah Palin, *Good Tidings and Great Joy* (New York: Broadside Books, 2013), 29.

33. http://newyork.cbslocal.com/2011/07/23/world-trade-center-cross -moving-to-permanent-home/.

34. http://www.faithstreet.com/onfaith/2013/05/02/of-course-the-911-cross -is-a-religious-symbol/12086.

35. http://abcnews.go.com/US/atheists-sue-cross-world-trade-center-museum /story?id=14169830.

36. Ibid.

37. http://www.ieyenews.com/wordpress/atheists-seek-recognition-in-911 -museum-display/.

38. In oral argument before the Second Circuit Court of Appeals.

39. http://www.ancient.eu/Ur-Nammu/.

40. http://sidurisadvice.com/Ur-Nammu.html.

41. http://definitions.uslegal.com/h/hate-speech/.

42. http://www.theologynetwork.org/unquenchable-flame/luther/the-first -commandment.htm.

43. Pastor Rune Enoe, http://www.landoverbaptist.net/showthread.php?t=16785.

44. http://www.gotquestions.org/Catholic-idolatry.html. Good write-up at a religious site.

45. http://www.casebriefs.com/blog/law/constitutional-law/constitutional-law -keyed-to-sullivan/the-religion-clauses-free-exercise-and-establishment /mccreary-county-v-aclu/.

46. http://www.casebriefs.com/blog/law/constitutional-law/constitutional-law -keyed-to-sullivan/the-religion-clauses-free-exercise-and-establishment /van-orden-v-perry/.

47. https://www.youtube.com/watch?v=bFPao6FHUPI.

48. Tenth Circuit Court of Appeals Decision 12/20/10, p. 7, n. 2.

49. https://www.youtube.com/watch?t=95&v=bFPao6FHUPI.

50. http://www.christianpost.com/news/survey-9-11-wtc-cross-does-not -violate-separation-of-church-and-state-53356/.

51. http://www.patheos.com/blogs/friendlyatheist/2012/02/20/utah-pays -nearly-400000-to-settle-road-crosses-case/.

Chapter 10: Relish the Future

1. http://www.usnews.com/news/blogs/god-and-country/2009/03/09/new -survey-those-with-no-religion-fastest-growing-tradition.

2. Public Religion Research Institute , American Values Atlas, 2014

3. Gallup, 2013, "In U.S., Rise in Religious Nones Slows in 2012."

4. Ibid.

5. 2015 PEW Data suggests that those for whom religion in "at least somewhat important in their lives" number 30 percent of *nones,* but since PRII's information is about *belief,* not *the importance of religion,* I use PRII's numbers to represent theists (people who have a belief).

6. http://religions.pewforum.org/reports.

7. http://www.psychologytoday.com/blog/the-human-beast/201204/atheism -defeat-religion-2038.

8. https://www.barna.org/barna-update/article/12-faithspirituality/260-most -american-christians-do-not-believe-that-satan-or-the-holy-spirit-exis#.U -0C1PldXyA.

9. http://www.pewforum.org/2015/05/12/americas-changing-religious -landscape/

10. http://www.census.gov/popclock/.

11. http://www.simpletoremember.com/articles/a/jewsdontbelieve/.

12. http://www.pewresearch.org/fact-tank/2013/10/02/how-many-jews-are-there-in-the-united-states/.
13. http://www.religionnews.com/2015/05/12/christians-lose-ground-nones-soar-new-portrait-u-s-religion/.
14. http://www.pewforum.org/2015/05/12/americas-changing-religious-landscape/.

Chapter 11: Moving Forward

1. http://www.marchofdimes.org/mission/polio.aspx.

Appendix 1: Free Will

1. http://www.alternet.org/story/147623/why_does_god_reveal_himself_to_some_people_and_not_to_others. This note added just as an FYI.

INDEX

ABOUT THE AUTHOR

David Silverman is the dynamic and outspoken president of American Atheists, the organization known as "The Marines of the Atheist Movement." He is the creator and executive producer of the first Reason Rally, the largest atheist gathering in history, which unified America's secular movement and brought together thirty thousand atheists on the National Mall in Washington, DC. Silverman is known as a harsh critic of religion and its influence in the lives of all citizens, and his tactics and TV appearances have earned the attention of believer and atheist alike. He has appeared on many major news programs, including *CNN Special Report: Atheists: Inside the World of Nonbelievers*, *The O'Reilly Factor*, *Stossel*, *Hannity*, *Ronan Farrow Daily*, *Varney & Co.*, *Scarborough Country*, *The Real Story with Gretchen Carlson*, CNN's *Paula Zahn Now*, *Fox and Friends*, NPR's *All Things Considered*, *Nick News*, and many more.

Silverman is on Facebook at facebook.com/davesilverman and on Twitter @mratheistpants.

More information on American Atheists (a nonprofit corporation) can be found at atheists.org.